The University of

D1823228

THE OPERATION AND REGULATION OF FINANCIAL MARKETS

Studies in Monetary Economics
Published by Macmillan.

THE OPERATION AND REGULATION OF FINANCIAL MARKETS
(*edited by Charles Goodhart, David Currie and David T. Llewellyn*)

ADVANCES IN MONETARY ECONOMICS (*edited by David Currie*)

ISSUES IN MONETARY ECONOMICS (*edited by H. G. Johnson and A. Nobay*)

READINGS IN BRITISH MONETARY ECONOMICS
(*edited by H. G. Johnson and A. Nobay*)

Series Standing Order

If you would like to receive future titles in this series as they are published, you can make use of our standing order facility. To place a standing order please contact your bookseller or, in case of difficulty, write to us at the address below with your name and address and the name of the series. Please state with which title you wish to begin your standing order. (If you live outside the United Kingdom we may not have the rights for your area, in which case we will forward your order to the publisher concerned.)

Customer Services Department, Macmillan Distribution Ltd
Houndmills, Basingstoke, Hampshire, RG21 2XS, England.

The Operation and Regulation of Financial Markets

Edited by

Charles Goodhart
Norman Sosnow Professor of Money and Banking
London School of Economics and Political Science

David Currie
Professor of Economics
Queen Mary College, University of London

and

David T. Llewellyn
Professor of Money and Banking
Loughborough University

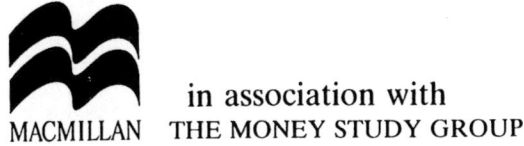

MACMILLAN   in association with
THE MONEY STUDY GROUP

First published 1987

Published by
THE MACMILLAN PRESS LTD
Houndmills, Basingstoke, Hampshire RG21 2XS
and London
Companies and representatives
throughout the world

Printed and bound in Great Britain by
Biddles Ltd, Guildford and King's Lynn

8   7   6   5   4   3   2
03 02 01 00 99 98 97

British Library Cataloguing in Publication Data
The operation and regulation of financial
markets.—(Studies in monetary economics)
1. Finance
I. Goodhart, Charles   II. Currie, David
III. Llewellyn, David T.   IV. Money Study
Group   V. Series
332   HG173
ISBN 0-333-43582-6

Contents

Acknowledgements

The production of this volume would not have been possible without the help of a number of people. Thanks are due to the Committee of the Money Study Group for their help in the editorial process, particularly to Anthony Courakis, who organised the Conference at Brasenose College, Oxford, where many of the papers were presented; and to Christopher Green, the Secretary of the Money Study Group.

Finally, the Money Study Group owes a great debt to the ESRC (Economic and Social Research Council) for its continuing financial support and encouragement over many years.

CHARLES GOODHART
DAVID CURRIE
DAVID T. LLEWELLYN

Notes on the Editors and Contributors

Richard T. Baillie studied economics and econometrics at the London School of Economics and has been Visiting Professor at the University of California at San Diego, Visiting Associate Professor at the University of Toronto and at Wayne State University, and Research Fellow at the Australian National University. His main research interests are econometric methodology for dynamic models and applied monetary and macro-economics. He is currently on the staff of the Economics Department at the University of Birmingham.

David Cobham is a lecturer in economics at the University of St Andrews in Scotland; he specialises in monetary policy and control and has published a number of articles in this field.

Anthony S. Courakis is an Official Fellow of Brasenose College, Oxford. He studied economics at the University of Manchester and Nuffield College, Oxford. Prior to joining Brasenose in 1974 he was a lecturer at Merton College, Oxford, 1971-4, a senior economist at the Inter-Bank Research Organisation, 1972-3, and a research officer at the Oxford Institute of Economics and Statistics, 1973-4. He has served as an economic adviser to the Bank of Greece and the Bank of Portugal, and as a member of the Greek Government Committee on Financial and Monetary Reform. A member of the Committee of the Money Study Group since 1974, he is also a founding member of the Greek Society for Economic Research and Managing Editor of the *Greek Economic Review*. His publications relate to bank behaviour, financial regulation, the demand for money, and monetary policy, and include articles in *Economica*, the *Review of Economic Studies*, the *Economic Journal*, and the *Oxford Bulletin of Economics and Statistics*.

Keith Cuthbertson is a lecturer in economics at the University of Newcastle. He previously taught at Thames Polytechnic and has worked in HM Treasury, and more recently at the National Institute of Economic and Social Research.

David Currie is Professor of Economics at Queen Mary College, University of London, and Director of the International Macroeconomics Research Programme, Centre for Economic Policy Research. He has published extensively in the areas of monetary economics, macroeconomics and international macroeconomics.

James Davidson is a lecturer in economics at the London School of Economics. He received the degrees of BSocSc from the University of Birmingham in 1973 and MSc (Econometrics and Mathematical Economics) at LSE in 1975. He has also taught at the University of Warwick.

Rodney Dickens was on secondment at the Bank of England over the period this research was undertaken. He subsequently returned to his job as an economist at the Reserve Bank of New Zealand, where he has been employed since 1980.

Charles Goodhart is the first Norman Sosnow Professor of Money and Banking at the London School of Economics. He was appointed in 1985, having previously worked for 17 years as an adviser at the Bank of England, specialising in domestic monetary issues. He is the author of a number of books and articles on monetary history and policy.

Christopher J. Green is Sir Julian Hodge Professor of Banking and Finance at the University of Wales Institute of Science and Technology. Educated at Oxford and Yale universities, he has been on the staff of the International Monetary Fund in the African Department, and has taught at Manchester University. Prior to taking up his present appointment, in 1985, he was an assistant adviser in the Economics Division of the Bank of England.

Maximilian J. B. Hall graduated from Nottingham University in 1975 and remained for a further two years to undertake a PhD on the monetary ramifications of local authority borrowing arrangements in the UK. In 1977 he was appointed a lecturer in economics at Loughborough University, where he has remained ever since, duly completing his PhD in 1978. He has lectured and published widely on domestic and international money and banking issues (his book entitled *Monetary Policy Since 1971: Conduct* *and Performance* was published in 1983) and since 1982 has acted as economic adviser to the Macao Business Centre.

Mervyn Lewis is Midland Bank Professor of Money and Banking, and Co-director, Nottingham Institute of Financial Studies at the University of Nottingham. His previous position was Reader in Economics at the University of Adelaide. He has visited University College, Swansea, and the University of Manchester, and has been Visiting Scholar, Economics Division, the Bank of England, and a Consultant to the Australian Financial System Inquiry. He has published four books on monetary economics.

David T. Llewellyn is Professor of Money and Banking and Head of the Economics Department at Loughborough University, and Chairman of the University's Banking Centre. He has previously worked at HM Treasury and the International Monetary Fund. He is also Consultant Economist to money and foreign exchange brokers Butler Till Ltd. He is a committee member of the Money Study Group and on the Editorial Board of *Banking World* and *Retail Banking International.*

Patrick McMahon is a graduate of Trinity College, Dublin, and has studied at Oxford and Birmingham. He has been Visiting Professor at the Universities of Kyoto, Bordeaux, Mannheim and Wayne State among others. His main research interests are macroeconomics, monetary and financial economics and applied econometrics, and he is currently in the Department of Economics at the University of Birmingham.

Jean-Marin Serre is maître-assistant in the Faculté des Sciences Economiques of the Université de Clermont I in France; he specialises in monetary and fiscal economics, and has contributed to the field of development economics as a member of the Centre d'Études et de Recherches sur le Développement International.

Mark P. Taylor was educated at Oxford and London Universities and is currently a lecturer in economics at the University of Newcastle upon Tyne. He has previously worked as a foreign exchange dealer in the City.

Introduction

David T. Llewellyn

The Money Study Group (MSG) was formed in 1969 with two main objectives. The first is to bring together people (in the United Kingdom and from abroad) who are concerned with the functioning of the British and international monetary systems, whether as academic scholars and researchers, economists working in the financial sector, or officials of the Bank of England and the Treasury. The areas of interest of the Group include monetary theory and policy, and the operation of financial markets, institutions and systems. The second objective is to promote research into monetary economics and, through its regular seminars and conferences, to provide a forum for the discussion of the results of research. The Group subscribes to no particular school of thought, and takes no collective position on policy and other questions.

This volume is the second of a new annual series of selected papers given to the regular meetings of the MSG and its Annual Conference held in September. The current volume includes papers given at its meetings in the 1984-85 academic year, and the conference held at Brasenose College, Oxford, in September 1985. Generally the MSG will not prescribe an annual theme and the selected papers may cover a wide range of topics within the broad area of monetary economics. On this occasion the papers have been brought together under the current title: *The Operation and Regulation of Financial Markets*. The volume is divided into three sections: *Regulation and Structural Change in Financial Markets, Modelling Money and Banking*, and *Modelling Financial Markets*. These areas clearly reflect the nature of much of the research currently being undertaken in monetary economics.

The first section covers particularly timely issues in the context of major structural and operational changes in the UK, US and international financial systems and changes in the regulatory environment. Financial systems in many countries are undergoing substantial structural and operational changes due in large part to various combinations of a more intensive competitive environment, official deregulation moves and the impact of technology. At the same time the pace of financial innovation has accelerated bringing with it changes in the risk characteristics in the financial system. The changes are likely to have important implications both for the structure of financial systems, the operation of financial institutions and the conduct and operation of monetary policy and prudential regulation.

The changes in many countries (but notably the UK and US) are affecting, for all institutions, the range of business operations, how services are being provided and the industrial structure of the financial services industry but, above all, the extent, intensity and nature of competition. In particular the basic trend is increasingly towards the breaking down of traditional demarcations between different sets of financial institutions. This is comparatively easy in the UK (certainly compared with the US) because the historic demarcations have been largely, though not entirely, self-imposed rather than forced by legislation. In fact, unlike in most countries, there has not been a well-defined legal framework defining and regulating the scope and nature of the business of financial institutions in the UK. Regulation in general has tended to be informal and discretionary with a large element of self-regulation. In some cases demarcations have been maintained by restrictive practices. Building societies are an obvious and major exception to this general rule in that their activities have been substantially circumscribed by legislation. Nevertheless, the specialist distinctions in the UK have had the full informal backing of the authorities.

More generally, financial intermediation and the provision of financial services are becoming increasingly internationalised in three dimensions: users of services increasingly have global options, suppliers of services have a widening range of international options, and institutions are increasingly diversifying their location internationally. In the process national financial systems are becoming subsets of a global financial system. This is most apparent in securities trading, as technology may have the effect of making physical location of institutions and markets less important than in the past.

Powerful pressures have recently developed on regulatory authorities throughout the world, but notably in the major financial centres, towards deregulation. In the first place, international competition can have the effect of diverting financial intermediation away from those national financial systems which are most constrained by regulation. The concomitant danger is that international competition in deregulation can emerge. Secondly, in the increasingly competitive environment, financial innovation spurred by aggressively competitive financial institutions and markets can have the powerful effect of circumventing regulatory constraints. Thirdly, in some countries (most notably in the UK) an ethos has developed that the free play of market mechanisms (albeit with some residual prudential constraints) is more likely to enhance efficiency and the interest of consumers.

Technology has also had a powerful impact in the process of deregulation as it widens the range of business options available to financial institutions and hence is a factor weakening traditional boundaries. It also has the effect of making location an increasingly less important consideration in the provision of financial services (most especially to the corporate sector) and accentuates the trend towards an internationalisation of finance. If the regulatory environment in other countries confers a competitive advantage on foreign institutions, pressure develops to adopt a similar regulatory arrangement. To the extent that technology has the effect of integrating financial systems, it contributes to a trend towards developing similar regulatory arrangements between countries. Overall, regulation in the financial system cannot now be regarded as exclusively a national issue with national regulatory arrangements framed without any reference to those in other major financial centres.

Regulation in the financial system is always a mixture of statutory, self-regulatory arrangements, moral suasion and self-imposed constraints. There has never been a comprehensive legal framework governing the regulation of financial institutions. The role of legislative regulations, however, has been considerably less dominant in the UK than in most other countries. The 1979 Banking Act in the UK was the first comprehensive legislation governing the business of banking. Financial regulation in the UK has tended to rely little upon the law, substantially upon the general authority of the Bank of England, and reinforced by voluntary arrangements based in part upon various forms of cartel and restrictive practices.

In the first paper Maximilian Hall offers a detailed account of the collapse in 1984 of Johnson Matthey Bankers and the controversial response of the Bank of England; the discussion is set in the context of the case for and against prudential regulation and supervision of financial institutions (most especially banks) and a detailed review of the system of banking regulation and supervision in the United Kingdom. Hall also considers some broader issues related to prudential regulation and supervision of banks in the light of the JMB affair.

The structure and operation of the British financial system changed substantially during the 1970s in the context of competitive pressures induced partly by measures of deregulation. Two major sectors, however, were not affected by deregulation: the Stock Exchange and domestic securities industry, and building societies. The Stock Exchange maintained its restrictive practices over pricing, single capacity and membership which had the effect of excluding banks and maintaining the historic demarcation between banking and securities business.

The structure and operation of the Stock Exchange and British securities industry are now, however, changing substantially, and this is the focus of the second paper, by Charles Goodhart. The UK has traditionally been sensitive about conflict of interest in the securities industry, as shown by the division of functions on the Stock Exchange. This institutional division has been underpinned by two restrictive practices of the Stock Exchange: the rules enforcing single capacity, that is, the separation of the functions of broker and jobber, and the restrictions on outside ownership, which meant that after 1982 and until March 1986, any entity not a member of the Stock Exchange could not own more than 29.9 per cent of any Stock Exchange firm. Single capacity operation was also buttressed by agreement over minimum commission charges.

All of this is now being dismantled and represents a process of deregulation that is not primarily a product of a change in the law (though it has the full support of the Bank of England and government) but of the force of external competitive pressures.

Charles Goodhart describes recent and prospective developments in the London Stock Exchange and securities markets where the structural changes are likely to be substantial. He considers the historical structure of the Stock Exchange, and the factors producing it, and the development of international competition which has contributed to the current structural changes and the injection of (bank) capital into the British securities market. In the final part of his paper the important issue of the role of information in the market is considered.

Structural change and deregulation are not unique to the UK. Similar trends have emerged in the US as a series of deregulatory moves (such as, *inter alia*, the Depository Insititutions Deregulation and Monetary Control Act of 1980, and the Garn-St Germain Depository Institutions Act of 1982), combined with the market impact of technology and the evolution of new strategies by financial institutions, have induced substantial structural change in the US financial services industry. Historically (since the 1930s) regulation has been designed to impose geographical limitation on the business of financial institutions and a strict demarcation between banking, insurance and securities business, following an interpretation that the banking failures of the early 1930s were associated with banks' securities trading. In fact there is little empirical evidence to support this interpretation, not the least because in general the banks that failed were not substantial traders in securities. Nevertheless, the tradition of regulation in the US has been to maintain a specialised function for financial institutions. The third paper by Mervyn Lewis reviews the structural changes occurring in the financial services industry in the United States, which are undermining the historical functional divisions partly imposed by regulations. This is done in the context of an analysis of the characteristics of financial firms and the nature of the demand for financial services. The paper makes the point that, contrary to the implicit assumption in much of US financial regulation, diversification has the normal effect of reducing risk rather than making financial institutions more vulnerable. The paper concludes with a useful summary of the arguments for and against financial supermarkets, which debate is as relevant in the context of current developments in the UK as it is to the US experience.

In the final paper of the first section David Cobham and Jean-Marin Serre observe that monetary growth has been significantly more variable in the UK than in France over both the medium term and the short term. They consider seven specific factors that might have contributed to this and conclude that differing influences are responsible for short- and long-term differences in variability, and that the relevance and power of some of the factors varies over the period considered. The paper ends by suggesting that the apparently more ambitious use of monetary policy in the UK may have been a perverse response by policy-makers to the difficulties of operating monetary policy in a more open economy where financial markets adjust more speedily than do goods markets.

The second section of this volume comprises three papers brought together under the title *Modelling Money and Banking*. The paper by Keith Cuthbertson and Mark Taylor provides an appraisal of the role of money as a buffer stock, and in a review of a number of buffer-stock models concludes that some of these models are not necessarily inconsistent with rational expectations hypotheses, and that the two approaches can be usefully combined. The analysis is presented in the context of micro-theoretic arguments, and consideration is given to the main methods applied to empirically implementing buffer-stock models. Policy implications are considered and the paper concludes: 'on all fronts we believe the (buffer-stock) approach has reasonable theoretical appeal and enough empirical support to warrant further research'.

The paper by James Davidson also adopts the buffer-stock approach, and models the demand for money in the context of a system of equations describing money supply, prices and income. Money is treated as the residual component of the short-run portfolio decisions of the non-bank private sector, but the deviations from the implicit long-run demand schedule, while they can persist (and such persistence is empirically estimated), act through a servo-mechanism to stabilise the system. The equations are estimated for the UK subject to appropriate cross-equation parameter constraints, under alternative assumptions about the definition of money.

In the next paper Anthony Courakis challenges the conventional view that compulsory balance sheet ratios imposed on banks (for example, cash ratios) are equivalent to a direct tax on deposit returns and have the effect of reducing the profit-maximising level of bank deposits. He shows that imposed cash ratios (even when no interest is paid on them) can have the effect of raising both deposit interest rates and the equilibrium volume of bank deposits. The analysis is developed on various premises, including allowing for real resource costs of intermediation, perceptions of loan default, different types of assets and liabilities comprised in bank portfolios, and the presence of other intermediaries in competition with banks. The over-all conclusion of the paper is that the effect on the volume of deposits of imposed cash ratios depends *inter alia* upon the characteristics of supply and demand for the assets and liabilities traded by banks, and that in general there exists some compulsory positive cash ratio that, other things being equal, implies a higher equilibrium volume of deposits than in the case of a zero ratio.

Three papers make up the third section of the volume under the title *Modelling Financial Markets*. Richard Baillie and Patrick McMahon focus upon rational expectations in financial markets and the efficient markets hypothesis and in this framework consider alternative models of the term structure of interest rates. The authors compare a simple distributed lag-type model (based on the notion of one-way causality running from short- to long-term interest rates) with a bivariate autoregressive model allowing for joint determination of short and long rates. This is followed by a discussion of rational expectations models of the term structure. Their conclusion is that the usual form of the rational expectations model of the term structure as adopted in the US literature is found not to be supported by the data of the bond market. It is not necessarily incompatible with alternative specifications of the rational expectations term structure.

Christopher Green considers the structure of interest rates from a different angle. He derives asset price expectation formation equations and argues that these can be used in empirical research aimed at circumventing the Lucas critique. The conclusion is that the mean-variance model with rational expectations can explain a significant proportion of the movement of UK asset returns in the estimating period 1972-7. Over the period the authorities avowed strategy was to 'peg' short-term interest rates and the results produced suggest that this was correctly perceived by private agents and incorporated into their calculations.

The volume concludes with Rodney Dickens's paper on the variability in UK asset markets since the mid-1960s. The paper presents the results of an investigation of the volatility of UK gilts, interbank, foreign exchange and share markets through the application of the ARCH model developed by Engle and which measures the dispersion around the conditional mean rather than about the sample mean. The paper notes that variability in the selected markets was 'relatively low, stable, and co-ordinated up until the early 1970s, (while) more distinct 'cycles' in variability were in evidence after this period'.

The collection of papers demonstrates the variety and quality of current research being conducted in monetary economics encompassing theory, empirical testing and the detailed formal analysis of financial markets and institutions. All of the papers have an 'applied' orientation and some have immediate policy implications. They all cover important issues and the Money Study Group, through its series of annual volumes, is pleased to be able to advance analysis and debate in these areas.

Part I
Regulation and Structural Change in Financial Markets

1 UK Banking Supervision and the Johnson Matthey Affair*[1]

Maximilian J. B. Hall

The rescue of Johnson Matthey Bankers (JMB) in October 1984 raises important issues for the prudential regulation and supervision of banks in the UK. The authorities responded to the event by proposing amendments to the supervisory system, but it is argued here that they are not sufficient to ensure that a repeat of a JMB-style rescue is avoided, nor do they deal adequately with a wider set of prudential issues that exists independently of the JMB case.

The outline of the paper is as follows. The case for prudential regulation and supervision of financial institutions in general, and for banks in particular, sets the scene, which is followed by a brief review of the system of banking supervision in the UK. The events and issues centred on the collapse and rescue of JMB are then described, followed by consideration of the authorities' response. The final part of the paper considers some of the broader issues related to prudential regulation and supervision of banks.

THE NEED FOR PRUDENTIAL CONTROLS

The necessity for prudential regulation is normally assessed in terms of the requirements of consumer protection and financial stability. The desire to protect the small or less financially sophisticated investor from fraudulent activities or ineptitude of management has led to the introduction of deposit insurance schemes and the requirement for an improved flow of information from those soliciting deposits. The economic benefits are perceived to lie in an improvement of the allocative efficiency of the financial system, due to both increased investor confidence and the improvement in information. Associated costs of regulation, however, are

*Paper presented at the Annual Money Study Group Conference, Brasenose College, Oxford, September 1985.

3

potentially high, and include: the direct costs of compliance with, and enforcement of, regulatory requirements; resource misallocation (to the extent that the regulatory authorities may judge a requirement to support 'non-viable' institutions to be in the interests of maintaining stability in the financial system as a whole); possible reductions in consumer choice (through the imposition of restrictions on the range of business activities); and operational inefficiency.

Preservation of financial stability is seen as a pre-requisite of economic growth, and is one reason for the closer scrutiny of financial *vis-à-vis* non-financial enterprises. The problem for central banks arises in deciding which, if any, financial institutions should be allowed to fail as the requirements of a sound financial system might at times be inconsistent with allowing the full mechanisms of a competitive market place to operate. In any event, the legitimate liquidity needs of the system as a whole should never be threatened – a requirement that demands the provision of an official 'discount facility' to deal with instances of loss of public confidence and other financial 'shocks'.

Several factors account for the general trend towards a proliferation and increasingly widespread use of prudential controls in the financial sector: (1) the internationalisation of banking operations (with new attendant risks, for example, country risk, foreign currency exposure, maturity transformation, risk concentration and overdependence on inter-bank sources of funds); (2) particular problems caused by higher and more volatile inflation and more volatile interest rates and exchange rates; (3) structural changes (often in response to deregulation in monetary control and of the business operations in the securities markets) in domestic financial systems creating the potential for the emergence of various forms of 'conflict of interest'; and (4) an intensification in domestic and international competitive pressures in the financial system (due partly to the breakdown of demarcations in the provision of financial services and the effects of technological innovations), which may threaten greater instability in the financial sector.

Given acceptance of the need for prudential regulation, the supervisory authorities must decide upon the most appropriate mix of statutory and non-statutory controls that satisfies prudential objectives while at the same time minimises inequities (by maintaining the competitive neutrality of regulation) and associated costs. The issue normally narrows to one of weighing up the advantages, in terms of flexibility, low administration costs and minimal interference with standard business practice, of self-regulation against the doubts over effectiveness that non-statutory regulation undoubtedly encourages. In general, self-regulation is preferred, with government exercising the necessary degree of moral suasion, with minimal back-up statutory powers, to ensure that objectives are fulfilled.

THE CURRENT SYSTEM OF BANKING SUPERVISION OPERATED IN THE UK

The present statutory framework for the supervision of 'banking' institutions (that is, Recognised Banks and Licensed Deposit-Taking institutions but, for the purposes of this paper, excluding discount houses) was established in the 1979 Banking Act. The core element of this legislation was that any company wishing to take deposits in the UK had either to be *authorised* by the Bank or specifically exempted as, at the time, was the case for building societies, local authorities, National Girobank, National and Trustee Savings Banks and the Bank of England. A distinction was drawn between Recognised Banks and Licensed Deposit-Takers, mainly on the basis of the range of services offered, although this implied no distinction in standing in the eyes of the Bank. Supervision itself centred on the measurement and assessment of liquidity, capital adequacy and foreign currency exposure. Ratio analysis provided the starting point for subsequent discussions with management with a view to implementing prudential controls in a flexible manner. A formal deposit protection scheme was also introduced. The Bank's system of supervision thus remained flexible despite the new statutory powers, with a wide measure of discretion remaining in the interpretation and application of the authorisation procedures and with the assessment of the adequacy of prudential standards carried out on an individual basis (although 'peer group' analysis is taken into account). The regular management interviews that follow the statistical analysis of the returns remain the cornerstone of the system. For UK-incorporated institutions these discussions normally take place quarterly but for the clearing banks and UK branches of overseas companies interviews take place roughly every six and nine months respectively.

Before considering the key elements of the system in more detail it is pertinent to emphasise the importance of the auditing process to the success of a system that does not involve a formal and regular examination procedure (unlike in the US and elsewhere) nor insists upon the auditing of prudential returns. The task of the auditor is to assess the authenticity of the facts (for example, the valuation of assets, liabilities and reserves) as presented in companies' accounts by the directors. Thus the first duty is to shareholders, although the reports are available to third parties, including banking supervisors. In some countries, such as Switzerland, banking law imposes a requirement upon auditors to convey any information they think relevant to banking supervisors but this has not hitherto been the case in the UK where such action would represent a breach of confidentiality. Indeed, the only action an auditor can take to alert supervisors to impending problems is to qualify the accounts but this is an extreme measure and rarely done. Effective supervision in the UK therefore relies heavily on the expertise of auditors, a situation that has only recently been called into question following the Johnson Matthey affair.

Returning to the authorisation procedures for the establishment of a deposit-taking institution, the first stage of the process is for applicants to complete questionnaires requiring details of the nature of the applicant's business or proposed business and for information about its managers, controllers and directors. In the case of applications from branches of overseas institutions, the Bank also seeks assurance from the relevant overseas supervisory authority that they are satisfied with the quality of its management and its financial soundness. Additionally, letters of comfort, designed to extend shareholder responsibility beyond that arising from limited liability status, are sought from any institution (bank or non-bank) or person controlling at least 15 per cent of the voting power of a bank. Similar assurances may be sought from controlling third parties. Subsequent to the formal application, discussions between the Bank and senior management of the institution are usually held to provide a deeper insight into the nature of the institution's business. Finally, applications are assessed in the light of statutory criteria laid down for authorisation in the Banking Act. Those companies refused authorisation have a right of appeal to the Chancellor of the Exchequer (under Section 11 of the Act), who is required to refer them to an independent body acting under the Tribunal and Enquiries Act, 1971.

The Bank has considerable discretion in the interpretation and application of the statutory criteria laid down for authorisation. For example, in determining whether an applicant should be classified as a Recognised Bank or a Licensed Deposit-Taker the Bank will base its decision mainly upon a review of the detailed information demanded in respect of each of the five categories of service set out in Schedule 2 of the Act, namely the provision of: (1) current and deposit account facilities or the acceptance of wholesale money market funds; (2) overdraft and loan facilities or the lending of funds in the wholesale money markets; (3) foreign exchange services; (4) finance through bills of exchange and promissory notes and for foreign trade; and (5) financial advice or investment management services and services in the securities area. In general, the 'recognition' categorisation will only be conferred upon those deemed to provide an adequate level of service in each of the five areas or a highly specialised banking service (such as provided by discount houses) but this requirement can be waived in exceptional cases. Similarly, the Bank has to make subjective judgements in the interpretation of the criteria relating to authorisation as a Licensed Deposit-Taker which, briefly, involve requirements that directors, controllers and managers are 'fit and proper persons', that at least two individuals effectively direct the business (as is also the case for a Recognised Bank) and that the business is conducted in a 'prudent manner'. The last mentioned requires an institution to meet certain specific demands relating to the adequacy of capital, liquidity and provisions for bad and doubtful debts together with some undefined requirements (Bank of England Annual Report, 1984, pp. 41–4).

Central to the supervisory process is the assessment and measurement of capital and liquidity adequacy. The question of capital adequacy was first addressed by the Bank in 1974 through the establishment of a Joint Working Party with the London and Scottish clearing banks. This duly reported in 1975 (*Bank of England Quarterly Bulletin*, September 1975, p. 240) recommending the use of two ratios, the *free resources ratio* (that is, the *gearing ratio*) and the *risk asset ratio*, in the assessment of capital adequacy. The first ratio related current, non-capital liabilities to an adjusted capital base (premises, equipment and other fixed assets, goodwill, investments in subsidiaries and associated companies and trade investments, unquoted investments and connected lending were all deducted) and was taken to represent the acceptability of an institution's capital to its depositors and other creditors. Accordingly, it was important that it could be constructed on the basis of published information (although the inclusion of any inner reserves and general bad debt provisions within the definition of capital militates against this). The second ratio was used as a measure of the adequacy of capital in relation to an institution's exposure to risk of losses, and related such risks to the capital available to absorb them. It was (and still is) this second measure which was regarded as the more relevant for supervisory purposes, although no norms were laid down for individual companies or groups of companies on the grounds that this would be inappropriate considering the great diversity of business operations between deposit-taking institutions.

These guiding principles were reviewed during 1979 by the Bank and, following circulation of a consultative document with the banking system, the present system of assessment was established (*Bank of England Quarterly Bulletin*, September 1980, p. 324). The Bank's approach remains a flexible one, with assessment conducted on a case-by-case basis, and pays due attention both to the interests of depositors with individual institutions and to the need to preserve confidence in the over-all system. It also reflects the acknowledged division of responsibilities (as determined within the Basle *Concordat*) among international supervisory authorities. This led the Bank to assess the capital adequacy of UK-incorporated deposit-taking institutions on a consolidated basis (that is, including the operations of all branches and wholly or majority-owned subsidiaries) and to ensure that authorised subsidiary companies operating in the UK were adequately capitalised in their own right. Although the gearing and risk asset ratios were retained, modifications and extensions were introduced, notably in respect of the definition of the adjusted capital base[2] (for both ratios) and the grading of risks incurred for the purpose of calculating the risk asset ratio. In the Bank's assessment of capital adequacy, this quantitative approach complements the Bank's qualitative judgements on such issues as the quality of capital, management strengths, profitability and business prospects and the spread of business.

The Bank's approach to *liquidity adequacy* was set out in a Bank paper issued on 20 July 1982 (*Bank of England Quarterly Bulletin*, September 1982) which represented the final version of papers previously circulated by the Bank of England in March 1980, March 1981 and the summer of 1981. In the early papers the Bank attempted to devise a scale of liquid assets cover for what were defined as 'maturity uncertain' and 'maturity certain' liabilities. In the latter case, the required liquid assets cover would have varied according to the maturity. Also, a distinction was made between what was defined as 'primary' and 'secondary' liquidity. In the light of substantial criticism of the papers, the Bank subsequently abandoned the suggested liquidity measure, based on the distinction between maturity-certain and maturity-uncertain liabilities, and both the 'primary' and 'secondary' liquidity requirements. The proposed detailed system of liquid asset cover was also dropped and, instead, the Bank adopted a case-by-case approach but with the caveat that 'it believes it possible to achieve a common basis of measurement which may then be applied after due consideration to . . . the particular circumstances of each bank', (*Bank of England Quarterly Bulletin*, March 1981, p. 41). This materialised in the 1982 paper (discussed below) as a measure incorporating 'a series of accumulating net mismatch positions in successive time bands'. Across the board norms were eschewed and the role of liability management in the liquidity management process was formally recognised.

The main objective of the Bank in the 1982 paper was, and remains, to ensure that banks (taken to subsume Licensed Deposit-Taking institutions (LDTs) throughout this section), are able to meet their obligations (both deposit withdrawals and lending commitments) on the due dates. Individual banks' liquidity requirements must generally be capable of dealing with *any* net shortfall in cash inflow, anticipated or otherwise. To this end, the Bank seeks to satisfy itself that individual bank management teams adopt a 'prudent mix' of liquidity forms, and a diversified deposit base appropriate to their individual circumstances. They must also have monitoring and control systems in operation that will ensure that such a policy is followed continuously. Across-the-board liquidity norms are not applied. The Bank looks at the liquidity of a bank's total business undifferentiated as to currency denomination, although, in certain circumstances, it may be deemed appropriate to assess liquidity adequacy by currency denomination (especially sterling) also.

The liquidity measure adopted by the Bank and used as a first step in the qualitative assessment of liquidity adequacy for an individual bank is based upon a cash-flow approach, with assets and liabilities (combined, irrespective of currency denomination) being placed in a 'maturity ladder', with the net positions in each time period being accumulated. The Bank describes the measure as 'a series of accumulating net mismatch positions in successive time bands'. Lending commitments are taken into account through their inclusion as liabilities in the appropriate time band, or as otherwise agreed. The differing degrees of marketability of assets (placed at the start of the ladder and not according to their maturity date) is recognised by applying varying discounts (the more marketable the asset, the lower the discount), against the (normally market) value of the assets. The treatment of loans only nominally repayable on demand (for example, overdrafts) has to be agreed individually with the Bank, and assets of a doubtful value are excluded or otherwise treated on a case-by-case basis. Contractual standby facilities negotiated with other banks are treated as sight assets, taking into account their remaining term and likelihood of renewal. Finally, on the liabilities side, deposits are including according to their earliest maturity, although account will be taken of the stability and diversification of the deposit base in establishing guidelines. Non-deposit liabilities maturing within one year are included but not contingent liabilities, unless they are thought likely to materialise.

A tangential component of UK banking supervision is *deposit insurance*. The Deposit Protection Board was set up by the 1979 Banking Act to administer the Deposit Protection Scheme. Under the Scheme, 75 per cent of the first £10 000 of a depositor's sterling deposits with any one member institution is guaranteed. The fund is financed by a levy on all authorised institutions in proportion to their deposit base, the initial contributions being limited to a minimum of £2500 and a maximum of £300 000. The initial target for contributions was set at between £5m. and £6m. but, if necessary, further sums can be called for. The scheme covers both corporate and personal depositors (but not persons associated with the institution) although the bulk of the former will probably not derive much satisfaction from the application of the *caveat emptor* principle above the £10 000 mark. Overseas institutions operating in the UK may be exempted by the Treasury from the Scheme if they can demonstrate that deposit protection arrangements provided by their home authorities guarantee as good a level of protection as that offered by the Scheme to deposits taken by their UK offices. The purpose of limiting the cover offered to 'small' depositors to only 75 per cent of their investment was to ensure that prospective investors retained an incentive to act prudently in their selection of investments. Otherwise a 'moral hazard' would be created whereby investors had a financial incentive to deposit with the institution offering the highest prospective yield, irrespective of the level of risk incurred by the institution in its business operations.

The measurement, monitoring and control of banks' exposure to movements in exchange rates is a further aspect of UK banking supervision. The Bank accepts (*Bank of England Quarterly Bulletin*, June 1981, p. 235) that the primary responsibility for the control of exposures arising from foreign currency operations rests with the bank's own management. But in order to discharge its supervisory responsibilities, the Bank seeks both to ensure that internal control procedures are adequate and to ascertain the extent of each bank's exposure with a view to relating it to other risks incurred and to its capital base.

The Bank's concern relates to all exposures arising from any uncovered foreign currency position in any currency. Net positions in single currencies are considered alongside the aggregate net position in all currencies. In agreeing (individually with each bank) dealing position guidelines, the Bank accepts the market distinction drawn between 'structural' (that is, those creating exposures of a longer-term nature) and 'dealing' positions (that is, those creating exposures as a result of 'normal', day-to-day operations). Accordingly, it excludes structural positions from consideration. The Bank, nevertheless, includes both dealing and structural positions in the aggregate foreign currency position included in the risk assets ratio used by the Bank in the assessment of capital adequacy, and expects to be consulted on any part of a position that a bank wishes to be classified as structural. Additionally, the institution's particular circumstances and expertise in foreign exchange operations will be taken into account before guidelines are formulated. UK-incorporated banks experienced in foreign exchange can generally expect to agree guidelines limiting: (i) the net 'open' dealing position (that is, the difference between assets and liabilities) in any one currency to 10 per cent of the 'adjusted capital base'; and (ii) net 'short' (that is, net foreign currency liabilities) open dealing positions of all currencies taken together (measured as the sum of its net short open positions, spot and forward) to 15 per cent of the adjusted capital base. The same arrangements apply to the operation of all UK banks' branches at home and abroad and, eventually, subsidiaries will be included to provide a consolidated assessment for capital adequacy purposes of banks' foreign currency exposures. In respect of the UK branches of foreign banks, all are given dealing guidelines unless their dealing operations are minimal.

The final two strands of banking supervision relate to the control of large loan exposures and ownership controls. The Bank operates a guideline whereby banks are expected to notify and justify any individual exposure to non-banks amounting to more than 10 per cent of its capital base (in July 1985 the Bank recommended the introduction of a complementary 25 per cent of capital limit on all individual exposures to non-banks and on loans to groups of 'closely-related' borrowers). In considering the acceptability of exposures, the Bank will take into account the standing of the borrower, the nature of the bank's relationship with the borrower, the nature and extent of security taken, and the bank's expertise in the area of lending undertaken. Exposures to borrowers connected with the bank will receive particularly close attention and, generally speaking, the greater the number of 'large' exposures the greater will be the required capital ratios. Limits are not placed on interbank, country, or sectoral exposures but, again, all exposures of more than 10 per cent of the capital base are subject to examination and may necessitate a higher capital coverage, especially where there is a high concentration of large exposures or where the risks are conspicuously high. Country risk is monitored by the Bank on a consolidated, world-wide basis, and the creditworthiness of individual debtor countries is also independently assessed. No standardised guidelines are specified, however, the Bank preferring to ensure that adequate internal assessment, control and monitoring systems exist, aiding this process through the dissemination of relevant information, (Cooke, 1982, pp. 11-12). In the case of loans to countries engaged in debt rescheduling, the Bank's response has been to engineer a rise in provisions through moral suasion.

Finally, with respect to ownership controls, banks are restricted to a maximum 10 per cent (raised from 5 per cent in September 1984) stake in money brokers, and other understandings exist between the Bank and the relevant government departments (for example, the Department of Trade in respect of links with insurance companies) governing the permissible degree of interlocking ownership with non-bank financial institutions. These guidelines and practices, which are designed to limit the risks associated with connected lending and cross-contamination are, however, likely to be altered as the pace of diversification quickens, a fact exemplified by the Bank's willingness to allow a bank to purchase a discount house during 1985 in preparation for trading in the revamped UK securities markets.

THE JMB AFFAIR

In October 1984, following an approach from the directors of Johnson Matthey plc, who believed that the establishment of the necessary loan provisions adequate to cover anticipated losses arising from the lending activities of their banking arm, JMB, would threaten the whole group, the Bank of England bought JMB and its subsidiaries for a nominal sum (£1) and wrote off a large chunk of their assets. Under the rescue plan, Johnson Matthey was required to put up £50m. to allow JMB to continue trading. On 7 November, after much dispute and, given the uncertainty of eventual provisions, a fruitless search for an outright purchaser of the company, an agreed package of indemnities was announced to cover the possibility that JMB's eventual loan losses might exceed its original £120m. capital base.[3] The package was necessary to keep JMB's lines of credit open and involved the participation of banks (the clearing banks, much to their annoyance, being required to contribute the bulk of the banks' share, set at £35m.), the other four members of the gold ring (£30m.)[4], accepting houses which were not members of the gold ring (£10m.) and the Bank of England (£75m.)[5]. Calls below these limits were to be met in the same proportions. The indemnities relate solely to JMB's commercial loan portfolio and participating banks will share in any 'profits' made on the eventual return of JMB to the private sector. Finally, on 22 November the Bank made a further loan, in the form of a deposit,[6] of £100m., to provide additional working funds.

Perhaps the most far-reaching issue raised by the JMB affair concerns a consideration of the criteria upon which a bank rescue may be justified. In deciding whether or not to rescue an insolvent institution, a central bank must weigh the requirement to preserve the stability of the financial system against the resource misallocation, welfare losses and *moral hazard* implications likely to result from interfering with the workings of the market place. Even for a market not characterised by the full requirements of 'perfect competition', welfare optimisation demands minimal interference with the process of entry to, and exit from, the industry (Baumol, 1982).

The rescue of JMB was the first 'lifeboat' to be launched since the much grander operation mounted during the 1974/75 'fringe banking crisis'

(Reid, 1982), when resources of up to £2.5bn or so were marshalled. On that occasion the Bank's intervention was justified in the following way:

> The Bank thus found themselves confronted with the imminent collapse of several deposit-taking institutions and with the clear danger of a rapidly escalating crisis of confidence. This threatened other deposit-taking institutions and, if left unchecked, would have quickly passed into parts of the banking system proper. While the UK clearing banks still appeared secure from the domestic effects of any run . . . their international exposure was such that the risk to external confidence was a matter of concern for themselves as well as for the Bank. The problem was to avoid a widening circle of collapse through the contagion of fear.
>
> (*Bank of England Quarterly Bulletin*, June 1978, p. 233, para. 25)

Similar arguments, especially relating to the likely damaging effect on external confidence, were advanced to justify the JMB rescue. First and foremost, the Bank argued (Bank of England, 1985) that a number of special factors contributed to rendering a liquidation of JMB (an option which was considered, but rejected) unacceptable because of the potential consequences for the banking system as a whole. It was rejected on the grounds that the Bank might not have been able to contain the likely ensuing confidence crisis and also because the provision of the necessary liquidity in the form of gold would have necessitated recourse by the Bank to the government-owned gold reserves held in the Exchange Equalisation Account or to government guarantees for the borrowing of gold from other sources. Although ruled out on the grounds of impracticability, given the short time available within which a decision had to be taken, it is not obvious why this type of liquidity provision should have posed such an insuperable problem. The Bank felt that it would be unable to convince the market in the early days of the crisis that Johnson Matthey's bullion business was trouble-free, with the result that JMB's failure might have precipitated liquidity problems for the remaining four members of the London 'Gold Ring'. In turn, the crisis of confidence might have spread to other British banks at home and abroad. Some evidence to support this view had apparently been gleaned on 1 October, even before JMB's problems had been announced, when banks in the Far East were said to be refusing to deal with first class British banks, some of which did not operate in the bullion market.

An international perspective was also considered and a relevant factor in this was the rescue by the US authorities of Continental Illinois, an event which appears to have had considerable impact on the Bank's reaction. Indeed, the US experience of a drift of international funds away from their banks in the wake of the Continental Illinois crisis is seen as indicative of the likely response to a collapse of JMB. To the extent that this would have involved a switch out of sterling, exchange rate pressures would also have been intensified.

The second strand of the case for rescuing JMB was the desire to preserve London as the major international bullion market. Failure of JMB would almost certainly have precipitated the collapse of Johnson Matthey plc, carrying the risk that London's position would have suffered irreparable damage, thereby threatening a reduction in future invisible earnings. [An added attraction of JMB to foreigners was its refining capacity and, of the 'Gold Ring' members, JMB was unique in operating such a process.]

The main difficulty for an 'outsider' in trying to compare the two events lies in assessing the scale of the problem present on the two occasions. The risk of further 'contagion' was self-evident in the 1974/75 crisis, with the potential to threaten even the clearing banks (National Westminster was at one stage moved to publicly deny that it would require lifeboat support itself). But even the Bank conceded it was not obvious why the collapse of JMB, engaged to only a comparatively minor degree in commercial banking activities, should have raised a similar spectre of large scale financial collapse. Secondly, the principles guiding the style of rescue were not explicitly stated in the latest event.[7] Nevertheless, Charter Consolidated, the largest shareholder at the time, was brought into the rescue and Johnson Matthey was asked to contribute an amount judged to be the maximum that could be made without seriously impairing its own creditworthiness. Unlike the Slater Walker Limited support package of 1975/77, however, no longer term claim on the parent's assets/profits was taken, partly as a result of the Bank accepting Charter Consolidated's participation on the latter's terms, namely that it was conditional on Johnson Matthey not incurring an open-ended commitment to JMB.

Whether or not the Bank exaggerated the potential dangers of a JMB collapse, a dangerous *moral hazard* has been created. For, although JMB's original shareholder, JMB plc, lost its investment and certain key executives were replaced, others, wholly or partly engaged in the provision of 'banking' services, might be encouraged to act less prudently than circumstances would otherwise dictate. The authorities are patently aware of this danger as indicated in several public statements by the Chancellor of the Exchequer and the Bank of England. But no amount of exhortation is likely to persuade market operators to ignore the Bank's actual deeds in the market place. Despite the existence of the banks' deposit insurance scheme, which might act to reduce the degree of 'automaticity' apparent in the Bank's response to difficulties experienced by 'banking' institutions, the Bank's inclusion of (net) holdings of banks' perpetual floating rate notes within a bank's capital base, given that the bulk will end up in bank hands, compounds the moral hazard problem by reinforcing the Bank's reluctance to let *any* 'banking' institution fail. Finally, as the Bank's actions suggest, if blanket protection of 'small' depositors is to be assured, then the benefits accruing from offering only limited coverage to depositors under the Deposit Protection Scheme will be nullified.

Other issues raised by the JMB affair concern the adequacy of existing authorisation procedures and subsequent surveillance of banks' operations through quarterly discussions with management, the role played by auditors in the supervisory process and the implications for the regulation of diversified financial conglomerates. Subsidiary issues relate to the competence of senior Bank supervisory staff (JMB was allowed to produce its March 1984 quarterly return, due in April, in June 1984 and then to postpone a meeting between its directors and the Bank, planned for July, until August), the adequacy of existing supervisory staff numbers and their training (the Bank admitted that JMB's regular returns did contain some clues to the developing crisis which might have been picked up earlier, for example, the rapid growth of the commercial loan book, the large and growing exposures to less than first class names and a declining risk assets ratio), and the adequacy of existing links between the Bank and the Treasury.

The fundamental weakness in existing authorisation procedures, whereby Recognised Banks are supervised less rigorously than LDTs, was highlighted by the JMB affair. Admittedly, until this case little evidence had emerged to call this aspect of banking supervision into question, but this does not necessarily mean that all other Recognised Banks have been adequately supervised. Rather, it may be the case that the scale of any problem existing elsewhere has, to date, been contained. Secondly, the appalling catalogue of incompetence unearthed by the Bank (Bank of England, 1985, pp. 34–5) calls into question the Bank's application of part of the authorisation procedures. For, by its own admission, the Bank positively vetted individuals for the purpose of running a banking operation who subsequently were found guilty of gross ineptitude in virtually every area of commercial banking practice. Surveillance practices, subsequent to authorisation, are also called into question, given the extreme incompetence displayed by JMB management over which the Bank has presided, the Bank's inability to ensure adequate loan diversification despite the existence of a 10 per cent of capital 'guideline',[8] and the Department of Trade and Industry's willingness to tolerate late filing of accounts.[9]

ROLE OF AUDITORS

Auditors occupy an awkward position within the supervisory process. Under the Companies Act they are required to report to the shareholders whether or not the accounts prepared by a bank's directors provide the required 'true and fair view'. In coming to a conclusion they will review the bank's systems material to its accounts (for example, internal audit and inspection systems) and examine transactions on a sample basis to validate the authenticity of the records (Fowle, 1985.) They will then consider the judgements made by the directors in highly sensitive areas (for example, in making provisions against bad and doubtful debts), discuss problem loans, loan provisioning, and so on, with senior management and, finally, report back to the directors, with recommendations where appropriate. If, at that stage, the auditors cannot agree with the directors that the accounts present a 'true and fair view' they can either resign or qualify the accounts, either of which risks precipitating a run on the bank. Without the client's permission, the auditor is unable, at any stage, to express fears to banking supervisors. Whether or not JMB's auditors noticed the internal control and managerial deficiencies, and accounting misrepresentations, is therefore not the only relevant point because, assuming they did, how strongly did they register their dissatisfaction with JMB's directors and were they right in signing an unqualified audit report? If the auditors are to be criticised by the Bank[10] the criticism must rest largely on any failure to spot internal control deficiencies and accounting misrepresentations, for the qualification of the audit would, in all likelihood, only have resulted in a sudden and haphazard collapse of the bank, thereby complicating any subsequent 'lifeboat' operation. The carefully-orchestrated rescue operation of the Bank that actually took place is obviously to be preferred.

The role of the auditor leads conveniently into the next issue, namely the desirability of continuing with a supervisory system that depends so heavily on the auditing process for its effectiveness. In the UK, banking supervision is carried out according to the legislation embodied within the 1979 Banking Act. Despite this statutory element, governing authorisation procedures and deposit protection, the Bank's system of supervision is still a flexible one, with a wide measure of discretion remaining in the interpretation and application of the authorisation procedures and with the assessment of the adequacy of prudential standards (for example, relating to capital, liquidity and exposure to exchange rate risk). The cornerstone of the system remains the management interviews that follow the Bank's statistical analysis of the required returns, with no requirement that the latter be audited. This approach contrasts sharply with that taken by bank supervisors in other countries which adopt a policy of formal bank inspections. But even there the system is not infallible (witness the collapse of Continental Illinois in the US in 1984) so, taking account of the Bank's previous track record, calls for the abandonment of the current, flexible approach in favour of a more formalised, inspection-based system are unlikely to be entertained. Nevertheless, the weak links of the present system should be strengthened (see below).

THE AFTERMATH

An important consequence of the JMB 'lifeboat' operation was the establishment of a committee (the 'Committee set up to consider the system of Banking Supervision') involving Treasury and Bank officials and an outside expert, to review banking supervisory procedures to determine if any changes were necessary. In particular, the committee was asked to consider the relationship between bank auditor and supervisor, the handling of risk concentration and assessment of asset quality, the statistical requirements imposed on subject institutions and the adequacy of existing staff resources and training programmes in the Bank's supervisory department.

The Committee made the following recommendations (Cmnd 9550, June 1985): (i) the replacement of the existing two-tier system of authorisation with a single Bank authorisation to take deposits; (ii) that legislative steps be taken to dismantle the barriers presently preventing discussions taking place between auditors and supervisors, with a view to allowing for a regular dialogue between the two parties; (iii) that exposure to a single non-bank borrower or interconnected group of borrowers should not exceed 25 per cent of a bank's capital; (iv) that banks should set up audit committees and appoint finance directors; (v) that internal control and reporting requirements be strengthened;[11] (vi) that the number of staff (especially accountants) engaged in the supervision department at the Bank be increased and given commercial banking experience; (vii) that the ceiling for deposit protection granted under the Deposit Protection Scheme be raised from £10 000 to £20 000.

Recommendations (i), (v) and (vi) are all straightforward yet necessary amendments and, as such, merit no further discussion. Item (iv) represents an attempt to improve upon the internal auditing process but stops short of requiring a full audit of prudential returns (spot checks were, however, recommended). Moves towards the Canadian system, whereby the authorities 'authorise' accounting firms for bank audit purposes and require frequent change in the auditing firms employed by individual banks might also usefully be considered. These measures would provide a means of improving audit standards and of reducing the risk of 'moral hazards' arising from the establishment of close affinities between banks and auditors respectively. Items (iii) and (vii) merit further consideration. (Although item (ii) is the most far-reaching and controversial reform suggested, the debate is not pursued further in this paper.)

The suggestion that the large exposure guideline be changed to 25 per cent of a bank's capital, with no legislative support, is curious to say the least in that JMB's problems are recognised to have largely arisen as a result of breaches of the old 10 per cent guideline. The Bank has admitted that breaches of this guideline by other banks were commonplace (in practice, the guideline represented a reporting threshold and point of enquiry) but a relaxation of the guideline to a 25 per cent level, even if *de facto* it becomes more of a ceiling, can hardly represent a tightening up of loan exposure control. Admittedly, the Bank still expects to be notified of any single non-bank exposure amounting to over 10 per cent of a bank's capital and, under normal circumstances, will probably insist on an appropriate capital cover; nevertheless, the ruling appears excessively generous (although not by international standards).

The final recommendation, that the maximum cover available to a depositor under the banks' Deposit Protection Scheme be doubled to £20 000, appears irrelevant to the JMB affair, although indexing (but in this case overindexing) of the cover is presumably justified in its own right. For, even with the higher figure, the necessity for a 'lifeboat' for JMB, as perceived by the Bank, would not have been reduced as the problem was a fear of a contagious liquidity crisis rather than an isolated bank collapse. Assuming that the purpose of the proposal is to improve the Deposit Protection Scheme, a more radical and appropriate reform would have linked the contributor's premium to the degree of risk incurred through its operations.

OUTSTANDING ISSUES

Capital adequacy

The most basic issue with respect to capital adequacy is the definition of capital itself. The Bank's approach has already been outlined in brief but more detailed justification for this is now called for. A major problem facing supervisory authorities around the world in recent years has been the reconciliation of a desire to improve the capital ratios of banks, at a time when the perceived risks of banking (especially on the international front) have risen appreciably (Group of Thirty, 1982a, 1982b), with the need to ensure adequate provisioning against bad and doubtful debts. The problem is compounded by fiscal considerations, which favour both subordinated debt at the expense of equity capital by allowing tax relief on interest payments but not dividends, and specific against general provisions by confining tax deductibility to the former. Moreover, fiscal changes can sometimes necessitate sudden revisions to banks' policies on deferred tax provisioning, and profitability considerations influence the banks' ability to boost capital through both equity issues and retained earnings.

The response of the UK clearing banks to these pressures has been fairly uniform and, to a large degree, determined by the Bank's approach to defining capital. Of particular significance here is the official line taken on subordinated loan capital and debt provisioning.

The Bank's treatment of loan stock issues in its 1980 paper differs from that which obtained since 1975. Its former view was that the function of loan stock (which had to be subordinated and medium- to long-term) was to finance part of the infrastructure of the business and not to provide a cushion against losses. This view rested on the observation that, unlike shareholders' funds, loan stocks are impermanent, do not offer flexibility with respect to servicing costs, and are not available to absorb losses without precipitating a liquidation. This observation, of course, still held true in 1980, but the Bank was by then more conciliatory, emphasising that, in spite of the drawbacks, fully-subordinated medium- to long-term loan stocks might reduce the threat to creditors' confidence in the event of an institution experiencing difficulties and so enhance its ability to survive. Moreover, where the loan stocks were long term and denominated in foreign currency, maturity and currency mismatches might be reduced. In the light of these considerations, the Bank decided to allow the inclusion of fully-subordinated loan stock, up to a maximum of one-third, within the capital base provided that they were of a minimum initial period to maturity of five years, did not incorporate restrictive covenants triggering early repayments, and were subject to an amortisation factor once passing within the five years remaining to maturity threshold. This last stipulation was designed to 'discourage unduly short initial terms, soften the impact on capital ratios when loan stocks mature and are not replaced, and reflect the diminishing comfort afforded'. Finally, the Bank demonstrated its determination to prevent an illusory boosting of capital for the banking system as a whole, in recognition of the fact that the bulk of bank issues are held by other banks, by insisting that all banks operating in the UK deduct their holdings of other banks' issues in calculating the size of their capital base. In so doing the risk of a domino-style collapse of the banking system is reduced.

Table 1.1   Gearing ratios of the English clearing banks: 1982–85

Bank	Gearing ratio (%)			
	end 1982	*end 1983*	*end 1984*	*end-May 1985*
Barclays	3.9	4.6	4.1	5.5
Lloyds	4.4	5.2	5.0	6.3
Midlands	3.9	4.5	4.4	5.0
National Westminster	4.6	4.9	4.5	6.0

Source: Published accounts and (for end-May 1985) estimates.

The Bank's limited seal of approval for subordinated loan stock issues was eagerly seized upon by the clearing banks in the early 1980s but by the end of 1984 most were near to or up against the stipulated ceiling. Accordingly, different means had to be found for raising capital ratios (all four English clearing banks suffered a decline in their gearing ratios during 1984 – see Table 1.1) to levels expected by investors and supervisors alike. To a limited degree, improvement was sought by restraining balance sheet growth and/or raising the quality of loans and the level of commission income for a given-sized balance sheet, but the major contribution still had to come from new capital-raising activities. Barclays broke the ice in March 1985 with a £513m. rights issue but the other clearing banks did not follow suit. Instead, they opted for perpetual floating rate note (FRN) issues after Lloyd's pioneering $750m. May 1985 issue which, for the first time, the Bank accepted as 'primary' capital.[12]

The Bank's earlier treatment of undated/perpetual FRNs was explained in a note circulated in November 1984 to members of the British Bankers' Association containing new proposals for measuring capital adequacy in the light of recent capital market innovations. A maximum of a half of primary capital could be held in FRN form provided that: (i) the issue never has to be repaid, except in the case of liquidation; (ii) the issue converts automatically into equity if the issuing bank gets into financial difficulties; and (iii) no cross-default clauses, negative pledges or clauses which trigger early repayment of the monies raised are contained in the terms of the issue. The market's initial reaction to the Bank's ruling was that the market in perpetual FRNs would collapse as anyone prepared to buy the notes in the form demanded by the Bank as an alternative to pure equity would probably demand a substantial discount, thereby making the issue prohibitively expensive for the banks. In the event the market could not have been more wrong, for the May 1985 issues, admittedly in slightly different form from that initially demanded by the Bank, were snapped up by investors at very fine margins ($\frac{1}{8}$ per cent to $\frac{1}{4}$ per cent above LIBOR (London Inter-Bank Offer Rate)). Given that a very high proportion of FRN issues ends up in bank hands (perhaps as much as 80 per cent), the (bank) purchasers were presumably of the view that the collapse of an English clearing bank was an extremely remote possibility and one which, at any rate, would only likely occur after their own demise! The collapse of Continental Illinois in the US in 1984 and the practice of central banks bailing out depositors but *not* shareholders of individual banks should caution against complacency, however. Indeed, the 'triple-B+' rating given to Midland Bank's issue by Standard and Poor's, the US credit rating agency, suggests a more reasoned investor approach has now set in following the initial euphoria.

Moving on to an assessment of the Bank's treatment of *debt provisioning*, the justification for including only general bad debt provisions (this was *not* the case before 1980 when specific provisions were included also) in the capital base is that provisions set aside for likely losses that have already been identified are not available to cushion future unidentified losses. This ruling, making allowance for the tax deductibility of specific reserves, favours general rather than specific provisioning for all except the relatively well-capitalised banks, which the English clearing banks certainly weren't in the early 1980s (see Table 1.1). Accordingly, only modest specific provisions (especially against 'international lending') were made by the clearing banks during the 1983/84 financial year. For the whole of 1984, however, the policy was reversed, with the bulk of the increase (£500m. on 1983) in bad debt provisions being made in specific form. As Table 1.2 indicates, this approach was adopted by each of the English clearing banks.

An explanation for this change in clearing bank policy on debt provisioning, in the face of continuing pressures to improve capital ratios, may lie in the banks' desire to boost recorded profits and hence maintain dividend payments in real terms, perhaps as a precursor to future rights issues. This highlights the problem facing bank supervisors in assessing the adequacy of debt provisions. The final decision of an individual bank will, subject to meeting the requirements of the 1981 Companies Act, always

Table 1.2   1984 debt provisions of English clearing banks (£m.)

Provisions	Bank			
	Barclays	Lloyds	Midland	National Westminster
Specific				
domestic	178	103	} 471	104
international	267	101		137
General				
domestic	} 80	} 65	} 145	} 110
international				
Total	525	269	616¹	351

Note: 1.   Of this total, £456m. was attributable to losses experienced by Midland's subsidiary Crocker National Bank. If the influence of Crocker National Bank is excluded from the figures, specific provisions total £150m. (down £38m. on the 1983 figure) and the general provision amounts to zero.

Source: Published accounts.

reflect a compromise between adequately reflecting the risk of losses likely to arise (and hence satisfying auditors, regulators and the long-term interests of shareholders), recording profits that are thought politically acceptable to the incumbent political administration (that is, levels which will dissuade the Treasury from mounting new revenue-raising exercises), and satisfying the short-run desires of shareholders and possibly facilitating the imminent fund-raising activities of the bank itself by declaring adequate dividends. The Bank faces an unenviable task in reconciling and weighting the often conflicting requirements of interested parties and coming to a conclusion on the adequacy of provisions made by banks.

A problem subsidiary to that of defining capital is how to take account of banks' off-balance-sheet activities within the assessment and measurement of capital adequacy. The recent rapid surge in such activities has demonstrated, yet again, that prudential control, like monetary control, is not immune to disintermediation, but supervisory authorities are only just beginning to come to grips with the problem. The response of the Bank to what the Governor has termed the 'securitisation' of lending (that is, the switch from making normal loans to trading in and underwriting security issues), and the mushrooming of activity in new markets (options, futures, interest rate swaps, forward rate agreements and interest rate protection packages), has been to advise caution. With respect to the latter set of activities, the Bank has expressed fears about the competence of management to exercise adequate internal control over the use of highly sophisticated computer programming techniques and a review is currently being held to enquire into the risks that can arise from the acceptance of contingent liabilities through these mediums. On the 'securitisation' of lending, the Bank has already acted (April 1985), demanding that 'note issuance facilities' (NIFs) and 'revolving underwriting facilities' (RUFs),[13] whether or not they have been drawn down, be treated as contingent liabilities for the purpose of calculating risk asset ratios (that is, bearing a weight of 0.5, half the amount allotted to a normal loan) and that the risks arising from the sale by banks of packages of assets be taken into account in the assessment of capital adequacy. Banks involved in the underwriting of commercial issues of short-term paper run the risk that, in adverse conditions, they are left holding worthless investments. Although participating banks do attempt to minimise their likely exposure to losses by confining facilities to borrowers with a high credit rating (for example, banks, 'blue-chip' companies and governments), and do charge commitment fees (commonly in the range $\frac{1}{24}$ to $\frac{1}{32}$ per cent), these are regarded as inadequate by the authorities to cover the risks involved.

A further problem relates to the assessment of capital adequacy for banks or banking groups engaged in a wide range of financial, and even non-financial, activities. One approach (one the Bank has indicated it will take to primary dealers in the new gilt edged market) is to 'dedicate' or ascribe part of business capital to particular areas of operation but this raises a number of issues. For example, to what extent do different business operations require separate incorporation rather than a simple earmarking of capital, and how should 'banking' status, with its attendant privileges and responsibilities, affect the attitude of regulators in their assessment of capital adequacy for conglomerates incorporating 'banking' operations? Finally, how should the adequacy of capital be assessed for a securities trading operation, an area in which banks are becoming heavily involved?

The final major issue outstanding on the capital adequacy front is the need, despite the risk of impairing flexibility (Dale, 1982, pp. 25-9), for greater harmonisation of the regulatory treatment adopted by supervisors around the world. This would prove beneficial on the following counts: (i) it would improve global resource allocation by allowing investors to make sensible comparisons of banks' capital positions whatever the banks' country of incorporation or place of operation;[14] (ii) it would reduce competitive inequalities faced by banks operating in an international market; and (iii) it would improve the stability of the international banking system by, for example, ensuring that all supervisory authorities adopt both the consolidation principle (and so remove the incentive for business to gravitate to areas of perceived supervisory 'laxity') and the guidelines of the Basle *Concordat* governing the division of supervisory responsibilities between parent and host supervisor.

Liquidity adequacy

The flexible approach taken by the Bank to the assessment of liquidity adequacy has effectively dealt with most of the criticisms of previous liquidity controls. These embraced the arbitrariness of designating a certain class of assets as 'liquid', with the associated distortive effects on relative yields, the impracticability of applying norms to the whole banking community, the illogicality of specifying requirements in the form of specific rather than average levels of liquid asset holdings, and the potential dangers associated with an overlap with monetary policy. Additionally, most concede that the Bank, as guardian of the stability of the financial system, has the right to ensure that internal control and monitoring procedures at least are adequate. Moreover, the existence of deposit protection schemes does not obviate the need for liquidity controls as the former protect only the nominal value and not the liquidity of deposits, bearing in mind that costs arising from delays in restoring the liquidity of deposits in the event of a financial collapse or assisted merger can be substantial.

If any criticisms are to be made of the liquidity arrangements, perhaps the most valid concerns the lack of any explicit 'cost-benefit' analysis, a feature common to the other strands of banking supervision. Of particular concern are the disintermediation incentives provided (for example, for business to move off-balance sheet or offshore) and the competitive inequities introduced, especially between locally-incorporated and foreign banks. Also, banks and supervisors alike must remain alert to increasing depositor sensitivity to interest rate and service differentials, a process accelerated by rapid technological advance, with concomitant ramifications for deposit stability.

Deposit insurance

The most basic, yet continuing, controversy with respect to deposit insurance relates to the very need for such arrangements. Arguments in favour embrace the following: (i) they help preserve the stability of the financial system by promoting investor confidence; (ii) that the protection of the nominal value of some monetary assets is a communal benefit (Santomero and Watson, 1977); (iii) that it is necessary to provide a safety haven for the small, and by implication, unsophisticated investor; (iv) that it is preferable for banks to pay explicitly for deposit protection rather than to receive it through government largesse in the form of an implicit government guarantee. Opponents, however, would emphasise the following: (i) 'moral hazards' may be created by discouraging the investing public from undertaking adequate appraisal of prospective risk-adjusted rates of return and by encouraging bank management to take higher risks for a given pattern of expected rates of return; (ii) the provision of an adequate risk-return spectrum of investment opportunity may be impaired; (iii) the costs incurred, in terms of funding and administering deposit insurance schemes, might outweigh the benefits which, at any rate, might be achieved by alternative means. As the success of the scheme depends on the strength of the contributing members (assuming the schemes are industry-run), deposit insurance cannot be used in isolation of other supervisory techniques to guarantee the nominal value of deposits. In this sense, deposit insurance imposes an additional burden on subject institutions unless measures are taken to reduce the supervisory effort elsewhere. For example, the existence of deposit insurance may obviate, to a large degree, the need for official lifeboats.

Despite the initial reluctance of the clearing banks, which argued that the introduction of deposit insurance would reduce the level of competition in financial markets and underwrote the unfortunate principle of the more efficient subsidising the less efficient or prudent, the Deposit Protection Scheme was eventually introduced with features designed to minimise the moral hazard dangers and overcome some of the other objections. For example, coverage is limited to a relatively low value of deposits (£10 000) and only 75 per cent protection is provided. The failure, however, to link the premium payable to the level of risk incurred by the insured institution (which might, for example, be readily obtained by standardising the risk assets ratio computed for capital adequacy purposes) detracts somewhat from these efforts. Moreover, it is not clear to what extent, if any, the existence of the scheme has allowed for an offsetting reduction in supervisory effort elsewhere.

CONCLUDING COMMENTS

The Bank of England issued two consultative documents on proposals to reform banking supervision on 19 July 1985. The recommendations include: abolition of the two-tier authorisation system for depqsit-takers, with the minimum net-asset requirement raised from £250 000 to £1 m.; limiting large exposures to single non-bank or 'closely-related' groups of borrowers to 25 per cent of capital (in addition, all exposures to non-banks of over 10 per cent are to be reported); broadening the powers of the Bank to obtain and disseminate information; introducing limited independent checking (for example, by the banks' auditors) of prudential information; making amendments to the Deposit Protection Scheme involving an increase in the level of protection offered, an increase in the minimum level of contribution, and removal of the Treasury's power to exempt overseas institutions under certain circumstances. These recommendations would plug some of the supervisory 'gaps' evident in the wake of the JMB affair but do not go far enough in improving the standards of prudential supervision in the UK. Bearing in mind the principles that should underlie any system of prudential controls, as for instance contained in the Campbell Report on Australia (Australian Government Publishers Service, 1981), the following measures might usefully be considered for adoption: (i) full auditing of prudential returns; (ii) the 'authorisation' of bank auditors; (iii) a review of existing authorisation procedures, additional to the ending of the two-tier system; (iv) linking a contributor's 'premium' under the Deposit Protection Scheme to the degree of risk incurred; (v) providing legislative backing to tighter loan exposure 'rules' (the sanction of de-authorisation appears a weak deterrent given it is rarely exercised); (vi) a raising of the weighting (currently 0.2) given to 'market loans with listed banks' within the computation of a bank's risk assets ratio, in order to reduce the risk of a domino-style collapse arising from interbank exposures and thus, hopefully, making it easier for the Bank, under certain circumstances, to allow 'banking' institutions to fail; (vii) limiting the diversification opportunities open to banks. Whilst the adoption of these measures risks impairment of the flexibility of prudential supervision, it would go some way to reassuring investors that self-regulation of financial markets will only persist as long as market operators demonstrate their ability to regulate themselves in a manner which satisfies the expectations of investors and supervisors alike. The recent Lloyd's underwriting scandals and the JMB affair suggest that a reaffirmation of a desire for *effective* depositor/investor protection is in order.

Notes

1. This paper does not incorporate any material made available after July 1985.
2. The capital base comprises: (i) amounts partly or fully-paid up on issued share (ordinary and non-redeemable preference) capital and

share premium; (ii) loan capital (up to a third of the total capital base net of outstanding goodwill and subject to straight line 'amortisation' in the last five years of life) which is fully subordinated to other creditors (including depositors) and which has an initial term to maturity of at least five years and involves no restrictive covenants; (iii) general bad debt provisions, less any associated deferred tax asset; (iv) general reserves (including 'inner' reserves) plus the balance on the profit and loss account; and (v) minority interests, when included in accounts as a result of the consolidation of subsidiary companies not wholly-owned.

3. In the event, the Bank decided in May 1985 that provisions of £245m. were necessary to cover the losses incurred. This resulted in the Bank and the other participants in the 'lifeboat' contributing half of the shortfall each. Although the scale of the provisions is thought adequate, this will remain subject to review on a quarterly basis until March 1986 when the indemnity agreement signed by the banks in March 1985 is due to expire.

4. JMB is a member of a group of five big gold bullion dealers which jointly 'fix' the price of gold twice-daily in London.

5. The Bank's contribution, if called upon, will come from the Banking Department's reserve which led the government to claim that taxpayers' money was not involved. However, a fall in these reserves might necessitate an increase in the tax on banks (that is, through an increase in the 0.5 per cent of eligible liabilities, non-operational cash requirement), which is likely to be borne by shareholders and consumers of financial services alike. Also lower banking profits by the Banking Department will result in a reduced contribution to the Exchequer.

6. In May 1985 this was converted into capital in the shape of £50m. ordinary shares, £25m. redeemable shares and £25m. subordinated loan stock dated 1995. The capital is to be recovered if and when JMB is returned to the private sector, which is expected to be in 1986.

7. The approach adopted by the 'Control Committee' of the Bank of England and the English and Scottish clearing banks during the fringe banking crisis was set out in the *Bank of England Quarterly Bulletin*, June 1978, pp. 233–9. Before agreeing to provide the support the Committee required to be satisfied that: (i) the company seeking support was currently trading solvently and, on the basis of best estimates possible at that time, was likely to remain solvent provided it received liquidity support; (ii) the company exhibited sufficient banking characteristics to justify support and had attracted a significant level of deposits from the public; (iii) the company did not possess any institutional shareholders whose interest in the company was such that they might properly be expected to provide the necessary support. Where other financial institutions were involved, either as significant shareholders or as large depositors, they would be pressed to contribute by increasing their lending or, at the very least, not withdrawing their deposits. A margin over LIBOR (1.5–

2.0 per cent) was generally charged, according to the perception of risk involved, although account was taken of the need not to prejudice the chance of the supported company severing its dependence on support funds and re-establishing its position in the market. Security, when available, was taken when deemed appropriate.

8. The Bank expects to be notified of any single non-bank exposure amounting to over 10 per cent of a bank's capital and, depending on factors such as the standing of the borrower, the nature of the bank's relationship with the borrower, the nature and extent of security taken, and the bank's expertise in the area of lending undertaken, will specify an appropriate additional capital cover. Breaches of the guideline are, however, commonplace, and the Bank condones this on the grounds that a 'rule' would be too constricting. Complicating factors in JMB's case were the non-reporting of certain large exposures and the persistent understatement of the size of the two largest exposures. In its 1985 Annual Report, the Bank claims that the reported figures for these two exposures at end-June 1983 were 15 per cent and 12 per cent of capital compared to the 'true' figures of 26 per cent and 17 per cent respectively, and at end-June 1984 were 38 per cent and 34 per cent compared to the 'true' figures of 76 per cent and 39 per cent respectively.

9. Leaving aside the JMB case, Financial Intelligence and Research (1984) found that one in five LDTs had not filed accounts for more than two years despite the Companies Act requirement that reports be filed within seven to ten months (depending upon the kind of business undertaken) of the end of the financial year.

10. Both the Bank and Johnson Matthey plc are suing JMB's auditors, Arthur Young, for substantial damages arising from their alleged negligence.

11. This is to include measures to ensure that statistical returns are lodged with the Bank on the due dates. The Committee suggests that late submissions prompt immediate action from the Bank in the form of a visitation and, perhaps, an inspection of the books.

12. A definition of capital, comprising the highest quality components, favoured by banking supervisory authorities in the United States and adopted by the Bank in 1984. In the UK context, it is defined as shareholders funds plus general reserves plus general provisions against loan losses plus minority interests plus (since May 1985) qualifying FRN issues.

13. NIFs and RUFs were first developed in the Euromarkets as techniques for underwriting the short-term security issues of corporate bodies, thereby ensuring the continued availability of short-term money through the medium term (seven to ten years) for corporate borrowers. They represent an attempt to reconcile lenders' preferences for liquidity with borrowers' preferences for medium-term finance. Typically, a group of underwriting banks will guarantee the availability of funds for the medium term by agreeing either to purchase any unsold short-term notes issued by the borrower at each roll-over date or to provide a stand-by credit. If the borrower is a

bank, the paper is normally in the form of a certificate of deposit and for non-bank borrowers, in the form of promissory notes. A contingent liability is therefore incurred by the underwriting bank as the borrower might, at some stage during the term of the contract, run into financial difficulties and even default.

14. This would require convergence on the definition of 'capital' and hence on the regulators' treatment of inner reserves, subordinated debt (including FRN issues), bad debt provisions, deferred tax provisions, minority interests, and so on. Harmonisation of accounting conventions and fiscal systems would thus be required.

References

AGPS (1981) *'Australian Financial System: Final Report of the Committee of Enquiry'* (Campbell Report), Australian Government Publishing Service (Canberra).

Bank of England (1975) 'The capital and liquidity adequacy of banks', *Bank of England Quarterly Bulletin*, September.

Bank of England (1978) 'The secondary banking crisis and the Bank of England's support operations'. *Bank of England Quarterly Bulletin*, June.

Bank of England (1980) *The Measurement of Liquidity*, consultative paper issued by the Bank of England in March 1980.

Bank of England (1980) 'The measurement of capital', *Bank of England Quarterly Bulletin*, September.

Bank of England (1981) 'The liquidity of banks', *Bank of England Quarterly Bulletin*, March.

Bank of England (1981) 'Foreign currency exposure', *Bank of England Quarterly Bulletin*, June.

Bank of England (1981) *The Measurement of Liquidity*, consultative paper issued by the Bank of England in the summer of 1981.

Bank of England (1982) 'The measurement of liquidity', *Bank of England Quarterly Bulletin*, September.

Bank of England (1984) *Bank of England, Report and Accounts*, June.

Bank of England (1985) *Bank of England, Report and Accounts*, June.

Baumol, W. K. (1982) 'Contestable Markets: An Uprising in the Theory of Industry Structure', *American Economic Review*, 72: 1–15.

Cooke, W. P. (1982) *'International Lending in a Fragile World Economy'*, paper presented to the *Societé Universitaire Européenne de Recherches Financières* Colloquium, Vienna, April.

Dale, R. (1982) *'Safeguarding the International Banking System: Present Arrangements and a Framework for Reform'*, paper presented at the *Societé Universitaire Européenne de Recherches Financières* (SUERF Colloquium), Vienna, April.

Financial Intelligence and Research (1984) 'UK licensed deposit-takers: financial status and performance (London, February).

Fowle, M. (1985) 'Should bank auditors and supervisors talk to each other?', *The Banker*, April.

Group of Thirty (1982a) *Risks in International Bank Lending* (New York).
Group of Thirty (1982b) *How Bankers see the World Financial Market* (New York).
Reid, M. (1982) *The Secondary Banking Crisis 1973-75* (London: Macmillan Press).
Report of the Committee set up to consider the System of Banking Supervision, Cmnd 9550 (HMSO, June 1985).
Santomero, A. M. and Watson, R. D. (1977) 'Determining an optimal capital standard for the banking industry', *Journal of Finance*, 32: 1267-82.

2 Structural Changes in the British Capital Markets*

Charles Goodhart

In this paper I shall describe certain recent developments in the London financial and capital markets, and try to draw from them certain more general lessons about the future directions of change.

In part, as a result of encouragement by the authorities, in part from self-interest, in part as a result of historical developments, the financial system in the UK during the early twentieth century became strictly compartmentalised, with groups of financial institutions providing similar, limited, well-defined intermediary functions, and forming themselves into separate associations, or 'clubs'. The authorities, notably the Bank of England, typically supported such 'club' formation. It has had obvious administrative advantages; it enables the authorities to deal with a handful of elected club officials, rather than a multiplicity of individual institutions. Moreover, the clubs can be required to design themselves and install a workable and adequate regulatory system, applying certain tests of professional competence for entry, and monitoring their members' continuing good behaviour on the basis of an agreed code of conduct. By such means much of the burden of supervision and regulation can be delegated to the 'club'. Moreover, the cartelised nature of the 'club', often including limitations on price and interest rate adjustment in particular, and competition in general, protected the profitability of the members, including the less efficient, and thus made failures, crises, and so on, less common.

Anyhow, soon after the start of the twentieth century, each of the institutional groups, such as the clearing banks, the building societies, the insurance companies, and so on, had a separate, limited, and well-defined functional role. Each distinct group tended to form its separate association, such as the Building Societies' Association, or the London Discount Market Association, which would set requirements for entry, and rules of

*I am extremely grateful to Bill Allen, Patricia Jackson, David Llewellyn and Hilary Stonefrost for guidance and support in preparing this paper. Not only are the remaining errors my responsibility, but so also are the idiosyncratic judgements.

31

behaviour, frequently including rules which constrained freedom of competition in pricing, and in setting interest rates, thus acting as a price-fixing cartel.

THE HISTORICAL STRUCTURE OF THE LONDON STOCK EXCHANGE

These features have been as apparent in the British capital market as elsewhere within the financial system in the UK. In the London Stock Exchange (LSE) the functions of the main agents have been compartmentalised and restricted. Thus the dealers, who wished to benefit from the various advantages of doing business there, advantages primarily arising from its size, liquidity and central position, but also certain fiscal advantages connected with Stamp Duty on transfers of listed shares, have had to belong to the LSE, which set rules of entry and rules of behaviour. Among these latter are that members of the Stock Exchange could only act in a *single* capacity, that is either as agents of clients who wished to buy, or sell, securities (the broker), or alternatively as principals who would buy, or sell, securities for their own books (the jobber). In order to have a well-functioning market, it is desirable for somebody always to be prepared to form the other side of an order from a client, via his broker, to buy or sell. Since the flow of buying and selling orders from clients will not exactly match, this requires that the market be made by a principal, prepared to buy or sell for his own book – in this case, in the LSE, the jobber. In order to strengthen the position of the jobber, and thus make the market broader and more liquid, the Stock Exchange required that all deals be put through a jobber, rather than competitively matched by one broker dealing either in-house, or with another broker. This would have been difficult to enforce, if there had been a strong competitive incentive for brokers to deal more cheaply amongst themselves than via the jobbers. In order to reduce this incentive, a key element of the Stock Exchange rule book required minimum commissions to be paid to brokers on Stock Exchange deals. This rule, however, raised the cost of dealing above that which more aggressive competition might have brought about, in particular for large block deals.

Although this was an obvious constraint on trade, its effect in underpinning single capacity dealing had a number of attendant advantages. The separation of agent and principal reduced the likelihood of conflict of interest. Thus, when a market operator is acting both as agent and principal, he will have an incentive to park securities, which have become an uncomfortably large proportion of his own portfolio, into the hands of his clients. Such conflicts of interest can be frequent; they can also at times be difficult to recognise clearly. For example, a financial institution directly involved with a company as a principal, for example, as a manager or underwriter of a new issue, will generally emphasise (to themselves) the good points of that company, and honestly not realise the existence of potential conflicts of interest in placing large amounts of such shares in the portfolios of customers over whose business the financial institution has some discretionary control. Such conflicts of interest already arise where a financial intermediary, for example, a merchant bank, acts both as a principal in some market operation, and also in a discretionary role as adviser and portfolio manager to clients. The ending of single capacity is likely to increase the potentiality for such conflicts: it made the Stock Exchange easier to police, and somewhat less subject to misfeasance, though temptations, and opportunities, to improper activities, for example, by advising unnecessarily frequent deals (that is, 'churning'), through the use of insider information, or even by straight fraud, were by no means eliminated by the maintenance of single capacity.

Furthermore, the separation of function on the Stock Exchange, as was broadly true elsewhere in financial markets in the UK, allowed the com-partmentalised functions to be carried out by agents with less capital than might otherwise have been necessary. This was partly because the limitation of function brought with it some constraint on the range of risks undertaken by the agent, reduced the extent of information required by the operators of the business, and increased the transparency of the firm to supervisors/regulators. Also, the cartelised system, and restrictions on entry, tended to allow higher average margins and more certain profits. Such risk limitation was obviously true of brokers. Since they were dealing purely as agents, and not as principals for their own book, their risk was strictly limited, while the existence of minimum commissions provided a known, and reasonably comfortable margin. So brokerage houses needed relatively little capital. Since little capital was needed, and in order to re-emphasise the personal and unlimited responsibility of the broker, the Stock Exchange restricted membership of the Exchange to unincorporated Partnerships until 1969. Thereafter, the Stock Exchange Council, recognising, as Sir Nicholas Goodison commented in the Bridge lecture of February 1985 (reproduced in *The Stock Exchange Quarterly*, March 1985), that brokerage firms needed to tap outside capital, changed the rules to allow firms to form themselves into limited companies, and to take in outside shareholders. But a limit of 10 per cent of a firm's capital was placed on any one such outside shareholder (which was raised to 29.9 per cent in

1982, this latter being just below the arbitrary point where the Take-over Panel in the UK reckons that effective control passes). But few firms, partly because of the fiscal advantages of remaining as partnerships, took advantage of this opportunity (until the floodgates opened after the prospective abandonment of minimum commission in 1983). In the statistics, indeed, brokers remain treated as part of the personal sector; not even as other financial intermediaries.

Although jobbers, dealing as principals for their own book, were subject to greater risk, the fact that all deals had to be put through their books meant that they were assured a higher turnover and better information, which gave them a larger regular dealing return than might otherwise have occurred under a more competitive system. Even so, there was regular concern whether the jobbers on the LSE were adequately capitalised. More-over, the LSE was becoming more highly concentrated, especially among jobbers. By 1980 there were only 14 jobbers. Indeed the Chairman of the Stock Exchange, Sir Nicholas Goodison, stated in the Bridge Memorial Lecture, that, 'In 1976 we had already been reduced to only five substan-tial jobbing firms. We knew, however, and we said it publicly, that any further reduction would put an intolerable strain on the single capacity dealing system'. Indeed, two jobbers, Wedd and Akroyd account for a substantial proportion of total business, especially in gifts deals.

It is difficult to obtain data on capitalisation of members of the LSE, since so many remain unincorporated partnerships, who need not file reports and balance sheets. Even so, it is widely admitted that such capital-isation is relatively low. One example is that Akroyd's, one of the two large jobbing firms, had a capital of about £40m. in 1983, which may, perhaps, be compared with Merrill Lynch's capital of over $1bn at the same date. Certainly the past structure of the London capital market allowed both the secondary market in the Stock Exchange and the primary market for new issues to be operated on a comparatively low capital base, for example, as compared with the US capital markets.

The future environment is likely to involve market-makers in a wider range of business, and thus more risk, and in a more competitive environ-ment with lower spreads – at least on larger transfers – and hence lower profit margins. This reduction in spreads should, however, be partly offset for market operators by a greater volume of turnover, as more deals are attracted to the LSE by the lower transactions costs (see the analysis by Mrs P. Jackson and Mr A. O'Donnell on 'The effects of stamp duty on equity transactions and prices in the UK stock exchange', *Bank of England*, Discussion Paper, 25 (October 1985)). Moreover, in some sectors of the capital market, for example, the gilts market, there may be over-capacity, at least at the outset of the change to the new environment. In this more competitive, possibly excessively competitive, and riskier, milieu, the firms involved would seem to require a considerably larger capitalisation than in past years, to survive the expected pressures and shocks.

PRESSURES FOR CHANGE

Thus, in the 1960s the British financial system was still characterised by a number of groups, or clubs, of financial institutions, with strictly limited and compartmentalised functions, largely cartelised price-fixing, and, in many areas, relatively low capitalisation. Since then this structural frame-work has been subject to much outside pressure, which has led to major internal changes. There have been various sources of such pressure. Among the most powerful have been technological advances in handling, transferring, collecting and accessing information. Consequently, the ease and speed of transferring information from one place to another has so increased as to allow the potential geographical range of effective competition to increase dramatically, for example, by providing better opportunities for arbitraging between markets. The ability of market makers to compete in offering cheaper and more effective markets in different geographical locations, even in different continents, has been increasing greatly. We are seeing the development, not only of a one-world money market, but also of a one-world capital market. Similarly, technological change, notably in the provision of information on screens via electronics, may be both altering and cheapening the form of the best practice, most efficient, method of market-making. The gap between the traditional method of market-making, for example, with cartelised fixing of commissions, on the one hand, and the most efficient alternative on the other, has probably become greater.

A second feature of recent years has been a generalised tendency towards deregulation and the removal of hindrances to the free working of market forces. Although in some respects this has arisen from the temper of the times, it has also been strongly influenced by the technological developments already mentioned. For these developments allowed financial institutions in many cases to move their business and operations outside the domain of the regulators. Unless the regulators reduced the excess burden that their regulations were felt to be imposing, then in many cases the institutions and markets which they were seeking to regulate would simply have disappeared, for example, have moved offshore. The evolution of the eurocurrency market is a prime example of this. Thus, in some cases, deregulation was necessary if certain financial institutions and markets were to continue to operate effectively domestically. A key, crucial, issue in this respect has been whether exchange control over capital flows across national boundaries has been maintained, or alternatively discontinued. So long as exchange control is preserved, the authorities within that country may continue to maintain the existence of protected, cartelised, high-cost financial markets and institutions, because then dissatisfied domestic customers cannot easily transfer their business abroad. This protection may, of course, be at the expense of having such domestic national institutions and markets fall increasingly far behind internationally competitive best practice. Nevertheless, it does defer the necessary date for change. But, once exchange control is removed, the pressures on all major countries to adapt to best practice, or find that their own markets and national financial institutions will wither, will become intense.

Exchange controls are also likely to act as an impediment to the entry of foreign firms into local capital markets, and thus reduce the impetus for innovation and efficiency that free entry can provide. London did develop as a leading euro-market centre while strict exchange controls remained in force, but this was an international entrepôt business in foreign currency excluded from the constraints of exchange control. In most cases markets will need to be mainly based on local, national business, and thus exchange controls will tend to reduce the spur to innovation and efficiency, not only by forcing residents to stay in these markets, but also by discouraging entry by foreign intermediaries.

INTERNATIONAL COMPETITION IN CAPITAL MARKETS

These developments have, of course, also been affecting the London capital market in recent years. Thus, the increasing internationalisation of capital markets has now allowed British customers, who in previous years would have, virtually automatically, had to use the London capital market (either the primary new issue market or the secondary market in the Stock Exchange), to have a choice between markets. Large companies can now not only obtain listings, but also envisage making their new issues, in part, or in whole, on other stock markets, notably in New York. Many UK companies have found it an advantage, partly in order to make a broader market in their shares, and so possibly to raise their equity capitalisation, to obtain a listing in America. This growing presence on the American capital market of British, and of other European, companies has not, however, been solely a one-way street; equally an increasing number of American (and Continental European) companies have become listed on the London Stock Exchange (in June 1985, 200 New York Stock Exchange (NYSE) companies were also listed on the LSE).

The initial step of obtaining a listing abroad is, perhaps, primarily an aspect of marketing strategy, obtaining both a wider market for the company's securities and an increased exposure for the company's name in that financial community. US institutions held foreign stocks worth $10-12bn in June 1985, probably about a ten-fold increase over the past decade. Such listing allows for the *possibility* not just of trading existing securities in the secondary market abroad, but also of using the primary capital market in the foreign centre to raise additional funds.

So, after the initial step of obtaining a listing, the extent of usage of alternative capital markets, in one country or another, then largely reduces to the essential question of the relative costs of operation. Even then, a combination of patriotism and political concern, in the wider sense, will tend to mean that a company domiciled in one country will continue to maintain probably the greater part of its capital market operations in its own country. Nevertheless, the most important question will be the relative cost of dealing in each country, including costs of registration, advertising, underwriting, and so on, and also any government taxation on such primary issues; similarly on the secondary market, the costs of commissions, and fees, and government taxes, such as Stamp Duty, or other form of taxes on turnover, that the government may levy on such transfers.

Currently anecdotal evidence suggests that the costs of dealing in secondary capital markets in the USA, notably in the NASDAQ (National Association of Security Dealers Automated Quotation) market, have been considerably lower than in London. In the NASDAQ market the cost of dealing has been reduced by competition between market-making dealer-brokers using the latest available electronic information systems. Such costs are considerably lower than those currently charged in London, where the more traditional broker/jobber system has still required a minimum commission for deals, until that becomes abandoned as part of the ongoing structural change. Moreover, the UK government has charged Stamp Duty on all deals on equities passing through the Stock Exchange. This was avoided in most transfers of UK securities in the US, since in that country the deals traditionally took the form of transfers of American Depositary Receipts (ADRs) rather than of the equities themselves, the registration of whose transfer in London would have attracted Stamp Duty. Consequently, dealings in some major UK stocks in US secondary markets became considerably cheaper than on the LSE, to such an extent that

some large deals between UK institutional investors were put through the
US markets, rather than London. For up to 20 per cent of some UK companies, for example, Dunlop, equity is held in ADR form. Partly because
of this threat of losing business to the US, the British government lowered
Stamp Duty from its previous level of 2 per cent to 1 per cent in the
Budget of 1984. Even so, the cost advantage of transacting in the secondary markets in the US is currently believed to be considerable. Thus,
transactions costs on the purchase of £10 000 worth of shares may still
amount to $2\frac{1}{2}$ per cent in the UK, compared with around 1 per cent in
the US and $1\frac{3}{4}$ per cent in Japan. On a £100 000 deal the transactions costs
could amount to $1\frac{3}{4}$, $\frac{1}{2}$ and $1\frac{1}{4}$ per cent in the three countries respectively.
The main factor behind the higher cost in the UK remains the 1 per cent
Stamp Duty. There are no transaction taxes in the US, and the tax in
Japan is only around $\frac{1}{2}$ per cent.

There are, perhaps, somewhat greater barriers to making comparative
international use of *primary* capital markets to raise additional capital
funds, at least in equity form. Thus, in the UK, the *Companies Act 1980*
(Sections 17–19), the Stock Exchange, and also the Investment Protection
Committees of the institutional investors, all require, in order to protect
the interests of existing shareholders, that all additional issues of equity be
offered to existing shareholders in a rights issue, unless a special General
Meeting of the shareholders is called to vote that a new issue can be made
in some other way. This procedure greatly adds to the cost and complexity
for a UK company of making an additional issue other than as a rights
issue. If the extra cost, time and effort of complying with foreign regulations, for example, as applied by the Securities and Exchange Commission
(SEC) in the USA, is also taken into consideration, one can see why the
option of raising new equity abroad is, so far, rather rarely taken. In a few
cases such an issue is made; a recent example is the issue of additional
shares in the US by Cadbury Schweppes. Aside from such various institutional constraints on making new issues in foreign centres, accurate data
on the comparative costs of making a new issue in one financial centre or
another are *not* available, but appear to be somewhat lower in the USA
than in London. There is some evidence to suggest that comparable issues
can be undertaken significantly cheaper (and more flexibly under the Shelf
registration arrangements), in New York than in London, or in other
European centres.

Besides such competition between London and the US capital markets,
there is also competition, notably on the corporate bond market (rather

than in the equity market, at least as yet), between London and the international capital market. Part of the apparent relative 'efficiency' of the euro-bond market will be owing to its comparative freedom from the constraints, limitations and controls imposed upon the more traditional domestic markets, a subject discussed further later. Anyhow, a sizeable segment of this euro-bond market is, of course, situated in London. So in this case we would not actually be losing business to a different geographical centre. Even so, in the absence of exchange controls , and given the possibility of interest rate swaps, exchange rate futures, and so on, the option is now open for a major company to raise funds in the international euro-bond market, as an alternative to raising a bond in its own domestic market. It can raise the funds in whichever currency denomination (i.e. in foreign currency bonds) it regards as most appropriate for its own business position and exchange rate profile; it can then transform the funds, should it so wish, back into the currency of the country in which it is primarily domiciled, using, perhaps, interest rates swaps to transfer the maturity position of its debt obligations to whatever its preferred profile might be. So, the international euro-bond market acts as a prime competitor for the domestic corporate bond market. Indeed, since about 1973 the UK domestic bond market has been stagnant, in part because corporate treasurers were scared to commit their companies to long-term high nominal fixed interest rates (in the 1985 Budget certain restrictions were removed from the issue of shorter term, 1–5 year, corporate debt). In place of such issues, corporate treasurers in the UK turned primarily to (medium-term, variable rate) bank finance; but they have also, increasingly in recent years, gone to the euro-£ and the foreign currency bond market, where the coupons and costs of issue have been lower and the market more flourishing.

More generally, finance directors and corporate treasurers of large companies in many industrialised countries have been turning to the euro-bond and foreign currency bond markets. A large part of this fast-growing market is sited in London. On 31 March 1985 there were 895 foreign-based and 72 UK-based euro-bonds listed in London with a value of $34,318 and $1,315 million respectively. Table 2.1 provides some data on recent growth and comparative size.

There are also now some initial soundings about establishing an international equity market, and various companies have begun promoting communications systems that could form the basis for such a market. But this is, as yet, at a preliminary stage.

Table 2.1   The growth of the international bond market

Outstanding value: end years	1975	1980	1984
Euro-bonds (1)			
($bn)	59.1[1]	123.0	261.8
% change on 1975		+108	+343
% change on 1980			+123
Foreign bonds (2)			
($bn)	N/A	86.9	120.7
% change on 1975		N/A	N/A
% change on 1980			+40
UK loan capital (3)			
(£m)	6609	5794[2]	7294
% change on 1975		−12	+10
% change on 1980			+26
US corporate and foreign bonds (4)			
($bn)	323.4	503.8	N/A
% change on 1975		58	N/A
% change on 1980			N/A

Notes: 1.   1976 – no data pre-1976
         2.   March, not December 1980
Sources: (1)   Orion Bank
             (2)   Orion Bank
             (3)   *The Stock Exchange Quarterly*
             (4)   *The Securities Industry in 1981*

THE CHANGING FORM OF THE LONDON STOCK EXCHANGE

The first dynamic of change, identified above, has been the development of new technologies, notably in the processing of information, which has allowed for new, more efficient and cheaper ways of making markets, and also for such markets to compete over a much wider geographical range, indeed internationally. In recent years this has increasingly affected the relative competitive position of the LSE. The second dynamic, also described above, has been that governments, partly in response, have reacted by a programme of deregulation, to remove some of the particular burdens and restrictive practices imposed on such markets, whether these were initially introduced primarily for fiscal reasons, for prudential reasons, or as a result of cartels operated for the protection of existing market participants. The reduction in Stamp Duty has already been noted. More important, in 1979 both the Labour and then the in-coming Conservative Government refused to exclude the Stock Exchange Rule Book and, within that, the key section requiring minimum commissions, from the ambit of the Restrictive Trade Practices Act (1973) (which had been extended to cover services by an Order in 1976). Subsequently, the Director-General of the Office of Fair Trading (OFT) referred the Stock Exchange Rule Book to the Restrictive Practices Court.

The prospective defence of the Stock Exchange was not so much that the minimum commission could be defended on its own, but that it was a key supporting element in the whole framework of the Stock Exchange. It was argued that without such a minimum commission there would be great competitive pressures on brokers to avoid the costs of putting deals through the jobber, for example, by matching deals, especially large block deals, either in-house or through a system of enquiry among other brokers that bypassed the jobbers. This would have rapidly destroyed the single-capacity framework, on which the present Stock Exchange was then based. Moreover, the role of brokers as principals, as would then rapidly arise, would mean that they would be taking much riskier positions, and would therefore need larger capitalisation. So the whole structure of the Stock Exchange was at risk.

However, it was concurrently becoming increasingly apparent that what was needed was a major structural change in London. In particular, the existing structure and market system was not sufficiently cost effective to match the competition from abroad. So, a planned and well-designed change of structure seemed necessary. Such a planning process would, as indeed transpired, be difficult enough to put through, notably because of the privileged market position and property rights of existing members of the Stock Exchange, which had been established by the existing arrangements and could be threatened by future changes, for example, by open access for outside firms to the LSE. But a confrontational legal battle, between the OFT and the Stock Exchange, before the Restrictive Practices Court was, in itself, no way to advance a *planning* process for establishing a more efficient capital market in London. So, before the case actually came to trial (it was set for early 1984), an agreement was reached, on 27 July 1983, between the Secretary of State for Trade and Industry (Cecil Parkinson) and the Chairman of the Stock Exchange (Sir Nicholas Goodison), whereby the government would exempt the Stock Exchange agreements from the scope of the Restrictive Practices Act (achieved by the passage of the Restrictive Trade Practices (Stock Exchange) Act (March 1984), while in turn the Council of the Stock Exchange agreed to abandon the minimum commission rules before the end of 1986 and to introduce lay members to the Council of the Stock Exchange.

Thereafter events moved swiftly. It became generally accepted that the abandonment of minimum commissions would lead rapidly to the ending of single capacity, and to the growth of market dealers with dual capacity to act both as agent and principal. In view of the potential for conflicts of interest that this might cause, and more generally in the aftermath of the Gower Report of January 1984, which had been established to consider the need for a more comprehensive regime for the protection of investors (in response to certain frauds and mismanagements among fund management companies, dealing in investments in property and commodities, such as Norton Warburg, M. L. Doxford and Co. Ltd, Imperial Commodities Ltd (Frewen), Exchange Commodities and Securities (Hunt), and so on, and concern over high pressure sales techniques in certain forms of insurance marketing), the government introduced a White Paper on Financial Services in January 1985. It is now embarked on a programme of legislation, to culminate in a Financial Services Act in 1986, designed to provide a broad framework of protection for investors over the whole range of the UK financial sector.

Under such external pressures the Stock Exchange has now decided that it must change its marketing form fundamentally, from its original single-capacity form, to a dual-capacity form, with broker/dealers. *Inter alia*, this latter change will require concurrently the introduction of an entirely different form of market-making, and new associated and supporting information systems. Because it will be a major structural break, the change cannot be introduced gradually. Instead it is all to be done on one 'big bang' day, which as agreed with the government, is due to occur at some time before the end of 1986.

Whereas, under the previous single-capacity system, the broker was largely protected from risk by being constrained to act as agent only, and could thus operate with a small capital base, the jobber, in his riskier role as principal, needed larger capital. Yet there was concern, well before the recent changes were mooted, whether the jobbers were sufficiently numerous and well capitalised. The increasing importance of the institutional investor has been raising the proportion of business passing through the LSE in large block deals. If the jobbers were to be able to absorb such large blocks without a defensive change in prices and widening of margins, they needed additional capital.

Moreover, the decline in the number of jobbers, and the privileged position accorded to them under LSE rules, enabled them to establish a wider spread between their bid and ask price. One of the objectives of the change in the market structure has been to increase the extent of competition between market-makers, thereby reducing their profit margins on turnover and the costs of transaction (although there should be an off-setting rise in volume). This increase in competition is thus likely to make the profitability on such dealing lower and more uncertain. Under such pressures, dealers finding it difficult to make adequate profits from pure market-making may be tempted to restore profitability by a riskier strategy of taking positions themselves. The new breed of market dealers will need a sufficient capital base to act as principal, as well as an agent, in a more fiercely competitive market where the institutional investor has become the key customer.

So there are several reasons for increased capitalisation in the London capital market. But the Stock Exchange was organised around *unlimited* partnerships. Such partnerships would, inevitably, have found it extremely difficult to raise additional capital from outside. So there was a need to change the structure of the Stock Exchange, in order to allow for outside ownership of member firms. This change has been taken in steps. As already noted, the first stage, taken in 1969, was to allow firms to form themselves into limited companies, and to sell their capital to outside shareholders, subject to a limit of 10 per cent on any one investor, raised to 29.9 per cent in 1982. Few firms, however, took advantage of this provision until after the abandonment of minimum commissions in 1983. Since then, as it became increasingly obvious that the whole structure of the LSE would have to change radically, an increasing proportion of (large) London brokers and jobbers have joined up with other larger financial companies, both UK and foreign, both banks and other securities houses, initially up to the 29.9 per cent limit, but clearly looking forward to the future in 1986 when outside firms will be able to take over the complete equity of existing members, and/or to set up new member firms. Indeed outside firms are already able to own 100 per cent of a member dealing separately in the new currency options market.

In contrast to the ability of many large London broking and jobbing firms to capitalise on their skill, know-how and customer base, on appar-ently highly favourable terms by contracting associations with outside financial institutions, both British and foreign, the smaller, less-well-known, and regional (outside London) Stock Exchange firms have generally not received take-over bids, at any price. They see themselves now facing a more competitive market, having received little, or no, compensation for their loss of property rights. Accordingly, there has been considerable jealousy between the larger and the smaller and regional firms. This has caused some difficulties in putting through the reorganisation of the Stock Exchange. A recent vote among the membership of the LSE produced a large majority, well above the 50 per cent constitutionally required, for a resolution to change the rules to allow 100 per cent single outside ownership of member firms. But a vote to change the Constitution of the Exchange, which would have enabled the transfer of ownership of the Exchange from the individual members to the member *firms*, which under the Constitution needed a 75 per cent majority, narrowly failed.

A similar case, for larger and better capitalised member firms, can be made, not only for the Stock Exchange, but also for the primary new issue market. For example, companies see considerable advantages in being able to arrange a new issue, for example, a new corporate bond, relatively quickly, which is easiest if it can undertake the transaction in its entirety with a single financial institution via the 'bought deal'. If the financial institution is large enough to undertake the risks, and subsequently to arrange the secondary placing of the bonds, the speed and flexibility, and therefore the ability to choose the right opportunity in markets, may be much enhanced (according to the efficient markets theorem, however, it should not be possible for advisers systematically to select better-than-average occasions). Even when the size of the issue is such that the sale arrangements, underwriting, and so on, have to be shared among many financial institutions, the greater placing power of larger financial entities has considerable advantages. At present it is difficult to realise such economies of scale in new issues in the London equity market. This is because the Companies Act 1980, together with the Stock Exchange and the Investment Protection Committees of the main groups of institutional investors, require that additional equity issues of listed UK companies have to be offered in additional tranches to current shareholders in the form of a rights issue. This hinders the adoption of cheaper, quicker and simpler means of issuing new shares for UK listed companies. On the other hand, it does protect the market position of existing shareholders.

Additionally, the existence of market-makers with much larger capitalisations may allow for changed methods of issue on the government bond market, the gilts market. Under the existing system the main market-makers have been two firms of gilt-edged jobbers, whose capitalisation under the circumstances was not large; the capital of one of these two firms, Akroyds, covering their dealing in equities as well as in gilts, was only £40m. in 1983. The shortage of strongly-capitalised operators in the primary market for gilts was an important factor in persuading the authorities to maintain the particular, 'tap', system of issuing gilts, whereby the Bank of England effectively has acted as the sole underwriter, on-selling such part of the stock as has not been taken up at the initial issue price into the secondary market after the tender, in quantities and prices that the market is able to absorb. Those stocks which are largely taken up by the (Issue Department of the) Bank of England for subsequent on-sale into the secondary market are known as 'tap stocks'. There have been fears that the market itself would simply not have been strong enough to have absorbed large quantities at auction, for example, on occasions when the news was unexpectedly bad, without the government broker in effect standing ready to support the market by effectively acting as underwriter of last resort.

This may now be changing. With the ability to operate in the gilts market being opened to outside firms (through separately capitalised subsidiaries), a large number of applicants have put their name forward to serve as primary dealers in the gilts market. On 17 June 1985, the Bank of England published the names of 29 prospective applicants to operate as primary dealers in the gilts market; these names included many of the largest banks and other financial institutions, not only in the UK, but also from the USA and the rest of Europe. The volume of capital that these entrants are capable of dedicating to this function is now extremely large (some £600-700m.). Indeed, the scale of capital that may be applied to this function (for the authorities are requiring such capital to be dedicated to a separate subsidiary for this purpose), raises the question of whether such primary dealers will be able to obtain an adequate return on such capital from the margins, which will in turn be compressed by competition, on turnover in this market. The prospective number of primary dealers in London, at 27, is broadly the same as the number on the New York bond market, but the value of marketable government debt outstanding in the UK is only about 10 per cent of that in the US. If the primary dealers cannot make a satisfactory return from their normal dealing operations, there is the possibility that they will try to boost their profits by taking larger positions. This will inevitably add to risk, and some players may take a wrong view. There is, thus, a considerable likelihood that at least some of those who have declared their intention of joining this market will suffer some considerable loss.

There is, therefore, a risk that market positioning could lead to loss, and reduce capital adequacy, even where the institutions are considerably larger, and better capitalised, than existing members of the Stock Exchange. The authorities are, however, requiring separately dedicated capital among primary dealers in the gilts market, and the amount of capital so prospectively applied seems so sizeable that market members could suffer considerable losses without putting the market at any risk. Such dedication of capital to the subsidiary should also reduce the risk of contagion, whereby losses in one part of the business imperil its other activities. Thus, if the parent company makes losses elsewhere, it cannot quickly and covertly reduce the capital standing behind its gilts operations – in order to finance losses elsewhere. Equally, the existence of a dedicated volume of capital in the gilts market should limit the extent of losses that the parent might, knowingly or unknowingly, finance in that particular subsidiary before either rectifying the situation, or withdrawing from the business.

But this raises several other important questions. First, capital is more efficiently and economically used when it can be transferred flexibly from one role and requirement to another. Is it, therefore, generally sensible to restrict an institution's capital into various limited and dedicated uses, making such capital untransferable? This issue was raised in a recent paper on the role of capital by Mr J. Barge in *The Banker*, July 1985, who argued that 'Emphasis on capital as a symbol of depositor confidence is in conflict with the function of capital to meet unexpected losses and, as a result, is inducing changes in the way banks are managed'. In this context, the requirement that capital be separately dedicated and maintained to sustain confidence in individual parts of the business may reduce the flexibility with which capital can be used overall to meet unexpected losses, and thereby amounts to a disguised increase in the firm's over-all required capital ratio, with potentially adverse effects on profitability.

Secondly, another question is whether multinationals, especially those domiciled outside of the country in which the market is situated, are really controllable by the authorities of that country. Is not their ability to transfer positions between the subsidiary and the parent company such that the authorities of the market are not really able to control the multinational at all? Indeed, in general, is it possible for one supervisor to control the over-all position of a multi-function, multinational, financial conglomerate? That concern may be among the reasons why the Bank has specified that the various gilts market entities should be separately-capitalised subsidiaries.

In some cases there has been concern among the domestic market traders that multinationals, particularly from the USA, may enjoy certain supervisory and other advantages, arising both from their size, and also from their supposed ability to hide their position from the host supervisors, to obtain competitive market advantages. It is said, for example, that the bond traders in certain Canadian markets are frightened that they would be overwhelmed by competition from the large US security market-makers. There may be certain undertones of similar concern in the UK. This raises a number of further questions, such as the extent of economies of scale and scope in such market-making. Could larger, more-heavily-capitalised firms be able to force out the smaller, local firms? Would they want to do so? Would they then become liable to anti-trust regulation, if they attempted to do so?

It is not yet apparent how many competitive market-makers will set up in the equity market. Indeed (in cóntrast to the gilts market, where the authorities appear to be modelling their future market system closely on that already in operation in New York), it is not yet clear exactly what *form* the equity market will take. There was considerable debate, following the publication of a Discussion Paper by the Stock Exchange in April 1984, on the options for establishing a new dealing system, for example, whether there should be one kind of market, based on competitive market-makers, for the more-actively-traded larger shares, and another, perhaps continuing to rely on a specialist jobber and maintaining single capacity, for the less-actively-traded smaller shares. The Council, however, in their Report on 'The choice of a new dealing system for equities' (*The Stock Exchange Quarterly*, September 1984), came down against this latter proposal, on the grounds that such tiering would be confusing, that it would be impossible to monitor single-capacity operations in the lower tier, and that the proposed system of competing market-makers would, in practice, allow a straightforward evolution from existing activities. In view of the likelihood that there would, perhaps, be few prospective market-makers in some areas (of less-actively-traded shares), and that these might feel exposed to having to take large positions in shares which could not easily be on-sold (or purchased) without large swings in prices, the Stock Exchange may allow the quoted bids and offers of the market-makers dealing in less-actively-traded equities to commit them only up to a limited amount, and/or to be indicative rather than binding. Eventually the Stock Exchange may introduce an automated small-order computerised matching system for the lower end of the market.

The Council expressed a general desire to maintain as gradual and steady an evolution in the equity market as was consistent with the radical changes imparted by the abolition of minimum commissions and the cessation of single capacity. Thus they considered an entirely electronic marketing system, the computer-based Aggregated Resources System (STARS), but rejected it, largely on the grounds that the leap from a personalised system centred around a market floor to an anonymous electronic system was too risky to undertake all at once.

INFORMATION AND THE STRUCTURE OF THE MARKET

The question of the form of market that might be adopted for trading the various financial assets depends on a number of factors, notably on the projected volume of turnover. Markets have several dimensions, for example, whether continuous during the trading day or having a limited number of fixes, or market auctions at particular discrete points of time during the day. In those markets which only operate at discrete points of time, perhaps only on one occasion during the day, it is relatively simpler to accumulate the orders and arrange an auction at which the maximum number of buying and selling orders can be crossed. If, however, dealing is continuous, then the need to match the irregular flow of buying and selling orders requires there to be a full-time counterparty, or market-maker.

Besides the fact that market-making involves some considerable expenses, in particular heavy set-up costs, which need to be recouped, the market-maker faces the problem that he may, at certain times, have less information, less good or less quick, than is available to other potential traders. Nevertheless, as market-maker he is committed to making deals. This means that, at the least, a modicum of better-informed customers are likely to be able to make a profit at the expense of the market-maker. Clearly this is the case when the customer has access to inside information. At the limit, this may be illegal; but prevention of insider dealing is difficult to monitor and police, and the definition of insider trading is fuzzy and uncertain. There are always bound to be some potential traders who will have better information about certain eventualities, which will affect the price of marketable assets, in advance of the market-maker. In so far as there will, therefore, be certain traders, with better information, who will make a profit at the expense of the market-maker, the latter will have to widen the margin, or spread that he maintains between his bid and offer prices, in order to maintain an adequate rate of return on capital or, alternatively, cease to deal at all. This suggests that there may be a trade-off between the rigorous application of severe regulations against insider trading, as the SEC tries to establish in the USA, which should allow for lower spreads and smaller transactions costs or, alternatively, a more lenient view towards insider trading but, in consequence, a less liquid, more costly market place. In so far as competition between international markets causes trade and transactions to migrate to the lower-cost market, there may be a case, in terms of general self-interest, for maintaining a strict standard of policing and prevention of insider trading.

But further, if *all* market information is made instantaneously available, then the market-maker will often be placed in a worse position than the occasional dealer, who is capable of trading in such shares, either as agent or principal, but has not committed himself to be a market-maker. An example of this would occur if the investors are able to observe flows in the market sufficiently clearly in order to be able to ascertain when the market-makers, in order to fulfil their commitment to make a market, have taken a large long or short position. In that case, the investor (not the market-maker), observing the market-maker's position, will realise how that market-maker will in future feel under pressure to trade, and therefore the likely future trend of prices. Another example may arise when a news shock arrives, which considerably alters the expected fundamental price of an asset. Often it will take time, and resources, to assimilate the full implications of this for 'equilibrium' prices. The uncommitted trader can withdraw from dealing during this process; the committed market-maker may have, reluctantly, to soldier on.

Thus, the role of taking on the commitment to act as market-maker, being prepared to provide a bid, or offer, for existing securities, under all circumstances (at least up to some relatively large, prearranged absolute limit), without knowing which way the counterparty to the deal was wishing to transact, means that the market-maker is in a relatively exposed position. Because of certain information asymmetries, whereby the trader, or dealer, transacting with the market-maker may actually have better information, that exposed position may lead to potential losses to the market-maker and therefore either to larger spreads, or the inability to establish a satisfactory market at all. An alternative route is to ensure that the market-maker, in turn, has certain (informational) advantages which provides him with a preferred, privileged position enabling him to make a sufficient rate of return in order to carry out the market-making function. The question of how much information to provide, to whom it is to be provided, at what cost it is to be provided, and when, is crucial in the establishment of a capital market. This is, however, a complex subject, which can only be touched on here. It has begun to be analysed in the academic literature, for example the paper by L. R. Glosten and P. R. Milgrom (1985), 'Bid, Ask and Transaction Prices in a Specialist Market with Heterogeneously Informed Traders', *Journal of Financial Economics*, 13. I hope and expect there to be increasing communication and interaction between academics and market practitioners in this area.

Anyhow, there is a spectrum of possibilities. The minimum of information needed to be revealed on any capital market would be the prices of deals and the timing of such deals, in order to allow customers to check whether deals arranged for them were actually made at existing market prices: beyond that, however, there is a range of further trading parameters that could be monitored, and on which information could be transmitted, either on real time, or after a delay. Such information would include the volume of trades, the inside bid/offer range on any security at any point of time; or the full range of bid/offer quotes from all competitive market-makers in the market. This again raises the question of to whom and when such information might be revealed. Traders and investors would reckon to save time and money, the greater the information that was revealed. At the least, the more information, the easier it should be to prevent and check fraud; and there is certainly need for sufficient information to undertake an audit trail, though to check for unfair pricing all that is actually needed is for the Exchange itself to have all the information, so that they can check one bargain against another. The LSE is building such a system into the new arrangements. Of course, the release of the information to investors is an added protection; it also probably encourages them to arbitrage more. But, as noted earlier, the better relative information ordinary investors, traders and dealers have, the more exposed will be the market-makers to suffering losses from having worse information than those with whom they are dealing. Accordingly, the more information that is available, in particular instantaneously, to investors, the more likely it may be that spreads in such markets would be large, and/or dealers fewer, returning to a more monopolised position; at the extreme it might be difficult to establish a market at all. On the other hand, in so far as the market-maker possessed some informational advantages, the transactions costs might be kept lower, and/or the number of competitive market dealers would be higher.

This raises a number of issues. For example, the ratio of insider trading to total turnover is likely to be greater in second-line equities than, for example, in the gilts market. The more widely held the issue, and the better policed is insider trading (as is supposed to be the case with official secrets), the higher the ratio of general trading to insider trading. So, market-makers among second-line equities are likely to be more exposed to insider trading than in a broader, more liquid sector of the market, such as the gilts market. In consequence, market-makers in second-line equities would need various privileges and informational advantages to induce them to make a competitive market with reasonably low spreads.

On the other hand, if there are satisfactory, well-functioning, alternative sources of information on the likely equilibrium price, and the factors affecting the price of the assets being sold, then it may be *less* necessary to provide information on market positions to the investor. Thus, there could be a greater need for more information on market positions to be provided to investors in cases where the security being traded is less-well-known and traded infrequently, than, for example, in the case of gilts or of the shares of the largest companies in the country.

The problem is that insider trading exposes both market-makers and other uninformed dealers to losses. One form that the loss to uninformed traders can take is a widening of spreads between bid-offer prices, and a reduction in the size of deals for which the market-maker's quotes will be good as the market-maker seeks to protect his own position. If, however, an attempt is made to reduce the exposure of the market-maker to adverse informational asymmetry by allowing him certain offsetting informational advantages (for example, sole knowledge of his own book), in the hopes that this may reduce the size of spreads and transactions, then the uninformed investor may be at a great informational disadvantage relative both to the informed trader *and* to the market-maker. Indeed, in such circumstances the ordinary investor might well need protection from being exploited by market-makers, as well as by insider trading.

As Mr George of the Bank of England said in his speech on 'The City Revolution' at the Financial Times/Banker Conference on 12 July 1985, with respect to this general problem, 'competition is the absolutely fundamental underpinning of investor – or indeed more generally of user – protection. [While] competition is a *necessary* condition for effective investor protection . . . [it] is not regarded by society generally as sufficient'.

In general the less information and regulatory clout the authorities have themselves, and the greater is the likelihood of privileged positions being abused in malpractice, the greater is the necessity for all investors to be provided with as much market information as can technologically be provided. On the other hand, the more competitive the market, the better-known the asset, the better-policed the market, the more it becomes possible to limit the information on market position among market-makers, in order to provide them with a milieu in which they can quote the finest and most competitive spreads at all times, even in difficult market conditions.

Naturally, the lower the costs of transactions, the smaller the spreads between bid and offer, the more likely it is that orders and transactions will be passed through that market, rather than through a higher cost market. Moreover, as was earlier emphasised, the development of a single-world capital market is going to sharpen competition between markets. But, if the pursuit of lower transactions costs should involve giving the market-makers some informational advantages, then the benefits to that market would be lost if the market-makers were to abuse that advantageous position and engage in malpractice. Besides the cheapness and efficiency of any market, there must be an overriding concern with the market's reputation. Concern with reputation will be at least as important as concern with efficiency in the more competitive world capital markets developing. However small the apparent spreads between bid and offer prices may be, markets will lose customers if it becomes widely believed that some customers have been ripped-off. It is, perhaps, not so much the large institutional investor, but the smaller customer, who is at risk of finding himself overcharged, and misused. This suggests that there is a continuing, perhaps a growing, need for rigorous laws on the discretionary management of customers' funds, by all the financial institutions involved with the discretionary handling of such funds.

CONCLUSIONS

There have been some recurring themes in this paper. The most important of these is the increasing international competition between markets situated in different countries. A second has been the blurring of dividing lines between financial institutions, enabling financial conglomerates to operate as 'universal banks' in many markets simultaneously. This raises the, still unresolved, question of the importance of size and the extent of capital needed for financial intermediation in general, and for market-making in particular. How important are economies of scale, and of scope, in financial markets? How strong is the tendency for the new-order flow to concentrate into the cheapest, most efficient, financial markets of good reputation and organisation?

Because of such centripetal tendencies, supported by economies of scale and scope, there is clearly some tendency for the one-world capital market to establish its physical base in a small number of sites, in different time zones, for example, London, New York and Tokyo; moreover, in each of these centres the major players may well tend to be much the same group of multinational, integrated financial institutions.

Since this trend is recent and newsworthy, it is also possible to exaggerate its global significance. Despite the move towards a one-world capital market, the largest proportion of world financial intermediation will continue to be undertaken locally within each country, intermediating between lenders and borrowers of that country. Information is crucial to intermediation, and local knowledge is generally superior. Physical separation between markets may also continue to be enforced by exchange controls. But the presumption must be that efficiency in financial intermediation is enhanced to the extent that agents have access to mechanisms outside their national borders, and national suppliers of financial intermediation services are exposed to global competition. In such a situation it is likely that: (i) international intermediation will tend to displace domestic intermediation with both savers and investors in the same country using international intermediation channels if international markets are more 'efficient' than particular national markets; (ii) the efficiency of national markets should rise as monopoly profits are competed away; (iii) the domestic system is likely to become less subject to discontinuities in providing a spectrum of financial intermediation facilities, as competition has the effect of accommodating a wider range of financial requirements, and (iv) domestic users of the financial system would secure whatever scale advantages derive from having access within the country to foreign financial institutions operating in a wider domain.

3 Personal Financial Services in the United States: A Transatlantic Perspective*

Mervyn Lewis

A FINANCIAL REVOLUTION?

The United States is not short of financial institutions. At the beginning of 1984 there were in operation 15 380 commercial banks, 4047 savings institutions (that is, savings banks and savings and loan associations), 2125 life insurance companies, 21 930 credit unions, 2775 finance companies, 4697 securities firms, 3474 general insurers, and 800 odd mortgage bankers. There were also 330 money market mutual funds on offer and about 500 mutual funds and investment companies.

Such a vast number of financial institutions in existence owes much to legislation which has historically sought to separate institutions according to both product and geography. Federalism and fear of a 'money trust' have shaped American political attitudes to the regulation of financial institutions. Under the Constitution, both federal and state legislatures have been held competent to regulate financial businesses. In consequence, insurance companies and most banks and savings institutions are subject to state laws and restrictions upon branching and activities, separate from, or additional to, federal laws. Longstanding antipathy to any concentration of financial resources and possible conflicts of interest has underpinned a desire that the 'regulatory system should encourage a degree of diversity among institutions, large and small, specialised and generalised, 'retail' or 'wholesale' orientated'.[1]

*This paper derives from a study tour undertaken in January 1985, with Professor B. Chiplin, of central banks and financial institutions in Chicago, Atlanta, Washington, Hartford and New York. The author wishes to thank the 33 people interviewed for their co-operation and assistance. Professor D. T. Llewellyn of Loughborough University provided helpful comments on an earlier version of this paper.

Regulators in the US have looked to a tripartite division of the major financial firms, on a functional basis, into banking and other depository institutions, insurance companies and securities firms. At both federal and state level there have been imposed geographical restrictions upon the operation of depository institutions, a separation of commerce from banking and insurance and securities dealings, and a legal 'compartmentalisation' of the provision of financial services amongst the three groups.

In the space of a few years in the early 1980s, these three planks have been eroded significantly, and there has been much talk of a financial services revolution. Securities houses have developed close substitutes for bank and savings deposits, and now offer transactions facilities. Life insurance offices have linked up with mutual funds and investment houses. Banks and savings institutions have got into the business of brokering and underwriting insurance, and also securities dealing and consumer finance. Commercial enterprises have become financial 'department stores', and established 'non-bank banks'.

This paper focuses upon personal financial services. By examining the special characteristics of the markets for these financial services and developments in the UK, it seeks a wider perspective on the changes occurring in the United States.

SOURCES OF CHANGE

It has been said that the US has some of the world's best banks and the world's worst banking system,[2] and one interpretation of developments in the 1980s sees the US in some respects merely catching up with the rest of the developed world (Vittas, 1985). Yet there are similarities between the US and the UK in terms of the experiences of banks and depository institutions generally. In both countries there has been a blurring of the distinctions between banks and other depository institutions, a breakdown between the retail and wholesale segments of the capital market, widespread payment of interest on monetary assets, and a diversification of savings institutions into other financial services. What factors have prompted these common experiences?

Deregulation has been important in both countries, with the Depository Institutions and Monetary Control Act of 1980 and the Garn-St Germain Act of 1982 in the US, while in the UK exchange controls have been abolished, banking controls and hire purchase controls lifted, and a liberalisation of the Trustee Savings Banks has occurred. But regulation both influences, and is influenced by, the environment, and many of the developments have been more in anticipation of, rather than the result of, deregulation. Notably, banks in the US are endeavouring to widen their insurance business, even though the provisions of the Bank Holding Company Acts forbidding such activities have not yet been repealed by Congress, and the same is true of building societies in the UK. New technology is often seen to be *the* major driving force for change in the financial services industry. Technology is certainly important, but more as facilitating change sought after for other reasons. Rather, the efforts of individuals, businesses, financial institutions and markets to adapt to inflation and the extraordinary high and variable interest rates that has accompanied inflation, and monetary policy to prevent inflation, seem to be the most potent forces propelling changes in financial behaviour in the US, and the same forces were at work also in the UK.

For all of the 1970s, what Kareken (1984) calls 'forced disintermediation' was a fulcrum of monetary policy in the US. Banks and thrift institutions were subject to interest rate ceilings on deposits. Certificates of Deposits (CDs) were exempted, allowing the banks to offer the wholesale sector of the financial market a deposit instrument bearing market-related yields. Opportunities for the retail sector were limited: life insurance companies offered long-term vehicles for savings; finance companies raised funds in wholesale markets; while access to the securities markets was circumscribed by minimum denominations and high transaction costs on small lots.

By allowing market rates of interest to rise, relative to the ceilings, the authorities could lever sufficient deposits from both banks and thrift institutions to keep occasional inflationary pressures in check, without disintermediating the regulated institutions out of existence. Controlled disintermediation could continue to work so long as (a) inflation remained subdued and interest rates fluctuated within a narrow band, and while (b) the retail segment of the financial system was divorced enough from securities markets to keep the loss of time and savings deposits within acceptable bounds. The latter condition relied in part on 'consumer ignorance' but, more significantly, on institutional rigidities persisting. The former condition depended on the economic environment.

Inflation in the US increased rapidly after 1978, and market interest rates soared. This change in the environ from low inflation and low and stable interest rates to high inflation along with high and unstable interest rates had a profound impact upon all areas of the capital market. While yields on Treasury Bills rose above 10 per cent per annum, and in some months approached 20 per cent per annum, banks and thrifts were constrained by Regulation Q to offer 5 to 5.75 per cent per annum. Life insurance companies offered products in which the savings element of the 'bundle' was based on a portfolio of fixed interest securities acquired years before when interest rates were low. In both cases, there was created a gap which was too large not to be filled.

Securities firms did so. Money Market Mutual Funds are a textbook example of a financial innovation induced to fill a niche in the financial structure. They enabled individuals to aggregate their retail-sized deposits and so take advantage of the higher interest rates available in wholesale markets. The great appeal of the funds lies in the market interest rates, low minimum subscription ($1000), ready redeemability and relatively low riskiness. Introduced in 1970, the funds were little used until 1979. At the beginning of 1979, 10 billion dollars were invested in the funds. By the end of 1979 the funds exceeded 50 billion dollars, and by the end of 1981 they exceeded 180 billion dollars. Table 3.1 shows that during 1981 the growth of the money market mutual funds rivalled that of pension funds, as households withdrew balances from savings accounts and cashed in life policies.

From the viewpoint of the evolution of the US financial system and subsequent developments, the importance of money market mutual funds as a catalyst is difficult to overstate, for a number of reasons:

1. By offering short-term repositories for savings and transactions balances (or very close substitutes for them), they forced the legislators to allow banks to provide interest on transactions accounts.

2. They eroded the earlier segmentation between the relatively unregulated wholesale, and closely regulated retail, sectors of the capital market, demonstrating that, given the opportunity, individuals were not at all unsophisticated in their investment habits.

3. They broke down the barriers, erected in 1933, between investment banking and commercial banking, sparking off the present 'boundary war' between the previously segmented banks, thrifts, insurance companies, securities dealers and financial conglomerates.

In the UK the gap between wholesale rates of interest and retail bank deposit rates was smaller and thus took longer to fill, but the process of change in the 1980s was similar nonetheless. Unit Trust managers teamed up with merchant bankers to offer cheque account facilities with market-related interest rates. Building societies and the smaller banks soon followed suit. This concerted attack upon the major banks' retail deposit base saw those banks in 1984 introduce local equivalents of US money market

Table 3.1 Annual change in financial assets of households (billions of dollars)

Year	Savings associations	Savings banks	Commercial banks	Credit unions	Life insurance reserves	Pension fund reserves	Credit and equity instruments	Money market fund shares	Total†
1960	7.6	1.4	2.7	0.5	3.2	8.3	6.2		31.6
1965	8.5	3.6	14.9	1.0	4.8	12.1	2.8		55.1
1970	11.0	4.4	27.0	1.2	5.5	18.4	− 1.2		75.1
1971	28.0	9.9	28.1	1.7	6.3	21.1	− 8.9		98.3
1972	32.7	10.2	29.0	2.5	6.9	22.6	6.0		122.2
1973	20.2	4.7	35.3	3.6	7.6	25.4	32.0		142.7
1974	16.1	3.1	34.1	2.6	6.7	29.6	36.6	2.4	138.5
1975	42.8	11.2	24.6	5.4	8.7	34.9	27.0	1.3	162.8
1976	50.6	13.0	37.9	6.0	8.4	44.0	23.9	0.0	199.5
1977	51.0	11.1	37.8	7.7	11.5	54.6	27.8	0.2	223.0
1978	44.9	8.6	40.4	6.4	12.0	61.8	56.2	6.9	259.7
1979	39.3	3.4	31.4	4.4	10.7	84.3	52.9	34.4	277.7
1980	42.1	7.5	67.7	8.3	9.7	106.5	28.4	29.2	307.4
1981	14.3	3.0	45.9	3.1	9.2	107.9	12.5	107.5	343.5
1982	39.8	5.3	64.2	11.2	7.2	143.0	43.6	24.7	349.5
1983	110.1	15.3	64.7	15.8	8.0	146.0	83.9	− 44.1	411.2
1984	112.4	7.8	96.0	12.1	5.2	128.1	84.7	47.2	516.7

† Includes checkable deposits and currency not classified elsewhere.
Sources: Federal Home Loan Bank Board; Federal Reserve Board.

accounts to compete with the transactions accounts offered, for the first time, by a range of other institutions.

Where do matters go from here? In the UK diversification is proceeding apace. Securities firms are linking up with banks and other institutions, following the decision to deregulate stock market trading. The building societies – the largest remaining group of financial specialists – are expected to follow the Trustee Savings Banks and evolve, along UK banking lines, into financial 'department stores'.[3] Opinion in the US is more divided about the extent of change. It is said by some commentators that, as inflation is brought under control, many of the forces and pressures for change which have so evidenced themselves will subside. Small banks, thrifts and insurance companies have many supporters in Congress. If Congress re-affirms the tripartite separation of major financial services, the merger movement now occurring, it is argued, will surely slow down. When the mood for experimentation passes, additional investments in diversification will have to justify themselves in the 'cold light of market performance'. Then traditional patterns of specialisation are expected to reassert themselves.[4]

In order to provide some perspective upon such views, this paper examines in the following sections the implications of the balance sheet structures of US financial institutions, and some characteristics of markets for personal financial services. Our examination suggests that the changes in the US have some fundamental origins, and the paper concludes by looking at the 'pros' and 'cons' for the development of financial 'department stores' or 'supermarkets'.

IMPLICATIONS OF BALANCE SHEET STRUCTURES

In the US the deregulatory and competitive process set in train by the spectacular success of money market mutual funds has resulted in 80 per cent of retail time and savings deposits at banks and depository institutions carrying market-governed rates of interest. In addition, over 30 per cent of transactions accounts offer explicit interest returns. Much the same process has occurred in the UK. Already 80 per cent of the deposits which make up the money supply M3 bear market-related interest rates. Thus both countries are moving towards regimes in which the great bulk of monetary assets bear market rates of interest. This development has important implications for the operation of monetary policy, and the behaviour of interest rates and financial institutions.

Our analysis is based on the generally accepted proposition that relative and not absolute interest rates influence asset demands (and supplies) and that it is the relative rates which must adjust to restore asset market equilibrium following a change in market conditions. When bank interest rates are regulated, relative interest rates between bank deposits and other assets can be readily altered. With deregulation, it becomes a matter of how bank deposit rates are determined.

Consider the following representation of the market for bank deposits,

$$D(r_D, r_A, r_K) \, W = D^s$$

in which D^s is the supply of deposits, and in which the demand for deposits, $D(\ )$, as a proportion of private sector wealth, W, depends on r_D, the banks' deposit rate, r_A, the yield on 'securities', and r_K, the yield on capital assets. Conventional price theory would presumably see the yield on deposits as determined by the interaction of demand and supply in the market for deposits. If so, an excess supply of deposits would to some extent be 'bottled up' in the deposit market via an equilibrating reduction in the bank deposit rates.[5] On similar reasoning, Tobin (1963, 1969) saw the flexibility of the interest rate on 'money' as destroying the potential for discretionary monetary policy.

Our argument proceeds along different lines. Payment of interest on bank deposits is possible due to the intermediation activities of banks, whereby bank deposits are used to finance holdings of other assets. These other assets are themselves substitutes for bank deposits in the portfolios of the non-bank sector. The demand for bank deposits, then, will depend upon the yield on deposits (r_D) and on these other assets (r_A, r_K), while in the context of a neoclassical theory of the banking firm,[6] competition among banks will necessitate that the deposit yield offered will depend upon the yields available on the assets held in the banks' portfolios.

A special factor comes from the 'moneyness' of bank deposits. Because of the use of bank deposits as money, destruction of an excess supply or their creation to meet an excess demand cannot occur readily for the economy in aggregate, except under specified conditions (pegged exchange rate, and so on). Without these, the market for deposits may be characterised by 'monetary disequilibria' with deposits being accepted but not willingly held.[7] Adjustment to deposit rates seems more likely if disequilibrium is worked out in other asset markets, and with market-related bank deposits an interaction is set up which will see larger absolute changes in interest rates result.

A process of restrictive monetary policy, designed to meet money supply targets, operates by raising interest rates until the public's demand for money is constrained to the target range. But the interest rate which has to be raised to do this is the differential between market rates (on government paper and other assets) and bank interest rates. When the authorities engineer a reduction in the money supply (via, say, open market sales), a process of asset readjustment ensues which raises the yield on the non-monetary (financial and physical) assets. If bank deposit rates are held down by interest rate ceilings, the absolute increase in competing yields is also a relative one and, for some increase in absolute yields, portfolio equilibrium will be re-established.

When bank interest rates are deregulated and the ceilings lifted, banks are free to match the market offerings by raising their own rates. This is because the return on banks' asset portfolios will increase with market rates and, under competitive conditions, the higher return will be passed on to depositors, thereby narrowing the yield differential. Thus, to achieve a particular change in relative yields, necessary for portfolio equilibrium, a larger change in the absolute level of interest rates is necessary. Equilibrium is ensured by the existence of reserve ratios and other factors which drive a wedge between asset yields and deposit rates, and by excluding capital assets from bank portfolios.[8]

Not only are interest rates likely to be more variable when bank deposit rates are flexible, they are likely to be higher on average. This conclusion comes about because the relevant change in the US is from an interest rate ceiling on retail deposits to removal of that ceiling. When the ceiling operates, bank rates can follow market rates downwards but cannot do so in an upwards direction above the ceiling. Removal of the ceiling implies more flexible bank interest rates, but only in one direction.

Ignoring this asymmetry, the argument translates into the familiar IS/LM analysis as an LM schedule which is less elastic with respect to absolute rates of interest, as the fluctuation of bank interest rates with market yields offsets to some extent the tendency of the demand for money to vary with 'the' rate of interest.[9] At the same time, the spread of flexi-rate loan contracts and the development of private hedge markets for interest rate futures, makes it likely that it is the 'permanent' interest rate which is relevant for investment decisions. Consequently, the IS curve is likely to exhibit a reduced elasticity with respect to current interest rate movements.[10] Control of the quantity of money acts as a more effective automatic 'stabiliser' of income in the face of real shocks, using Poole's (1970) framework, but at the cost of larger induced fluctuations in the general level of interest rates.

Thus, even if inflation subsides, variability of interest rates seems likely to continue, due to the changed environment when banks, savings institutions and credit unions offer the payment of market-related interest rates on transactions deposits. This development, in turn, forces changes to be made on the other side of the balance sheet. Here there are some important lessons from the experiences of the thrifts (and savings and loans associations in particular) and the life offices in the United States. At the same time, there exist marked contrasts with these institutions' counterparts in the UK.

In the US both savings and loan associations (S & Ls) and life offices began the decade of the 1970s with basically a single liability and a single asset. In the case of the S & Ls, the liability was a generic savings deposit offering a fixed rate of interest, and the single asset was a home mortgage (which in 1970 constituted 85 per cent of assets). With the life insurance assets, there was not so much a single asset as a set of assets having the same characteristics, namely long-term and with a fixed nominal return, which constituted 84.3 per cent of assets in 1970. On the liabilities side, sales of whole of life policies made up 82 per cent of new policies written.

Secondly, both found the demand for their basic product was eroded during the years after 1970. In the case of life insurance offices, money paid over on life insurance premiums stood at 3.12 per cent of disposable personal income in 1970, virtually unchanged for 25 years. Thereafter, the ratio declined to 1.99 per cent in 1984. Within that category, whole of life policies declined to 22 per cent of amounts written.

Thirdly, both institutions found that they are subject to 'disintermediation'. For the life offices, that took two forms. Lapses and surrenders for both old and new policies have doubled since 1970 to 12 per cent of all policies in force in 1984. Whole of life policies have also been effectively unbundled by customers into their cost of protection and savings elements, by writing short-term life policies with the offices and undertaking the accumulation element with other institutions.

Fourthly, both groups are unsure about where to go. Savings associations have been able to offer attractive instruments on the liabilities side of the balance sheet, but have been less successful in terms of freeing up their assets to match the interest rate commitments they have undertaken, due to regulatory provisions which effectively prevented variable rate mortgages being written until 1981, and since then, because of consumers' resistance to variable rate mortgages (Goodman and Luckett, 1985). Net worth has declined to what would be crisis levels in the absence of federal insurance. The development of collaterised mortgages has eased the position to some extent, but the associations face fundamental decisions about the extent to which they will remain as intermediaries of house-holds' fixed asset accumulation.

For life offices, the outward signs are less apparent but the decisions facing them are, if anything, just as fundamental, yet may be less easily resolved. The industry, for its basic products, bundles together protection against specific 'risks' (for example, early death, disability) with various forms of long-term asset accumulation. But the sort of wealth accumulation which can be offered depends ultimately on the assets which the offices hold, and these assets continue to be fixed interest rate nominal claims - at end 1984, 82.4 per cent of assets were of this form. Risks of default and losses on individual securities, for example, mortgages, can be pooled and diversified but the basic nominal character of the assets, and thus the guarantees, cannot be altered. Whether the nominal bonds or mortgages backing life policies can provide the basis for bonuses which take the policy earnings close to a real guarantee for savings accumulated depends on the accuracy of the inflation premium built into nominal rates of interest.

An alternative route to providing policy-holders with a real guarantee is for the offices to hold assets which are claims, directly or indirectly, to real streams of goods and services in the form of the earnings of industrial and commercial enterprises, or holdings of real estate and property capable of being rented out or sold. Regulations, at state level, covering the type of assets in which life offices can invest prevent them pursuing this route as thoroughly as has been the case with life offices in the UK, as Table 3.2 shows. Thus to an observer from Britain, the US life offices have so far not addressed the inherent contradiction between the type of long-term guarantees which households need under inflationary conditions and those claims which the offices provide.

For both the S & Ls and life offices the problem was the inflexibility of the intermediation being carried out. Inflexibility arose, not because the institutions were specialised, but because intermediation was being carried out in ways which could not adapt readily to the changed circumstances of the 1980s. Had the savings associations been able to adjust rates, like the UK building societies, which were equally specialised, yet have been a major success story, most of the problems would have been avoided. Life offices were equally mis-matched, relative to UK counterparts, in having an asset portfolio in nominal terms in an environment which called for them to be able to offer real guarantees on their policy liabilities.

But the general lesson is that diversification does reduce risk. The UK building societies demonstrated that it is possible to have flexibility of interest rates with specialisation, but there may arise circumstances when

Table 3.2   Distribution of assets of life insurance companies at end 1983

Type of asset	US life companies percent of total	UK life companies per cent of total
Government securities	11.7	29.2
Corporate securities		
Bonds	35.4	3.9
Stocks	9.9	40.8
Mortgages	23.1	3.7
Real estate	3.4	17.9
Policy loans	8.3	0.4
Miscellaneous	8.2	4.2

Notes: 1.   UK 'corporate stocks' include unit trusts.
2.   UK 'real estate' includes only land, property and ground rents in UK.
3.   UK assets are valued at market values: US bonds would be at amortized values.
Sources: American Council of Life Insurance *Life Insurance Fact Book Financial Statistics*, HMSO.

that degree of flexibility may not suffice. Diversification of assets and liabilities across types and customers does reduce exposure and allow firms to respond to circumstances which cannot be predicted in advance. Banks, more than other institutional groups, have shown adaptability, largely because of their diversified balance sheet.

For this reason alone, diversification can be expected to continue. As Table 3.3 shows, the US banks and depository institutions still offer a narrower range of services than do the British banks.[11] In the UK, building societies, despite some ingenious efforts at getting around the constraints of their legislation, still offer a much narrower product range than the British banks. New legislation to widen their powers will be implemented in 1987. Some impetus for moves to diversification on both sides of the Atlantic comes from considering some of the special characteristics of financial products.

CHARACTERISTICS OF MARKETS FOR FINANCIAL SERVICES

Some understanding of recent developments can be gained by considering (a) the characteristics of financial firms, (b) the motives for demanding the products of financial firms, and (c) the inability to patent services.

Table 3.3 Comparison of product lines of selected financial institutions in the USA and UK

	USA						UK		
	National Bank	Federal Savings and Loan	Merrill Lynch	Prudential-Bache	Sears Roebuck	American Express	Clearing Bank	Trustee Savings Bank	Large Building Society
Cheque book/transactions account	Yes	Yes	Yes	Yes	Yes	Yes	Yes	Yes	Yes
Savings account	Yes	Yes	Yes	Yes	Yes	–	Yes	Yes	Yes
Certificate of deposit	Yes	Yes	Yes	Yes	Yes	Yes	Yes	Yes	Yes
Government insurance	Yes	Yes	Yes	Yes	Yes	–	Yes	Yes	–
Credit cards	Yes	Yes	Yes	Yes	Yes	Yes	Yes	Yes	Yes
Home mortgages	Yes	Yes	–	–	Yes	Yes	Yes	Yes	Yes
Consumer credit loans	Yes	Yes	Yes	–	Yes	–	Yes	Yes	Yes
Commerical loans	Yes	Yes	Yes	Yes	Yes	Yes	Yes	Yes	–
Investment banking	–	–	Yes	Yes	Yes	Yes	Yes	Yes	–
General insurance banking	–	–	Yes	Yes	Yes	Yes	Yes	Yes	–
Life insurance broking	–	–	Yes	Yes	Yes	Yes	Yes	Yes	–
Insurance underwriting	–	–	Yes	Yes	Yes	Yes	Yes	Yes	–
Mutual funds management	–	–	Yes	Yes	Yes	Yes	Yes	Yes	–
Discount stock broking	Yes	Yes	Yes	Yes	Yes	Yes	Yes	Yes	–
Investment manager/advisor	Yes	Yes	Yes	Yes	Yes	Yes	Yes	Yes	–
Real estate broking	–	–	Yes	–	Yes	Yes	Yes	–	Yes
Offshore services	Yes	–	Yes	Yes	–	Yes	Yes	Yes	–
Travel agency	–	–	–	–	–	Yes	Yes	Yes	–
Data processing services	–	Yes	–	–	Yes	–	Yes	Yes	–

Source: Committee on Banking, Finance and Urban Affairs, House of Representatives, and Annual Reports.

(a) Characteristics of financial firms

Firms operating in the financial industry produce services and, in general, a number of diverse services. In the case of non-service firms, it is possible to examine the internal production methods and processes without immediate reference to the firm's customers. But the products of financial firms, like those of other distributive firms, cannot be produced in advance and stored on the shelf awaiting sale. They are intangible and non-storable. In this respect it is incorrect to talk of the production of financial services separately from the delivery system. A service does not exist until it is 'consumed', and the production activities of financial firms cannot be divorced from the interface between the customer and the firm.

Recognition of this simple, but nevertheless fundamental, point enables us to identify four ways in which financial firms may differ. As in the case of manufacturing firms, the production facilities may be located in one establishment or spread across several plants. But, at the same time, potential customers are geographically distributed and demand a variety of services, while differing costs are incurred in achieving the customer-firm interaction required for the services to be produced. Consequently, we may envisage four methods of expansion in size available to financial firms.

(i)   The simplest case, corresponding to traditional ideas of large-scale operations, is where more of the same activities are conducted from the same location in a concentration of activities in a *large-scale plant*. Here there is a greater provision of essentially identical services within a particular geographical market.

(ii) A second method of expansion is similar to the first, except that the services are provided to a new market – call this *multi-market expansion from the same plant*, for example, an institution serving the wholesale market moving into retail activities, or vice versa.

(iii) A third mode of expansion involves the establishment of activities in multiple locations, thus 'bringing the service to the customer' rather than vice versa. We call this *multi-plant operations*. Here physical location is important to the customer, and by establishing multi-plant operations the firm reduces the 'external costs' (transport, time, effort) incurred by the customer in obtaining services from that firm. As compared with (ii), the importance of physical location stems from the magnitude of these external costs relative to the services provided. Location is likely to increase in importance as the frequency of transaction-yielding services between customer and firm increases and the average size of transaction decreases. Clearly transactions related to day-to-day payments fall into this category.

(iv) A fourth form of expansion involves the extension of the range of services provided (or activities conducted) by the firm, that is, *diversification of services*. This expansion may arise because of customers' demands for a range of services. Joint provision of these services may reduce the external cost to the customer, *despite the firm possessing no other comparative advantage*. Here we have the basis of banks' provision of agencies for insurance. Alternatively, skills developed in providing particular services may be well suited to use in other activities, for example, insurance companies using their investment skills to manage mutual funds. Diversification can take various forms: within the firm, as in 'universal banking' in Germany or Switzerland, by multi-firm activities, as in the holding company form of organisation, or in other ways, like franchising or networking.

Expansion of US financial firms by the third and fourth route listed above was restricted by the regulations compartmentalising firms by product and geography. As the population has become more geographically mobile both intra- and inter-state, the potential has increased too for *existing* producers of the services to lower customers' external costs. Simultaneously, improved technology has made it cheaper for firms to expand by these routes, and thus to find ways around geographical and product barriers. But because the barriers continue to restrict movement, those firms with existing non-financial geographical distribution channels (for example, Sears Roebuck), or with a widely-distributed financial product line (Prudential, Merrill Lynch), possess an ability to enter consumer banking. What such firms lack, in comparison with banks, is deposit insurance.

Deposit insurance is significant because of the second important characteristic of financial firms, which distinguishes them sharply from many other providers of services. Most financial institutions trade promises to pay in the future against current receipts. In contrast to commodity market transactions which involve a contemporaneous two-way exchange of commodity and means of payments, with no obligation for a future transaction, and in which the identity of the transactors is often irrelevant, financial contracts are crucially dependent on the characteristics of the transactors.

We can think of there being two dimensions to the intertemporal characteristic of financial services. As we have said, what is being purchased with an insurance contract or a bank deposit is a set of promises. The value of a 'set' of promises to the purchaser depends partly on what it is that is promised, and partly on the likelihood that the promises will, when they fall due, be fulfilled. On both scores the purchaser will be looking to buy some guarantee of quality. As far as the former is concerned, the purchaser is usually expected to be the best person to make the appropriate evaluation. But so far as the latter is concerned it is often difficult for the purchaser to make an accurate assessment. The further it is in the future that the promises are expected to fall due, the more difficult the task, yet the purchaser may not always get a second chance. Since the costs to the individual of a mistaken assessment are very high and if the costs to society of arranging for collective assessment are not high, we can readily appreciate why governments have provided purchasers with some assurance that the promises to pay become actual payments.

Provision of one such guarantee, deposit insurance, has historically been limited to banks and thrift institutions. With the 'non-bank bank' loophole, non-financial firms are now able to obtain deposit insurance and also access to the payments system by acquiring a non-bank bank. This is why the loophole has generated such notoriety among banking lobbies and a rush for applications by potential acquirers of banks.[12]

With non-payment services, the purchaser will be looking for some other indicators to establish whether the promises are (a) reasonable and (b) likely to be delivered. These indicators might be the size of the institution ('safety in numbers'), its longevity (past survival being used as a guide to further survival), and its repute (with the firm seeking to trade on its good name by 'branding' tied suppliers). The latter seems to apply particularly to Sears Roebuck and American Express, and in the UK to the clearing banks' provision of services like real estate broking.

(b) Substitutability of financial services

There is a vast array of personal financial services presently on offer. But most of these services are directed, in one way or another, towards satisfying three basic financial needs of persons. These are:

1. Payments services, that is, providing means of paying for, and acquiring, goods and services.
2. Consumption transformation, enabling individuals to rearrange the purchase of goods over time.
3. Financial security, ensuring the continuance of consumption in the face of changed economic circumstances.

Payments services generate a desire for instruments which (i) serve as a medium of exchange, enabling consumers to acquire goods, (ii) serve as a medium of payments, to effect payment of the goods acquired, and (iii) since purchases and sales are not synchronised, act as a temporary store of purchasing power. A chequeing deposit with a bank may perform all three functions. But the functions can also be 'unbundled' and carried out by separate vehicles. Thus a credit card issued by Visa, Mastercard, American Express or Sears may serve as the medium of exchange enabling the individual to obtain the goods. A bank cheque deposit or a Negotiable Order of Withdrawal (NOW) account at a savings institution (both of which may be accessed via a securities firm or insurance conglomerate) may be used for the actual payment. A time deposit or a money market mutual fund may serve as the temporary abode of purchasing power in between receipt of income and payments for the goods.

Rearrangement of consumption expenditures over time may be through borrowing and lending or by saving and investment (including the direct holding of real assets like housing or land). Lending can be by bank or thrift deposits, credit union shares, life insurance savings schemes, mutual funds, holding of shares and securities and so on, conditioned by the preferences of the individual and the time horizon of the financial need.

Financial security can be obtained in two basic ways. One is by undertaking savings, or having accumulated past savings and investments available in forms which can be drawn upon to sustain consumption in the face of economic losses. The other way of obtaining financial security is to take out insurance against the specific factors generating loss, that is, insurance against premature death, robbery, fire, accidents, injury, unemployment, ill-health, exchange rate variations, interest rate fluctuations, commodity price movements, and so on.

Much of the cross-industry 'boundary wars' of the past years is little more than a discovery by institutions of the extent to which financial services of various kinds can be substituted towards these three basic ends. Securities houses, which traditionally sold vehicles for longer-term savings, found that with sufficient pecuniary incentives one of their basic products, the mutual fund (unit trust), could be modified and allied to the provision of payment services. Banks and thrifts responded to this competition with new depository instruments which provide a better avenue for medium-term savings plans. All three - banks, thrifts and securities firms - provided in this way substitutes for the products of life offices.

The experience of life offices illustrates perhaps better than any other the substitution process. Life offices could offer financial security solely by means of one-year term insurance (or temporary life insurance) contracts, with annual premiums rising sharply in line with the age of the life covered. But more usually a contract period of a number of years duration is specified and a constant annual premium is determined, and the policy fulfils a dual function of providing both death cover and an avenue for savings. Over the life of the contract, a stream of constant annual premiums is handed over to the insurer, which holds and invests these funds on behalf of the insured. There is close affinity with a self-disciplined 'target saver' building up deposits in a time or savings account and, eventually, on a planned day, closing the account.

In the US case this analogy is especially apt since most funds are invested in fixed interest securities. This pattern of investment exposed the bundled-up policies, and particularly the savings element, to alternative competition when market rates of interest and inflation rose in the late 1970s. Consumers can unbundle the policies themselves by writing short-term insurance policies with life offices and undertaking the savings services with other institutions.

For the insureds, this 'do-it-yourself' unbundling of the death cover and savings elements allowed flexibility to rearrange insurance cover and savings provision without incurring the heavy commissions and high en-cashment costs of traditional life products. There was little inconvenience since many mutual funds firms are allied with or own insurers (Merrill Lynch, American Express). In the flexibility offered, we see the spur for insurers to copy the arrangement, indeed to institutionalise it, by means of *universal life* policies, while the second factor has undoubtedly provided an incentive for them to continue the diversification into other financial services.

(c) Service competition

Because there are many ways through which the three basic financial needs discussed above can be provided, a specialist cannot rely upon the unique-ness of the product. This point is reinforced by the ease with which product ideas can be copied. Successful innovation in finance cannot be patented, nor can the knowledge be bundled up and sold for royalties. As with other service industries (the self-service supermarket concept, for example), there is nothing to prevent imitation, and product cycles are short. Nevertheless, there remain some benefits from being either first in, or amongst the first in, with a new idea. The search for those, sometimes transitory, gains is likely to see thrown up an almost bewildering array of new financial instruments, along with much repackaging of old ones.

Much experimentation will occur as firms seek after the magical mix of services and products which will triumph over that mix offered by com-petitors. Some firms might be expected to have a clearly thought-out strategy. Most will happen upon an appropriate mix of services by trial and error, and the rationale will be provided ex post. Many developments are defensive. Since firms do not know in advance which combinations of products and mix of service will succeed, they will seek to establish a market presence in all experiments. Firms will exhibit 'toe-hold' behaviour, each following the other so as to avoid missing out altogether on a possibly profitable avenue of business.

We should also expect the entrants (or experimenters) to be those firms whose entry and exit costs are lowest. These are other financial firms, rather than those without experience in the provision of financial services. For financial firms, entry and exit can occur on a more limited scale that does not entail creation or disappearance of an entire organisation. A financial institution can add a new product by widening its existing range, and can abandon one of its lines should it prove to be unprofitable. This does raise the question of how permanent are some of the 'boundary incursions'. Based on the developments occurring in the United States, several observations can be made on the 'pros' and 'cons' of various forms or organisational structure of financial enterprises.

FINANCIAL SUPERMARKETS OR SPECIALISTS?

Does the future of personal financial services provision lie with the 'big battalions', or will there remain niches for small firms, specialising in geographic areas or particular products? We examine this issue by summarising the case *for* and *against* financial 'supermarkets' or 'department stores'. Some of the points have been made already.

Arguments for financial 'supermarkets'

Most of the reasons come under the description of economies of 'scope'.[13] Economies of scope exist when two or more goods can be produced jointly for a total cost which is less than the combined cost of producing the same amounts of each good separately. Because of economies of joint production, standardised depository, loan, brokerage and insurance products may be produced in combination more cheaply than a number of specialised producers could produce the same products on a stand-alone basis. Remembering that financial products are services, necessarily requiring interaction of the customer and firm, and involve intertemporal trades, we have the following factors favouring supermarkets. From the viewpoint of the customer:

1. Offering a range of services in the local office may provide the con-
    venience of one-stop shopping to customers and reduce their incon-
    venience and travelling costs when acquiring a package of services.
2. By branding, a known and trusted supplier can reduce consumers'
    search costs.
3. Dealing with a large and diversified firm provides safety in numbers
    and continuity of supply.

From the viewpoint of the **financial firm**:

4. There may be economies of scale in information in assessing the credit
    standing and monitoring the accounts of households which consume
    many services. Households which use the services of a financial firm
    provide it with information as to their credit-worthiness and reliability
    which can be utilised when providing other and future financial
    services.
5. Technological developments have increased the role of multi-purpose
    capital equipment in producing financial services – computerised
    record-keeping and transactions, telecommunications links with
    customers and markets. Diversification permits the cost of this equip-
    ment to be spread across additional product lines.
6. As *Automatic Teller Machine (ATM)* usage has grown, branch net-
    works and distribution systems have excess capacity. Because of
    competition, these cannot readily be closed down, so that diversifica-
    tion is a way of putting this excess capacity to use.
7. Economies of marketing and advertising may be realised when offering
    a set of related services to actual and potential customers.
8. Diversification allows flexibility in resource use across numerous
    activities and protection of the balance sheet in the face of unexpected
    changes in the economic and financial environment.

Arguments against financial 'supermarkets'

To begin with we list some reasons to be sceptical about the permanence
of the diversification trend:

1. With increased competition, as product and geographical barriers built
    up by regulation and custom are eroded, we should expect to observe
    once-for-all entry until excess profits are competed away. We should
    expect existing producers of financial services to be potential low-cost
    entrants into other markets. They can enter related markets on a more

limited scale, and exit again at low cost. Once the excess profits are competed away, the rationale for further entry will evaporate.

2. Much of what is hailed as new, innovative and path-breaking in technologically-based financial services is little more than 'splicing and repackaging' of products of other firms, for example, variations on the theme of the cash management account formula which in America has worked for Merrill Lynch, but not so well for imitators. Some American observers believe that the biggest changes are behind us, so that future technological change will be gradual – evolutionary, not revolutionary.

3. American banks have long entered other related areas such as consumer financing, mortgage lending, insurance agencies, underwriting credit life insurance via bank holding company affiliates. A number of studies of these operations have found little evidence that they increased the rate of profitability or reduced risk.[14]

4. There has been little evidence of the magical synergy which the conglomerates have sought after. Often the whole seems to be less than the sum of the parts.

5. Much of the move towards conglomeration appears to be defensive. No one really knows what area or combination of services is going to work. Therefore in America everyone who is big enough to do so is setting up a dozen or more experiments in order to establish a minimum presence in most areas. In that way firms are positioned so that they can jump on a bandwagon should one develop. The same remarks could be made of some of the developments occurring in Britain too.

In addition there are some attitudes of **consumers** which might slow down the process of diversification:

6. Consumers are unlikely to want to disclose all of their financial affairs to the one firm. Further, they are likely to want to diversify future lending prospects across potential suppliers. For these reasons they may want to spread financial business across several financial firms.

7. Pressure for the 'do-it-yourself' financial movement may continue. In the past consumers have put funds into banks, savings institutions and life insurance companies with little, if any, control over the disposition of this money in terms of where it is invested, the mix of security and safety, and the type of remuneration. In the early 1980s American consumers found that by shifting assets between mutual funds and transaction balances, and unbundling the protection and savings elements of life policies, they could do much better by 'mixing and matching' themselves than the professionals did on their behalf. The

D-I-Y approach to financial management is likely to continue, especially amongst the middle market segment. British experience too would seem to indicate that consumers prefer a D-I-Y approach.

From the viewpoint of **financial firms** the following factors may limit the tendency to conglomeration:

8. There is a potential for co-operative ventures. Most of the major developments have involved sharing, such as the Clearing House Inter-Bank Payment System (CHIPS) and the Clearing House Automated Payment System (CHAPS). Sharing of facilities enables firms to reap economies of scale and allows customers to have the greater convenience of a wider network.
9. Cultural and remuneration differences exist between the various providers of financial services. Officers in banks and savings institutions are normally salaried whereas insurance salesmen and securities brokers are on commissions. Investment bankers and securities dealers are used to a free-wheeling independent mode of operation which does not gel well within a hierarchical structure. These differences create much envy and conflict when they are integrated.
10. Finally, success or failure seems likely to depend much upon the management structure and organisation of the firm. How many products can branch managers or agents be expected to have knowledge of, let alone explain to potential customers? In Britain, for instance, can branch staff really explain all of the 300 products offered to customers? How much can chief executives of diversified organisations grasp?

CONCLUDING REMARKS

Discussion in the US on future developments has proceeded on somewhat different lines, and the consensus there is that firms will evolve into one of three forms:

1. A nationwide distributor, offering a full line of differentiated products through a broad geographic network (for example, Citicorp, Bank America, Merrill Lynch, American Express, Prudential-Bache and Sears are evolving in this direction).
2. A low cost, few frills producer, offering one low cost product, or perhaps a few related products, but with little servicing. (Discount

brokers, 'captive' consumer financiers and firms like Dreyfus, may be examples.)

3. A speciality firm or 'boutique', offering highly differentiated products and services targeted to particular groups of customers who appreciate the information provided and quality service supplied. (Bankers Trust, J. P. Morgan, are current examples, but other firms like Cigna have developed departments to do this.)

We have suggested some special characteristics of financial services which distinguish them from 'ordinary' products. Due to the potential to lower customers' transport and inconvenience costs, a supplier of a 'basic' service is going to look to tie secondary service lines to it (for example, a bank providing insurance). Even specialists seem unlikely to specialise in one product, rather one product range seems more likely. Financial institutions trade in promises, and potential customers will be looking to buy some guarantee of their delivery along with the product. Safety in numbers is one way of doing so, and this seems likely to favour the large producer offering a full line of differentiated products nationwide. Some financial institutions have been accused of reckless growth in order to generate the size needed to gain *de facto* insurance from the authorities. These special factors suggest a higher concentration in financial markets, borne out by experience in the UK.

Nevertheless, for reasons outlined earlier, we believe that there will continue to be a role for the smaller, specialised financial institution and that there are limits to the success of conglomeration, as true for financial as for other firms, if only on managerial grounds. US experience very strongly illustrates the importance of institutions having a flexible and diversified balance sheet. Reinforcing this attribute is the likelihood of interest rate variability continuing, due to the change of monetary regime. However, developments in futures markets, interest rate swaps and mortgage and commercial pools now enable diversification of balance sheets at much lower costs than previously. There is also much scope for the sharing of technological developments. Finally, although pacemakers like Sears and Citicorp grab all the headlines, it must be said that most of the 50 000 or more financial firms in the US are conducting much the same sort of business as they have done for many years.

Notes

1. Volcker (1981, p. 838). The structure of US regulation of financial institutions is examined in Benston (1984). General surveys of the structure of the US financial system have been made recently by Akhtar and Fryndl (1984) and Friedman (1984).
2. See Wallich (1984).
3. Developments in the UK are surveyed by Llewellyn (1985) and Lewis and Chiplin (1985).
4. For a clear statement to this effect see Lovett (1984). See also the statement by Volcker (1981).
5. See Weale (1985).
6. Santomero (1984).
7. The idea of monetary disequilibrium is developed in Artis and Lewis (1981), Laidler (1983) and Goodhart (1984).
8. These results are derived in Davis and Lewis (1982, 1983).
9. This is the conclusion also of Kasriel (1985).
10. This appears to be the conclusion drawn by Hester (1981).
11. Some information for the US institutions is derived from the Committee on Banking, Finance and Urban Affairs, House of Representatives, April 1984, reproduced in Aspinwall (1985).
12. The Bank Holding Act places restrictions upon the activities that companies which own banks are able to undertake, preventing banks from being allied with insurance companies, securities firms and commercial enterprises. The Act defines a bank as an institution that *both* accepts demand deposits and makes commercial loans. A bank acquired by, say, an insurance company is able to foreswear one of these two functions, remain a bank qualifiable for deposit insurance, yet avoid the holding company restrictions and effectively link up insurance and banking business.
13. The importance of economies of scope in the US financial system is emphasised in Kane (1984).
14. See Kaufman, Mote and Rosenblum (1984).

References

Akhtar, M. A. and Fryndl, E. J. (1984) 'Some features of financial asset accumulation in the United States', *Federal Reserve Bank of New York, Research Paper* 8412.

Artis, M. J. and Lewis, M. K. (1981) *Monetary Control in the United Kingdom* (Oxford: Philip Allan).

Aspinwall, R. (1985) 'Shifting institutional frontiers in financial markets in the United States'
in Fair, D. E. (ed.) *Shifting Frontiers in Financial Markets* (Dordrecht, Martinus Nijholl).

Benston, G. J. (1984) *Financial Services: The Changing Institutions and Government Policy* (Columbia University: American Assembly).

Davis, K. T. and Lewis, M. K. (1982) 'Can monetary policy work in a de-regulated capital market?' *Australian Economic Review,* January-March.

Davis, K. T. and Lewis, M. K. (1983) 'Monetary tactics and monetary targets: a guide to post Campbell monetary policy', *Economic Papers,* April.

Friedman, B. M. (1984) 'Financial intermediation in the United States', *National Bureau of Economic Research,* Working Paper 1451.

Goodhart, C. A. E. (1984) *Monetary Theory and Practice: The UK Experience* (London: Macmillan Press).

Goodman, J. L. and Luckett, C. A. (1985) 'Adjustable-rate financing in mortgage and consumer credit markets', *Federal Reserve Bulletin,* November.

Hester, D. D. (1981) 'Innovations and monetary control, *Brookings Papers on Economic Activity,* 1.

Kane, E. J. (1984) 'Technological and regulatory forces in the developing fusion of financial services competition', *Journal of Finance,* 39: 759–71.

Kareken, J. H. (1984) 'Bank regulation and effectiveness of open market operations', *Brookings Papers on Economic Activity,* 2.

Kasriel, P. L. (1985) 'Is deposit rate deregulation a Rx for M1?' *Economic Perspectives, Federal Reserve Bank of Chicago,* September–October.

Kaufman, G. C., Mote, L. R. and Rosenblum, H. (1984) 'Consequences of deregulation for commercial banking', *Journal of Finance,* July.

Laidler, D. E. W. (1983) 'The buffer stock notion in monetary economics', *Economic Journal,* 94: 17–34.

Lewis, M. K. and Chiplin, B. (1985) 'Deregulation and the competitive pressures upon British banks', Conference on Bank Structure and Competition, *Federal Reserve Bank of Chicago.*

Llewellyn, D. T. (1985) 'The evolution of the British financial system', *Gilbart Lectures on Banking,* Institute of Bankers.

Lovett, W. A. (1984) 'The revolution in U.S. banking', *Challenge,* November/December.

Poole, W. (1970) 'Optimal choice of monetary policy instruments in a simple stochastic macro-model', *Quarterly Journal of Economics,* 84.

Santomero, A. M. (1984) 'Modelling the banking firm: a survey', *Journal of Money, Credit and Banking,* 15: 576–616.

Tobin, J. (1963) 'Commercial banks as creators of "money"', in Carson, D. (ed.) *Banking and Monetary Studies* (Homewood, Illinois: Irwin).

Tobin, J. (1969) 'A general equilibrium approach to monetary theory', *Journal of Money, Credit and Banking,* 1(1): 15–29.

Vittas, D. (1985) 'Financial innovation in the United States: pulling ahead, catching up or leap frogging', *The Banker,* May.

Volcker, P. A. (1981) 'Statement before Committee on banking, housing and urban affairs', *Federal Reserve Bulletin,* November.

Wallich, H. (1984) 'U.S. bank deregulation: the case for orderly progress', *The Bankers,* May.

Weale, M. (1985) 'Changing regimes of monetary control', *2nd Journées Internationales d'Économie Monetaire et Bancaire* (Nice: Sophia Antipolis).

4 The Variability of Monetary Growth in France and the UK, 1970–84*

David Cobham and Jean-Marin Serre

I

The starting point of this paper is a particular difference between the functioning of the monetary systems and policies of France and the UK: monetary growth, as is shown below, has been significantly more variable in the UK than in France. The paper tries to explain this difference.[1]

Comparative analysis of different countries can be expected to throw light on some of the more general features of their economic systems and policies which are usually taken as part of the given background in studies that deal with one country alone. But for comparative analysis to be interesting and fruitful, there must be both enough similarities between the countries concerned to make it possible to exclude a certain range of potential explanatory factors and enough differences to make possible a contrast between some of their general features.

From this point of view there is much to be said for a comparative study of France and the UK. On the one hand they are both medium-sized developed market economies in what could be considered the second rank of the international league table. They are both relatively open, at least in terms of trade. And they have both experienced a comparable rise in the importance of monetary policy since the 1960s, with unpublished monetary targets being introduced in France from calendar year 1973, and in the UK from late 1973, and targets first published for both countries in 1976.

*The authors are grateful to David Llewellyn and George Zis for useful comments on an earlier draft, but retain full responsibility for the content and omissions of the present version (revised January 1986). The research on which this paper is based was financed by a grant from the Economic and Social Research Council under the title 'The variability of monetary growth in France and the UK: causes and effects' (ref. B00232055).

On the other hand France used a form of direct credit control, the *encadrement du crédit*, throughout the period 1973-84, while the UK abandoned direct credit controls in 1971 and used an indirect control (the corset) only intermittently between late 1973 and the summer of 1980. France has had a traditional attachment to balanced budgets and a history of much lower budget deficits than the UK, while financial markets and the market for government bonds in particular are wider and more developed in the UK. The French state has had a much stronger grip on its financial system, even before the 1982 bank nationalisations, through its ownership of the three largest deposit banks, through its control of the Caisse des Dépôts et Consignations which handles the savings collected through the large network of the Caisses d'épargne, and through a range of specialised state lending institutions. The sterling exchange rate was fixed only for the first two and a half years of the period considered here, while the franc was fixed at least to some of its European partner currencies for nearly three-quarters of the period. Finally, and more generally, French economic growth, both for the post-war period as a whole, and from 1970 to 1984, has been significantly faster than that of the UK.

The next section therefore introduces the phenomenon to be explained, outlines a simple model of money-supply determination and considers both the kind of potential explanatory factors to be examined and the kind of evidence available. Section III examines two explanatory hypotheses related to the objectives of monetary policy. Section IV considers two factors related to the framework of monetary control in the two countries. Section V examines three hypotheses related to more general features of their economic and monetary systems. Section VI draws some conclusions and suggests a hypothesis regarding UK policy for future research.

II

The phenomenon to be explained in this paper, that is, the difference in the variability of monetary growth between France and the UK, can be clearly seen in Table 4.1. Two measures of variability, the standard deviation (σ) and the standard deviation divided by the mean (σ/μ), are given in the table, for annual data, and for quarterly data, and for a range of monetary aggregates. For the UK these are M0, M1, £M3 and PSL2. For France M0 is not given because the frequent changes in required reserve ratios have made this aggregate both uninteresting and highly unstable.[2] French M1R (resident M1) is the aggregate that corresponds most closely to M1 in the UK, and M3R (resident M3) corresponds roughly to PSL2 in

Table 4.1   Variability of monetary growth in France and the UK

France		M1R	M2	M2R	M3R
Annual data					
Row					
1 1970 to 1983	σ	2.60	2.65	3.03	2.65
	σ/μ	0.22	0.19	0.22	0.19
Quarterly data					
2 1970 Q1 to 1983 Q4	σ	1.33	1.05	1.09	0.86
	σ/μ	0.48	0.31	0.33	0.26
3 1970 Q1 to 1972 Q4	σ	1.39	1.04	1.05	0.78
	σ/μ	0.46	0.26	0.26	0.21
4 1973 Q1 to 1976 Q4	σ	1.58	1.00	1.02	0.87
	σ/μ	0.60	0.27	0.28	0.24
5 1977 Q1 to 1981 Q1	σ	1.12	0.78	0.79	0.65
	σ/μ	0.45	0.26	0.27	0.21
6 1981 Q2 to 1983 Q4	σ	1.27	1.08	1.09	0.71
	σ/μ	0.42	0.39	0.41	0.27

UK		M0	M1	£M3	PSL2
Annual data					
7 1970 to 1984	σ	3.90	4.48	6.09	3.36
	σ/μ	0.42	0.38	0.45	0.26
Quarterly data					
8 1970 Q1 to 1984 Q4	σ	1.57	1.94	1.80	1.11
	σ/μ	0.71	0.68	0.56	0.36
9 1970 Q1 to 1973 Q4	σ	2.35	2.36	2.30	1.26
	σ/μ	1.14	0.97	0.51	0.34
10 1974 Q1 to 1976 Q4	σ	1.10	2.04	1.55	1.07
	σ/μ	0.37	0.70	0.71	0.43
11 1977 Q1 to 1979 Q4	σ	0.74	1.75	1.21	0.91
	σ/μ	0.23	0.46	0.40	0.28
12 1980 Q1 to 1984 Q4	σ	0.73	1.52	1.25	0.93
	σ/μ	0.54	0.59	0.43	0.32

Notes: Basic data expressed as percentage (annual and quarterly) growth rates. σ = standard deviation; σ/μ = standard deviation divided by mean.

Sources: *Rapport annuel* 1982 and 1983, Conseil National du Crédit. *Economic Trends Annual Supplement*, 1985 edn; *Economic Trends*, April 1985; *Bank of England Quarterly Bulletin*, various issues; data supplied by Bank of England.

the UK. Both M2 and M2R (resident M2) are given because they have both been targeted (M2 from 1973 to 1983; M2R from 1984); they correspond (M2R more closely) to M3 in the UK.

The results given in the table start from 1970 because that is the earliest year for which reliable and comprehensive French data are available. The subperiods for which quarterly results are given in the table have been identified on *a priori* grounds. For the UK these subperiods correspond to (a) 1970-73 - from the start of the period to the end of the pure Competition and Credit Control (CCC) phase; (b) 1974-6 - post-CCC but (more or less) before published monetary targets; (c) 1977-9 - the phase of *annual* published targets; and (d) 1980-84 - the phase of longer period targets under the Medium Term Financial Strategy (MTFS). The French subperiods consist of (a) 1970-72 - when direct credit controls were not in use; (b) 1973-6 - direct credit controls and unpublished monetary targets; (c) 1977 Q1 to 1981 Q1 - direct credit controls and published targets under the Barre Plan; and (d) 1981 Q2 to 1983 Q4 - direct credit controls and published targets under the Mitterrand government.

Comparison of the annual results (rows 1 and 7) shows that monetary growth has been significantly more variable, on either measure, in the UK than in France, particularly for the broad money supply definitions (M2 and M2R, sterling M3) which have been targeted. The same phenomenon is evident in the quarterly results for the over-all period (rows 2 and 8): here the variability on the second definition (σ/μ) is higher in both countries than on the annual results, as would be expected, since the annual data in effect incorporates a smoothing of quarter-to-quarter fluctuations.[3] There is a tendency for the variability of the broader aggregates to be lower, which is also as would be expected, since at least a part of movements in or out of the narrower aggregates will leave the broader aggregates untouched. Comparison of the subperiods for France shows relatively little variation, except for some tendency for variability to fall in terms of σ in the third subperiod and to increase in terms of both measures in the fourth subperiod. The UK subperiods on the other hand are characterised both by significantly higher variability in general than the French data and by a more marked tendency for variability to change between subperiods, being lower in the third and fourth subperiods. The figures for the broader aggregates in the fourth subperiod for each country are those where the difference in variability between the countries is smallest.[4]

The aim of this paper is to analyse the causes of this difference in the variability of monetary growth, and for this purpose it is necessary to construct an analytical framework in the form of a simple but very general model of money supply determination. The model to be used here is essentially that which is commonly employed (though often in a less explicit form) in both countries, both by the monetary authorities and by private analysts. It involves as a first step regarding monetary growth as the product of the growth in, and the interactions between, the credit-side counterparts of monetary growth. For the UK we have the familiar relationship:

change in £M3 =
public sector borrowing requirement (PSBR)
— net sales of public sector debt to private sector
+ sterling lending to private sector
— change in banks' net non-deposit liabilities
+ net external flows.

For France the corresponding relationship for M2[5] is conventionally given in terms of stocks rather than flows, and without distinguishing the budget deficit and its non-monetary financing, as follows:

M2 = claims on Treasury (net)
+ bank lending to the economy
— banks' stable resources
+ gold and foreign exchange (net)
— adjustment items,

where the 'economy' is the private (non-financial) sector plus nationalised industries and banks' stable resources are roughly equal to their non-deposit liabilities.

The second stage of the analysis is simply to view each counterpart as itself determined by a range of factors, and here it is convenient to distinguish between *mechanisms of monetary endogeneity*, whereby developments in the economy have effects on the counterparts of monetary growth, and *elements of monetary exogeneity*, whereby the counterparts are affected by the specific policy decisions of the monetary authorities. The principal endogeneity mechanisms which are relevant here include (i) the effect of economic activity on the budget deficit, (ii) the effect of economic activity on the demand for bank credit and hence on bank lending, (iii) the effect of fluctuations in confidence in financial markets on private sector purchases of government debt, and (iv) the effect of the balance of payments under fixed exchange rates on the external counterpart of monetary growth. The principal exogeneity elements include (i) the effect of credit controls on bank lending, (ii) the effect of policy decisions regarding the terms and conditions of government debt on the net sales of the latter, (iii) the effect of budgetary policy on the budget deficit, and (iv) (at least in some situations) the effect of official intervention in the foreign exchange market on the external counterpart. Finally, the main possible interactions between the counterparts include, on the one hand, semi-automatic mechanisms such as the effect under fixed exchange rates of the growth of the domestic counterparts on the growth of the external counterpart, or the effect of changes in the PSBR on the financial surplus of the private sector and hence on its borrowing from the banks; and on the other hand, mechanisms which depend on the policy decisions of the authorities such as a tendency for more government debt to be sold when the budget deficit is higher, or for bank lending and the budget deficit to increase together as the result of an integrated demand-management policy.

The third stage in the analysis relates to the relative strength of endogenous and exogenous effects on monetary growth. In the absence of the time and space to undertake and present a thorough empirical examination, it will simply be asserted here first that, in both countries, over the period considered, the authorities *have* been capable of determining, within certain margins, the medium-term (say one year) rate of monetary growth if they so wished; and secondly, that they have in general done so, such that the exogeneity elements have been the primary determinants of monetary growth over the medium term and longer periods, while in the short term the endogeneity mechanisms have often been important or even predominant influences on monetary growth.[6] This difference between medium- and short-term control presumably reflects official perceptions of both the greater costs of strict short-term controls and the greater probability of minor short-term fluctuations being reversed.

Given this analytical framework, in which monetary growth is determined by the growth of the counterparts which are themselves subject to 'endogenous' and 'exogenous' influences, what sort of explanation of the causes of the difference in the variability of monetary growth between France and the UK can be suggested and examined? A first category is explanations which focus on the objectives underlying the 'exogenous' elements: were the authorities, for example, more determined to reduce monetary growth more sharply in one country than another? A second category refers to the means by which objectives are translated into exogenous effects on monetary growth: were French credit controls more effective than the combination of fiscal control and debt sales used for much of the period in the UK? A third category includes wider features of the financial system of the two countries: was the demand for money, for example, more unstable in the UK in a way that caused the monetary aggregates to fluctuate more widely?

These three categories of explanation form the subject of the next three sections of the paper. First, however, it is necessary to say something about the kind of evidence which can be used to evaluate the various explanations. Standard econometric analysis is excluded because the sample of observations is much too small: the phenomenon to be explained is a phenomenon of a group of observations that is at the very least a subperiod of the data, and given the length of the over-all period it would not be sensible to subdivide it into more than four, or perhaps five, subperiods, while addition of extra countries would pose additional problems of its own. However, the use of subperiods makes it possible to bring some arguments to bear, and the analysis of the variability of the counterparts can also contribute. Beyond that a wider range of qualitative and quantitative information and arguments can be adduced, including both general points about the monetary and financial systems of the two countries and particular points about specific episodes. Whether the conclusions, such as they are, are any more or less firmly established than the conclusions of typical econometric tests, is left for the reader to decide.

III

One possible explanation of the difference in the variability of monetary growth is the possibility that the monetary targets in the UK have been more variable, so that the greater variability of monetary growth would represent the intended outcome of policy decisions. It is, however, easy to show that this has not been the case: on the two measures of variability used here French monetary targets (1973-84; $\sigma = 2.6$; $\sigma/\mu = 0.22$) were actually *more* variable than UK targets (1976/77-84/85: $\sigma = 1.1$; $\sigma/\mu = 0.12$).[7] In terms of the actual numbers, the French target rose from 15 per cent in 1973 to 15-16 per cent in 1974; it declined very gradually from 13 per cent in 1975 to 11 per cent in 1980; it rose to 12 per cent in 1981 and 12.5-13.5 per cent in 1982, before falling to 9 per cent in 1983 and 5.5-6.5 per cent in 1984. The UK target followed a fairly similar course, falling from 9-13 per cent in 1976-7 to 6-10 per cent in 1981-2, rising to 8-12 per cent in 1982-3 and declining gradually thereafter. This explanation can therefore be rejected.

A second possible explanation is that (a), monetary policy has been more 'ambitious' in the UK in the sense of trying to exert a stronger influence on the economy, so that monetary growth has been more variable in the UK because the authorities have tried to use the instrument of monetary policy more widely. It could also be suggested that (b), the greater pressure on the economy caused by the authorities' more ambitious policy decisions has led to a stronger reaction from the economy via the mechanisms of monetary endogeneity, so that monetary control has been less precise. It has already been argued that monetary targets in the UK have been if anything more gradualist than those in France, in terms of the comparison between successive targets. It is also known that French monetary targets were gradualist in terms of the relationship between the target and the forecast for the growth of nominal income in the target period. The French targets were set with explicit reference to these forecasts, which are available: the 1973 and 1974 targets were above the Gross Domestic Product (GDP) forecast by decreasing amounts, the targets from 1975 to 1978 were on average just under 1 per cent lower than the GDP forecasts, and the targets from 1979 to 1984 were around 2 per cent less than the forecasts. Comparable forecasts for nominal GDP over the target period are not readily available for the UK before 1982, so that it is not possible to compare the gradualism of the targets in these terms.[8] However, the concept of 'ambitiousness' of monetary policy relates in any case more to the difference between a given target and nominal income growth in the *previous* period, and perhaps also monetary growth in the previous period, for it is a question of how much the authorities expect to *change* the course of the economy. Table 4.2 presents the data for these two measures of ambitiousness in France and the UK: the average 'gap' between monetary target and lagged GDP growth, and to a lesser extent that between target and lagged monetary growth, is higher for the UK, and these gaps are also considerably more volatile. It could also be suggested that at least since 1979 monetary policy in the UK has been expected to operate on its own with little support from other policies such as incomes policy, while in France the various policy instruments have been more closely co-ordinated. Thus there is some evidence to support part (a) of this explanation. The concept of ambitiousness and the reasons for the greater ambitiousness of UK policy are considered further in Section VI.

As regards part (b), there are a number of endogeneity mechanisms that are likely to work in this way: attempts to exert pressure on the economy may, for example, lead companies to increase their overdrafts to finance an unexpected and unwanted accumulation of unsold stock, or they may increase unemployment and the budget deficit. And there is at least one episode in recent UK monetary experience which fits well into this perspective: the large PSBR overshoots of 1979-80 and 1980-81[9] had much to do with the unexpectedly rapid increase in unemployment, which in

Table 4.2   Measures of the 'ambitiousness' of monetary targets
in France and the UK

	Monetary target minus lagged monetary growth		Monetary target minus lagged nominal income growth	
	mean	*s.d.*	*mean*	*s.d.*
France, 1973–84	−1.7	2.4	−1.4	2.4
UK, 1976/7–84/5	−2.2	4.5	−4.6	5.6

Notes: Calculations are from the centre point of the target ranges where relevant.

Lagged monetary growth is the growth of the targeted monetary aggregate over the previous target period.

Lagged nominal income growth is the growth of GDP at current market prices over the four quarters to the 4th quarter of the previous calendar year for France, and to the 4th quarter of the previous financial year for the UK.

The UK targets for October 1978 to October 1979 and for June 1979 to October 1980 have been excluded to make some rough allowance for the overlap due to the use of rolling targets.

Sources: *Economic Trends Annual Supplement*, 1985 ed; OECD *National Accounts*, 1985; this table is also given in Cobham and Serre (1986).

turn had much to do with the severity of the pressures imposed on the economy by the combination of the fiscal and monetary squeeze and the (possibly associated) appreciation of the exchange rate; while the acceleration of bank lending to the private sector in this period can be viewed as a perverse short-term response to the squeeze.[10]

The suggestion of part (b) is on the whole more relevant to the question of the apparently poorer 'monetary marksmanship' of the UK monetary authorities, and it is considered in that connection by Cobham and Serre (1986). However, it may also have some contribution to make to the explanation of the difference in short-term variability of monetary growth. On the other hand, the hypothesis of part (a) refers primarily to the difference in the medium-term variability of monetary growth.

IV

A third possible explanation of the phenomenon is that the use of direct credit controls in France, as opposed to the intermittent use of an indirect control only (since 1971) in the UK, has enabled the French monetary authorities to maintain a more stable rate of monetary growth. In terms of the model of money supply determination outlined above, in France bank lending is dominated by exogenous policy decisions while in the UK the endogeneity mechanisms have much more scope. Moreover, it is possible that the French authorities have been more willing to use their policy instruments to stabilise monetary growth because the cost of doing so in terms of interest rate variability is lower in France where credit is rationed directly.

The importance of bank lending to the economy (France) or to the private sector (UK) can be seen in Table 4.3, which shows the standard deviations and means of each of the counterparts of monetary growth, using quarterly data for the same subperiods as in Table 4.1.[11] It is clear that bank lending to the economy has been the most variable single counterpart in France, for three out of four subperiods;[12] it has also dominated the rate of monetary growth in terms of the means of the counterparts. On the other hand, bank lending to the economy in France has been considerably less variable than bank lending to the private sector in the UK, where all three of the main domestic counterparts have had high standard deviations in each subperiod (and the external financing counterpart in at least two subperiods), with bank lending being the most variable on this measure in the first two, but not the last two, subperiods; and all three have made important contributions to the rate of monetary growth in terms of their mean values. This evidence suggests that the lower variability of bank lending in France may be responsible for a part but by no means all[13] of the difference in the variability of monetary growth.

However, for the explanation to go through it also needs to be shown that it is the *encadrement du crédit* which has been responsible for the lower variability of bank lending in France, rather than, say, some difference in the intrinsic ex ante volatility of the demand for bank credit in the two countries; and there are a number of points to be made here. First, the *encadrement du crédit* does not provide a completely rigid control of bank lending. It involves norms for the growth of bank lending which are set annually, but applied on a monthly or quarterly basis, and the banks are liable to steeply rising penalties in the form of supplementary reserve obligations if they exceed these norms. However, the system incorporates a number of elements of flexibility: banks may transfer between each other

Table 4.3 Variability of counterparts in France and the UK

(a)		France			
Counterparts (quarterly changes)		1970 Q1 to 1972 Q4	1973 Q1 to 1976 Q4	1977 Q1 to 1981 Q1	1981 Q2 to 1983 Q4
Claims on Treasury	σ	0.67	0.85	0.82	0.69
	μ	0.00	0.51	0.12	0.81
Bank lending to the economy	σ	1.39	1.16	1.00	0.99
	μ	4.53	3.99	3.58	4.20
Banks' stable resources	σ	0.52	0.52	0.66	1.19
	μ	−0.87	−0.53	−0.57	−1.09
Domestic counterparts	σ	1.80	1.48	0.78	1.81
	μ	3.67	3.97	3.14	3.91
Gold and foreign exchange	σ	0.71	0.77	0.30	1.30
	μ	0.89	−0.08	0.29	−0.37
Adjustment items	σ	1.03	1.10	0.79	1.28
	μ	−0.53	−0.22	−0.40	−0.73
M2	σ	1.04	1.00	0.78	1.08
	μ	4.04	3.67	3.02	2.80

(b)		UK			
Counterparts		1970 Q1 to 1973 Q4	1974 Q1 to 1976 Q4	1977 Q1 to 1979 Q4	1980 Q1 to 1984 Q4
PSBR	σ	1.75	1.35	1.31	2.28
	μ	2.00	6.13	4.68	3.13
Net sales of public sector debt to private sector	σ	1.58	1.59	1.47	1.17
	μ	−1.64	−3.42	−4.58	−3.28
Δ sterling lending to private sector	σ	2.77	1.86	1.17	1.45
	μ	3.94	1.57	2.88	4.09
Δ domestic counterparts	σ	3.65	1.64	2.41	1.48
	μ	4.31	4.28	2.98	3.94
Δ banks' non-deposit liabilities	σ	0.73	0.42	0.36	0.53
	μ	−0.52	−0.62	−0.36	−0.86
External financing	σ	2.11	1.09	1.89	0.73
	μ	0.68	−1.49	0.45	−0.13
Δ £M3	σ	2.30	1.55	1.21	1.25
	μ	4.47	2.17	3.06	2.94

Notes: Basic data expressed as percentages of money stock (M2 for France, sterling M3 for UK) outstanding. σ = standard deviation; μ = mean.
Sources: As for Table 4.1.

or across time any unused rights to make loans (*économies de crédit*) which arise from the underfulfilment of the monthly norms for bank lending; they can also lend in excess of those norms without penalty if the excess lending is offset by increases in their 'stable resources' (roughly, their non-deposit liabilities); various categories of credit (for example, export finance) have been exempted from the controls at different times; and lending in foreign currencies is not restricted. These elements of flexibility may well contribute to the viability of the system, but they also reduce its effectiveness particularly with respect to short-term control.[14] Secondly, the effects of the *encadrement* have varied over time: the Bank of France's indicators of the extent to which the system 'bites' (Enfrun and Pecha, 1983), the amount of credit rationing shown up by studies such as Debonneuil and Pages (1984), and the extent to which the *encadrement* norms have been utilised, all fluctuate significantly over the period. Thirdly, the *encadrement* was not operating during the first of the four subperiods shown in Tables 4.1 and 4.3, but although bank lending to the economy was slightly more variable in that subperiod monetary growth was not. (However, monetary growth was somewhat less variable in the third subperiod when the *encadrement* is thought to have 'bitten' more consistently; and other things may well not have been equal between these four subperiods.) Fourthly, a replication of the analysis of Tables 4.1 and 4.3 for the UK for an earlier period, when direct credit controls (of a different sort) were in operation, reveals that the standard deviations for monetary growth were generally lower in absolute terms but considerably higher relative to the means, than in the first subperiod shown in the tables, while no clearcut difference in the behaviour of bank lending to the private sector relative to that in the later subperiods emerges.[15] Finally, since both the rate of growth of nominal income and the public sector deficit have fluctuated less in France than in the UK, it is likely that the ex ante demand for bank credit has been less volatile in France.

The points made in the last paragraph all tend to suggest that the *encadrement du crédit* was by no means solely responsible for the lower variability of monetary growth in France, particularly as regards short-term variability. Against this, however, it must be said that the *encadrement* is widely regarded in France as having been effective in limiting monetary growth, despite all its admitted disadvantages in distorting the pattern of resource allocation, inhibiting competition between banks and so on. The appropriate conclusion to draw is probably that the system worked but not very precisely; thus it would have contributed to reducing the medium-term variability of monetary growth but had perhaps rather less effect on the short-term variability. However, this raises the question of why the system has not, it seems, been subject to the amount of evasion that British monetary economists would expect on the basis of UK experience with direct credit controls in the 1960s. One reason is that with financial markets less developed, particularly in the earlier part of the period, and the monetary financing of the state typically small, nearly all monetary creation was channelled through bank lending to the economy so that on a technical level the opportunities for evading the credit controls were more limited. A second reason is that the authorities continuously modified the system in an effort to preserve some flexibility, but at the same time to close any loopholes that emerged; in so far as the French tradition of *dirigisme* is relevant here, it seems to have been so by leading the authorities to be exceptionally vigilant and effective in policing the system rather than by imbuing the bankers with any noticeable inhibition against evading it. However, these two points constitute an insufficient answer to the question, and it will be reconsidered in Section VI.

A fourth possible explanation of the phenomenon is that the larger UK budget deficits, and the greater role of public sector transactions in the UK, have made monetary control more difficult by allowing room for a number of endogeneity mechanisms to operate, and therefore have led to a larger variability of monetary growth. Table 4.3 shows the high variability of both the PSBR and net sales of public sector debt to the private sector in the UK, and their important contribution to the over-all rate of monetary growth, while the corresponding French counterpart, claims on the Treasury, has been on average relatively small and rather less variable. Moreover, the correlation coefficient between PSBR and debt sales in the UK is such that, even if these two are combined in one counterpart – a 'public sector contribution to monetary growth' which is roughly equivalent to the French 'claims on the Treasury' – this counterpart is still significantly more variable than the French one.[16] However, there are a number of caveats to be made here.

First, the French monetary data count the nationalised industries as part of 'the economy', whereas the UK data refer to the whole of the public sector. Secondly, the French tradition of balanced budgets has always been followed more closely in published forecasts than in the outturn, and it depended in any case on the practice of *débudgétisation* which involves hiving off certain activities with their accompanying deficits and placing them outside the confines of the state as defined for budgetary purposes. Thus, not too much should be made of the smaller budget deficits in France. Thirdly, the corollary of larger deficits in the UK is the greater development of the market for government bonds. In particular it is clear that by the end of the period the UK monetary authorities were able to manipulate their sales of debt efficiently and flexibly so as to off-set, not only fluctuations in the PSBR, but also those in bank lending to the private sector, in the latter case often through 'overfunding'. The French authorities, on the other hand, although they probably had direct access to more funds from personal savings via the Caisse des Dépôts et Consignations than the UK authorities had via the sale of National Savings debt, had much less easy access to bond finance, particularly in the earlier part of the period.

Thus the effect of the difference between the countries in public sector deficits and transactions is likely to have varied between subperiods. In the first two subperiods French deficits (with the exception of 1975) were relatively small and often negative, and the UK authorities' tactics in the gilt-edge market were either still relatively passive or of the early Duke of York type such that debt sales were often highly unstable from quarter to quarter; so the difference between the countries is likely to have contributed to the difference in medium-term, and particularly short-term, variability of monetary growth. But in the third, and particularly the fourth, subperiod, when French deficits were larger and increasingly financed by bond sales and the UK authorities had greatly improved their debt sales tactics, this factor is likely to have been less important for the medium-term variability of monetary growth, though it may still have contributed something to its short-term variability.

V

A fifth explanatory factor is the greater instability of the demand for money in the UK. For a given initial rate of monetary growth, upward shifts in the demand for money are likely to increase the pressure on the economy and lead to some tendency for monetary growth to rise via the endogeneity mechanisms. At the same time, if the authorities perceive the shift for what it is, they are likely to relax their money supply target in order to preserve some underlying objective of their monetary policy such as an (implicit) target for nominal income growth. Thus, an upward shift in the demand for money makes the monetary target less appropriate, and therefore liable to be overshot, which would tend to increase the medium-term variability of monetary growth; it also makes precise monetary control more difficult, which would increase short-term variability.

It is clear that the demand for money has been considerably more unstable in the UK than in France over this period. The UK experienced a sharp reduction in velocity (for £M3) in 1972–3, a return to the trend level by 1976, and then another sharp fall in the early 1980s, and it has become impossible to identify a stable demand function of the traditional kind for £M3, the targeted aggregate, over the period. The 1972–3 movement is widely regarded as the result of a supply shock (Artis and Lewis, 1981), but that of the early 1980s must have originated on the demand side. In France, on the other hand, there have been no sharp movements in velocity, and a recent Organisation for Economic Cooperation and Development (OECD) comparative study found it relatively easy to identify a stable demand function for M2. Indeed, the authors commented, 'Perhaps somewhat surprising in this context is the stability of the M2 equation in France, since this aggregate has been targeted by the central bank, mainly through the use of quantitative controls (which tend normally to distort the M2 aggregate through a process of disintermediation)'. (Atkinson *et al.*, 1984, p. 163).[17]

There seems therefore to be considerable support for the hypothesis that the greater instability of the demand for money in the UK has contributed to the greater variability of UK monetary growth. However, it is worth noting from Table 4.1 that the variability of £M3 was no higher in the fourth subperiod which includes one of the strong movements in velocity, than it was in the third subperiod where no such movement is thought to have occurred. This suggests that the authorities managed to develop an ability to respond to demand shifts, and that instability in the demand for money is essentially a minor and occasional factor in the explanation of the difference in the variability of monetary growth.

A sixth explanatory factor is the greater exposure of the UK economy to external disturbances. By the early 1980s the two countries were more or less equally open in terms of the ratios of imports and exports to GDP, but the UK had been as open as this for a long time, whereas the French economy had become much more open over the two previous decades.[18] More importantly for present purposes, the UK monetary system has been much more exposed to international pressures than the French: the latter had stricter exchange controls and a series of subsidies and other devices to 'disconnect' French domestic interest rates from world levels; while the greater use of sterling as a reserve currency and the larger amounts of sterling held outside the UK mean that the UK is likely to have been more exposed to pure 'currency substitution'[19] movements in and out of its currency than France.

Thus, it can be argued that the UK was more exposed to external disturbances. It is also the case, as shown by Table 4.3, that the external counterpart of monetary growth has been more variable in the UK in every subperiod except the fourth, when the UK exchange rate was allowed to float more cleanly while France experienced serious balance-of-payments deficits as a result of the Mitterrand expansion. Even in this subperiod it can be argued that the external disturbance of appreciation in 1980-81 caused very large pressures within the UK economy and monetary system, pressures that manifested themselves in monetary terms in an increase in bank lending to the private sector as companies drew on their overdrafts. The UK has also experienced much more conflict between its monetary target and its (implicit) exchange rate target than France, despite the fact that France has had the firmer exchange rate targets (in the form of fixed parities).

The UK's greater exposure to external disturbances seems likely therefore to have made monetary control more difficult and the variability of monetary growth larger, though the direct effects of this factor must have fallen mainly on the short-term rather than the medium-term variability of monetary growth. It has long been clear that flexible exchange rates do not effectively insulate a country in the short term from nominal shocks, or in any term from real shocks, in the rest of the world. The present analysis suggests that, at least in monetary control regimes other than strict monetary base control, flexible rates do not make it easier to control monetary growth either. This is presumably a reflection partly of the effect of exchange rate fluctuations on monetary growth via the endogeneity mechanisms, and partly of the 'disciplinary' effects on policy of exchange rate fixity.

A seventh explanatory factor relates to the gap between the speeds of adjustment in financial markets on the one hand and in goods and services markets on the other. This gap has been highlighted in studies of exchange rate overshooting, where it turns out that the combination of fast-acting financial markets and slow-moving goods and services (especially labour) markets leads to exaggerated, 'overshooting', movements of financial variables such as exchange rates in response to changes in monetary policy.[20] Now it can also be suggested that the gap in the speeds of adjustment between different markets is likely to produce, in response to various shocks, internal movements in the monetary system comparable to the overshooting of exchange rates; but that, given the extent to which the central banks of both France and the UK have typically operated on quantities as well as prices, some of these internal movements will be of quantities rather than prices and as such will directly affect the growth of the monetary aggregates. If it were the case that the gap in the speeds of adjustment was larger for the UK, this rather complicated argument would predict a greater (short-term) variability of monetary growth in the UK.

It does seem likely that financial markets should adjust more quickly in the UK than in France, for they are generally wider, less controlled and more developed in the former, and that the labour market in particular should adjust more slowly in the UK where, for example, there is a much higher density of trade union membership than in France.[21] These possibilities need to be tested and the rest of the argument needs to be developed at much greater length than can be done here, but there seems to be some prima-facie evidence to support the importance of this factor.

VI

Of the seven possible explanatory factors considered in the preceding sections, only the first, that of greater variability of monetary targets in the UK, has been rejected outright. Of the remaining six, the greater ambitiousness of monetary policy in the UK, and the use of direct credit controls in France but not in the UK, are relevant to the explanation of the difference in the medium-term variability of monetary growth. The greater magnitude of public sector deficits and transactions in the UK is relevant to the explanation of medium-term variability in the earlier part of the period, and of short-term variability throughout. The greater instability of the demand for money in the UK is essentially an occasional factor. And both the greater exposure of the UK economy to external disturbances and the larger gap in speeds of adjustment between financial and labour markets in the UK are primarily relevant for the explanation of the difference in the short-term variability of monetary growth.

Thus, with five out of seven factors making some contribution, in qualitative terms at least, the explanation of the difference in short-term variability seems to be relatively straightforward. Moreover, it does not seem unreasonable to explain the changes in the variability of monetary growth in the two countries between subperiods in terms of improvements in the framework of monetary control in the UK, notably the development of debt sales as an efficient and flexible instrument, on the one hand, and in terms of a greater unsuitability of the *encadrement du crédit* in France to a situation of larger budget and external deficits, together with the recent movement towards a less gradualist and more ambitious use of monetary policy, on the other.

To explain the difference in the medium-term variability of monetary growth, however, it seems necessary to rely for the most part on only two factors, namely the use of direct credit controls in France, but not the UK, and the greater ambitiousness of monetary policy in the UK, and (at least) two particular questions are provoked by the attachment of so much weight to these factors. The first is the question posed and partly answered above, as to why the *encadrement du crédit* did not, apparently, stimulate more than a relatively limited amount of evasion. The admittedly partial answers offered to this question above referred to the process of continuous modification of the system by the Bank of France and to the relatively limited opportunities for evasion due to the channelling of nearly all monetary creation through bank lending to the economy. But a third point can be added here: the suggestion that the *encadrement* worked as well as it did precisely because of the relatively unambitious purposes to which it was put, precisely because the authorities were not trying to use monetary policy alone to exert major pressures on the economy or to bring about major changes in its course. Thus this factor can usefully be tied up with the other factor which is being invoked to explain the difference in the medium-term variability of monetary growth.

The second question is – why should monetary policy in the UK have been more ambitious? There are three ways of answering this question. First it could be argued that this ambitiousness is merely a logical consequence of the combination of equally or less variable targets with poorer 'monetary marksmanship': given that the authorities overshoot one target the next target is bound to be 'tighter' with respect to lagged monetary growth. Secondly, it could be argued that the UK has experienced a wider range of governments in terms of their objectives for economic policy and their perceptions of the workings of the economy, though it should be said that closer examination of the swings in French governments, from the Chirac expansion through the Barre Plan to the Mitterrand reflation and deflation, casts some doubt on this argument.

Thirdly, and more interestingly, it could be argued that the greater ambitiousness of UK policy is a response to some specific characteristics of the UK economy. In particular it could be argued that certain aspects of the UK monetary and economic system – especially those which have been cited above as explaining the greater short-term variability of monetary growth in the UK – make unambitious and stable policies more difficult to operate because any deviation in either direction from some intended 'moderate' course is likely to be immediately amplified. Thus there is a kind of 'knife-edge' to the operation of macroeconomic policy in the UK, which stems above all from the efficiency and openness of UK financial markets, for this is the common denominator of the sixth and seventh explanatory factors considered above, exposure to external disturbances and differential speeds of adjustment. It is itself partly responsible for the fifth factor, the instability of the demand for money, and it is highly relevant to the workings of the fourth factor, the size of public sector deficits and transactions. Moreover, it is possible that the perception of this knife-edge has made policy-makers tend to prefer less moderate policies in one direction or another which run less risk of being turned into a policy of the opposite kind.

Some illustration may be helpful at this point. The period considered in the paper includes for the UK two episodes of 'non-moderate' policies which were adhered to for a surprisingly long time despite an accumulation of evidence as to their undesirable effects: the Heath–Barber expansion of 1971–3 and the Thatcher deflation of 1980 onwards. It is not clear whether the governments concerned intended policy to be, respectively, quite as expansionary and quite as deflationary as it turned out to be. But at least policy did turn out to be, respectively, expansionary and deflationary. By contrast the period between these episodes involved an attempt to follow a 'moderate' and stabilising course which more than once turned out to be contractionary when it had not been intended to be (for example, 1974–5) or inflationary when it had not been intended to be (for example, 1976).[22] On the other hand, French policy over this period was predominantly 'moderate' and the episodes of 'non-moderation' such as the Chirac and Mitterrand expansions were brief.

It has been argued above that the difference in the medium-term variability of monetary growth between the two countries is dominated by a difference in the ambitiousness of policy, since the effectiveness of French direct credit controls was partly contingent on the unambitiousness of French policy. The suggestion now being made – and it can be no more than that – is that UK policy has been more ambitious because of some greater potential for instability in the UK economic system, which is in turn related to the greater efficiency and 'liberalness' of UK financial markets, relative to the perhaps greater 'inefficiency' of the UK labour market. Thus the higher (medium-term) variability of monetary growth in the UK may be a response to the difficulties of operating monetary policy in an economy where financial markets adjust very quickly but goods and services markets rather slowly. If so, however, it can be argued that this is a perverse response, partly because of the adverse effects on the economy of the instability of policy but also because ambitious monetary targets tend to provoke a reaction from the economy through the endogeneity mechanisms such that in quantitative terms they are inherently more difficult to achieve.

Finally it should be noted that France is now experiencing a period of reform and deregulation which is likely to bring her financial markets much closer to those of the UK in terms of their flexibility, their capacity for innovation and their openness to structural change. This process has already raised questions about the significance of particular monetary aggregates comparable to those discussed in the UK since the late 1970s.[23] It is also likely to increase the short-term variability of monetary growth in France, again bringing France closer to the UK. And it may create the temptation for policy makers to go for ambitious policies which increase the medium-term variability of monetary growth as well.

Notes

1. There is also a considerable difference in the accuracy with which the monetary authorities in the two countries have been able to hit their monetary targets. This difference is examined in Cobham and Serre (1986), a companion piece to the present paper, which also gives an outline of the development of monetary policy and control in each country over the period. On this development see also Cobham (1985).

2. See, for example, Frochen and Maarek (1981) and Guillaumont-Jeanneney (1982).

3. The results for four quarter moving totals, which incorporate a more consistent smoothing, indicate for both countries a somewhat smaller variability, but are otherwise comparable to those for annual data.

4. Results for a wider sample of countries – the Group of Seven – using annual data 1970–81 (from *International Financial Statistics Yearbook*, 1982) show that for 'money' + 'quasi-money' the UK had the highest, and France the lowest, variability out of the seven (the only exception being the σ measure for the USA), while the results for 'money' alone are less clearcut, with several countries showing higher variability on one or both measures than the UK but France still having the lowest.

5. M2 and its counterparts are used here because of difficulties in obtaining consistent series back to 1970 for the slightly different counterparts of M2R, the aggregate which is now targeted and which is probably preferable on *a priori* grounds both as control variable and as indicator of policy. Seasonally adjusted quarterly data for 1984 on the counterparts of M2 were unavailable at the time of writing and may not be produced. The differences between the UK and French official presentations of the relationship between monetary growth and counterparts are essentially matters of convention.

6. Some support for this statement can be found in Cobham (1982) and Artis and Lewis (1981, pp. 46–8) for the UK; on France see Serre (1979), Guillaumont-Jeanneney (1982, pp. 216–32), and David (1984); see also the discussion of the experience of monetary targeting in the two countries in Cobham and Serre (1986).

7. The targets are listed in Cobham and Serre (1986); in making these calculations the 'overlapping' targets in the UK case have been omitted as in Tables 1 and 4 of that paper and Table 4.2 below.
8. The nominal GDP forecasts available from 1982 are very close to the (£M3) monetary targets, but if some allowance was made for the expected trend growth in the velocity of sterling M3 then the relation between targets and GDP forecasts would probably be comparable to that in France since 1979.
9. Respectively 4.5 per cent and 7.8 per cent of sterling M3 outstanding.
10. Other factors relevant to this episode are discussed below. The general possibility of bank lending rising in response to a squeeze as companies increase their overdrafts is stressed in Bain and McGregor (1985).
11. σ/μ is not given in this table because what is relevant here is the contribution of the individual counterpart to the variability of monetary growth rather than its own variability. This contribution depends not only on the variance of the counterpart but also on its covariance with the other counterparts; various ways of taking account of the latter have been tried but the results were not interesting and are not reported here.
12. The exception is 1981 Q2 to 1983 Q4 where both stable resources, a negative item closely related to bank lending, and gold and foreign exchange were more variable.
13. Unless some very particular interactions among the counterparts are assumed.
14. See Serre and Cobham (1986) for further details on the *encadrement du crédit*. See also the study by Serre (1985) which obtained a significantly negative coefficient on an *encadrement* dummy in a New Classical-type monetary growth equation (annual data 1959–83), indicating that monetary growth has tended to be slightly lower when the *encadrement* was operating.
15. For £M3, for example, σ and σ/μ for the periods (a) 1964 Q1 to 1969 Q4, (b) 1965 Q1 to 1967 Q1 – when credit ceilings were operating, and (c) 1967 Q4 to 1970 Q4 – when credit ceilings were again in force, are as follows: (a) 1.27; 0.85, (b) 1.43; 0.89 and (c) 1.18; 0.80. However, other things may not have been equal as between these subperiods and those for which results are given in the tables.
16. For the four subperiods given in Table 4.3 the values of σ for this public sector contribution to monetary growth are 1.50, 2.00, 1.86 and 2.33 respectively.
17. For a similar study see David (1984, pp. 63–82). Simple confirmation of the basic empirical point is provided by calculations of the variability of French velocity (GDP/M2) and UK velocity (GDP/£M3), for annual data 1970–84: for France $\sigma = 0.10$ and $\sigma/\mu = 0.05$, for the UK $\sigma = 0.34$ and $\sigma/\mu = 0.11$. French M2 may have been influenced by the government's 'savings' or 'money demand' policies operated since 1978, and designed to encourage private sector savings, and increase the role in the financial system of the capital

markets and of other forms of non-bank financial intermediation; and by policies designed to improve company profits and reduce companies' dependence on bank credit (Biacabe, 1984). But the difference in the variability of monetary growth between the two countries is obviously a more solid phenomenon, relating to earlier subperiods as well, and to narrower and wider measures of the money supply which are less likely to be influenced by such policies.

18. See Estrin and Holmes (1984) for further details.
19. See Melvin (1985) for some recent work in this area whose results appear to suggest a somewhat higher degree of currency substitutability for sterling than for the franc.
20. See the papers in Eltis and Sinclair (1981), especially those by Beenstock, Budd and Warburton (1981) and Buiter and Miller (1981).
21. Barker, Britton and Major (1984) have argued that real wages are less flexible in France because of the more institutionalised system of indexation, but it is nominal wage flexibility which is relevant here and, in general, lower real wage flexibility implies higher nominal wage flexibility. It could also be argued that in the 1980s French incomes policy has speeded up the process of price adjustment in the labour market while the absence of an incomes policy in the UK contributed to the extent and duration of the loss of international competitiveness initially associated with the sterling appreciation of 1979–81. For comparison of French and UK financial markets see Morgan and Harrington (1977).
22. Similar difficulties attended an earlier Labour government's attempt to reduce the balance of payments deficit (caused by another 'non-moderate' policy) gradually and without savage deflation, in 1964–7.
23. See, for example, Biacabe (1984).

References

Artis, M. J. and Lewis, M. K. (1981) *Monetary Control in the United Kingdom* (Oxford: Philip Allan).

Atkinson, P., Blundell-Wignall, A., Rondoni, M. and Ziegelschmidt, H. (1984) 'The efficacy of monetary targeting: the stability of demand for money in major OECD countries', *OECD Economic Studies*, 3 (autumn): 146–76.

Bain, A. D. and McGregor, P. G. (1985) 'Buffer stock monetarism and the theory of financial buffers', *Manchester School*, 53: 385–403.

Barker, K., Britton, A. and Major, R. (1984) 'Macroeconomic policy in France and Britain', *National Institute Economic Review*, 110 (November): 68–84.

Beenstock, M., Budd, A. and Warburton, P. (1981) 'Monetary policy, expectations and real exchange rate dynamics', in Eltis and Sinclair (1981).

Biacabe, P. (1984) 'La politique monétaire en France', *Revue d'économie politique*, 94: 639–48.

Buiter, W. H. and Miller, M. (1981) 'Monetary policy and international competitiveness: the problem of adjustment', in Eltis and Sinclair (1981).

Cobham, D. (1982) 'Domestic credit expansion, the balance of payments and exchange rate, and inflation: some aspects of UK monetary policy, 1963-78, unpublished PhD thesis, Manchester University.

Cobham, D. (1985) 'A disequilibrium monetarist approach to the assessment of monetary control regimes', University of St Andrews, July, mimeo.

Cobham, D. and Serre, J-M. (1986) 'Monetary targeting: a comparison of French and UK experience', *Royal Bank of Scotland Review*, 149 (March): 24-42.

Debonneuil, X. and Pages, H. (1984) 'Encadrement du crédit et rationnement', *Cahiers économiques et monétaires*, 18: 125-64.

Eltis, W. A. and Sinclair, P. J. N. (1981) *The Money Supply and the Exchange Rate* (Oxford: Oxford University Press).

Enfrun, B. and Pecha, J. (1983) 'La nouvelle méthode d'élaboration de l'indicateur de morsure de l'encadrement du crédit', *Bulletin Trimestriel de la Banque de France*, 47 (juin): 55-88.

Estrin, S. and Holmes, P. (1984) 'International trade and the external constraint', London School of Economics and University of Sussex, mimeo.

Frochen, P. and Maarek, G. (1981) 'Réflexions sur le concept de base monétaire en France', *Cahiers économiques et monétaires*, 11: 5-41.

Guillaumont-Jeanneney, S. (1982) *Pour la politque monétaire* (Paris: Presses Universitaires de France).

Melvin, M. (1985) 'Currency substitution and Western European Monetary Unification', *Economica*, 52: 79-91.

Morgan, E. V. and Harrington, R. (1977) *Capital Markets in the EEC*, (Farnborough: Wilton Publications).

Serre, J-M. (1979) *Les théories de l'offre de monnaie*, Thèse d'Etat, Faculté des Sciences Economiques de l'Université de Clermont I.

Serre, J-M. (1985) *Neutralité de la dette publique et effets macro-économiques des 'chocs financiers'*, Thèse complémentaire, Faculté des Sciences Economiques de l'Université de Clermont I.

Serre, J-M. and Cobham, D. (1986) 'The new system of credit control in France', *Business Economist*, 17(2): 31-44.

Part II
Modelling Money and Banking

5 Buffer-Stock Money: An Appraisal*

Keith Cuthbertson and Mark P. Taylor

1 INTRODUCTION

In the recent literature there has been a revival of interest in the role of money as a buffer stock, that is, as an asset that acts as a 'shock absorber' enabling agents temporarily to postpone otherwise costly adjustments to alternative economic variables such as employment, investment and output. In broad terms this approach has been prompted by problems encountered in trying to estimate stable 'conventional' demand for money functions, in understanding the 'long and variable lags' of monetary policy and in the phenomenon of interest rate (and hence exchange rate) overshooting under monetary targets. Running in tandem with the buffer-stock notion has been the wide application in macroeconomics generally of the rational expectations (RE) hypothesis and 'market clearing' RE models of the New Classical School, where a key distinction is drawn between anticipated and unanticipated events. Although the buffer-stock approach is often dubbed 'disequilibrium money', we argue below that certain buffer-stock models are not necessarily inconsistent with RE and, indeed, that one can usefully combine the two approaches. There is also a recurring debate in the literature (Laidler, 1982) concerning the interpretation of estimated demand-for-money functions: are they demand functions, or do they represent reparameterised real balance equations (where causation runs from money to the arguments of the demand for money function)? The notion that buffer holdings of money are voluntarily held in the short run and then dissipated in a slow real balance effect clearly has attractions both as an explanation of 'temporal instability' in demand for money functions and in contributing to an explanation of 'long and variable lags'.

*This paper represents joint work. The authors wish to acknowledge helpful comments from Charles Goodhart and Ross Milbourne. Cuthbertson also acknowledges helpful discussions with Mike Artis while a Hallsworth Fellow at the University of Manchester.

One response to the temporal instability in demand-for-money functions over the 1970s has been the 'reopening of the pre-1973 agenda' (Judd and Scadding, 1982) whereby different combinations of a set of independent variables are incorporated into the short-run demand function.[1] This has produced some improvement in the temporal stability of some demand for money functions but much remains unexplained. For example, in a survey of US results Judd and Scadding (1982) report that proxy variables for financial innovation in the provision of bank deposits improve the performance of equations explaining the demand for M1. For the UK, Grice and Bennett (1984) find that incorporating wealth and the expected return on long-term debt improves the statistical performance of the demand for broad money (£M3).

'Conventional' demand for money functions usually include lagged dependent variables. Partial adjustment or adaptive expectations are often invoked as a rationalisation here. However, the partial adjustment mechanism constrains the lag structure unduly at the outset of the empirical investigation, while the adaptive expectations hypothesis is only optimal in somewhat restrictive circumstances.[2] Error correction models (ECM, Hendry, Pagan and Sargan, 1984) have less restrictive lag structures and allow partial adjustment and adaptive expectations as special cases, but the parameters are usually a convolution of expectations and adjustment effects and therefore may be subject to the Lucas (1976) critique. While the lagged dependent variable provides much of the statistical explanation in conventional demand-for-money functions, Laidler (1982) has argued that this variable cannot be rationalised in terms of partial adjustment when the money supply moves independently of demand, and there is continuous market clearing. Such independent supply shifts would occur under monetary targets, but are also likely to happen when the authorities set interest rates, since 'shocks' to the Public Sector Borrowing Requirement (PSBR) and bank advances (that is, the credit market hypothesis, Brunner and Meltzer, 1976) may result in increased money balances (at unchanged interest rates). Thus the notion that individuals are always on their short-run demand function, together with the presence of a lagged dependent variable with a large coefficient, both implies 'implausibly' long adjustment lags and an 'implausible' degree of overshooting in the arguments of the demand for money when the money supply moves independently of demand.

Resolution of the above problems provides a major challenge for monetary economists, and in this paper we present an appraisal of the contribution provided by considering money as a buffer stock and also by incorporating forward-looking behaviour into asset-holding decisions.

The literature in this area is vast and we do not intend to provide an exhaustive survey. Rather we present an overview of the main themes that have emerged, and although we discuss the micro-theoretic foundations of the approach, we concentrate on analyses of the empirical literature, including some of our own recent contributions. To broaden the accessibility of what may sometimes appear to the non-specialist economist as a rather bewildering array of disparate econometric models, we concentrate on the economic behaviour underlying the models, and relegate the detailed econometric points to notes and references to the source material.

We proceed as follows. In Section 2 we present the micro-theoretic arguments behind buffer-stock models and this is followed, in Section 3, by the main body of the paper which gives a synoptic account of the four main methods of empirically implementing the approach. We dub these: single equation disequilibrium money models, complete disequilibrium money models, the shock absorber and forward-looking models. In Section 4 we draw out the policy implications of these models and present some suggestions for further empirical refinements of the approach. We end with a brief summary.

2 MICRO-THEORETIC FOUNDATIONS

To illustrate the intuitive ideas behind the buffer-stock notion, consider the probable behaviour of firms in an uncertain environment. The costs of marginal adjustments to prices, wages, production and real stock levels may be very substantial relative to the 'interest foregone' by holding excess money balances. 'Shocks' to the firm's production and employment plans are likely to result in a change in cash balances which will be willingly held in the short run until the shocks are perceived as either permanent or temporary. Similarly, shocks to the money supply, for example, caused by an increase in the supply of bank advances may lead to unexpected changes in money holdings by other agents, when the advances are spent. In the buffer-stock approach, disequilibria originating in either demand or supply are explicitly considered. The speed with which firms adjust their 'excess' holdings of money may depend upon (a) their initial holdings, (b) the width of the 'band' within which money balances are allowed to fluctuate, (c) the review period for decisions, (d) the transactions costs of moving into other assets, goods, or in altering the production process, and (e) the source of the change in money balances and a view as to whether they are permanent or transitory (Goodhart, 1984). Taking up the last point, if the source of the change in 'buffer money' is concentrated rather narrowly, then even though each individual agent may adjust fairly quickly, the system as a whole may take considerable time to adjust as 'buffer money' is passed on to different agents.

If the money transactions technology is highly efficient and it is relatively costless to transfer between 'money' and 'near money', then buffer assets are likely to consist of a wider set of assets than transaction balances. For large firms in the UK, the automatic overdraft system may also be used as a buffer stock. Excess money may be used to reduce overdrafts. Cash shortages may also lead to increased overdrafts as the spread between money rates and the cost of overdrafts is relatively small for large firms. Thus, it may be liquidity that acts as the 'buffer stock' for large firms rather than simply 'money'.

For persons, the relevant interest spread between liquid assets and credit in the UK is rather large and automatic overdrafts are somewhat uncommon. Therefore, buffer assets are likely to consist of gross liquid assets, particularly money, and perhaps building society deposits. However, in countries where short-term credit is widely and easily available – for example, in the US and increasingly so in the UK (bank credit cards) – liabilities may also perform a buffer role.

At a more theoretical level, models of the precautionary demand for money (Miller and Orr, 1966; Akerlof and Milbourne, 1980; Milbourne, Buckholtz and Wason, 1983) provide a useful framework in which to analyse certain aspects of the buffer-stock approach. A characteristic of such models is that actual money balances are allowed to differ from 'return point holdings' by an amount that is unforeseen and unplanned. The individual agent allows his money balances to move between certain upper and lower limits and only when the latter are attained are money balances (instantaneously) adjusted to their return point(s). Planned (or average) money holdings are determined by the brokerage cost, the opportunity cost of money and some measure of the variability of net receipts. For example, in a particular version of Whalen's (1966) precautionary demand model (which assumes very risk averse behaviour), average money holdings $\bar{M}$ are given by

$$\bar{M} = \left(\frac{2\sigma^2 b}{r}\right)^{\frac{1}{3}}$$

where σ^2 = variance of transactions, b = brokerage fee and r is the opportunity cost of holding money balances. Except in some very restrictive cases the relationship between the variance of receipts and the level of income is likely to be highly complex. Having derived the level of *average* money balances, precautionary models allow the size of 'buffer holdings' to depend on the 'width' of the upper and lower bands, and the size of unanticipated receipts in any period (Goodhart, 1984; Milbourne, 1985). Note that 'buffer money', in the short run, is willingly held at unchanged interest rates.

What happens in such a model when there is an unanticipated increase in net receipts in the aggregate (consequent on, for example, an increase in government expenditure)? Some agents will hit their upper threshold and reduce their money balances to their 'return point holding' while others will accommodate an increase in buffer holdings. The net effect depends on the initial distribution of money balances across agents (since the 'shock' is unanticipated, the upper and lower thresholds will for the moment remain unaltered) but there is a presumption that aggregate buffer holdings increase, particularly if money balances are not continuously monitored. If the shock results in a permanent change in money balances, then a slow 'real balance' effect will ensue, altering prices, interest rates, and so on, and hence the 'return point' itself. Theories of the precautionary demand for money only explicitly analyse the increased voluntary holdings in the first stage of the above process but clearly a full buffer-stock model should also incorporate real balance effects.[3]

The precautionary demand model incorporates some rather restrictive assumptions. There is no explicit model of expectations and forward-looking behaviour, the dynamics of adjustment, and costs of monitoring money balances.[4] Moreover, the difficulties of measuring the (aggregate) variance of net receipts has rendered direct formal testing of the model the exception rather than the rule. The hypothesis might seem more amenable to testing at the micro level of the individual agent, but problems of confidentiality (for example, bank/customer relations) have largely precluded this option. It is unfortunate, but nevertheless true, that, in the empirical implementation of the buffer-stock notion, the precautionary demand model provides an intuitively appealing framework rather than an explicit equation suitable for estimation.

3   APPPLIED WORK ON BUFFER-STOCK MONEY: FOUR APPROACHES

3.1   Single equation disequilibrium money models

Estimates of demand-for-money functions for almost any developed country have a sizeable autoregressive component which has frequently been interpreted as reflecting slow adjustment of short-run to long-run desired money holdings. However, when such equations are inverted to obtain the market-clearing level of (say) the interest rate, the latter will grossly overshoot its long-run equilibrium value, in response to an exogenous change in the current period money supply. This has led various authors (Artis and Lewis, 1976; Laidler, 1982) to interpret these estimated 'demand-for-money' parameters as representing a slow real balance effect and to advocate inverting the demand for money function *prior to estimation.* The chosen argument of the 'demand function' then adjusts only slowly towards its long-run equilibrium value. If the supply of money is independent of demand factors, agents are temporarily forced off their *long-run* function because of slow adjustment in either interest rates, output or the price level (for example, Artis and Lewis, 1976; Laidler, 1980; Goodhart, 1984; Wren-Lewis, 1984). For example, Laidler (1982) demonstrates that a model in which the long-run equilibrium price level p_t^* is determined by the long-run demand-for-money function (with arguments $f(x)$)

$$p_t^* = m_t^s - f(x)$$

together with partial adjustment of prices

$$p_t - p_{t-1} = b(p_t^* - p_{t-1}) \quad 1 > b > 0$$

may be re-arranged to provide a conventional (real) partial adjustment model of the demand for money:

$$(m - p)_t = b f(x) + (1 - b)(m - p)_{t-1} + u_t$$

where $u_t = (1 - b)\Delta m_t$.

Artis and Lewis (1976) estimate a number of 'inverted' long-run demand-for-money functions assuming either slow adjustment in interest rates or nominal income. For the UK, using quarterly data up to 1973, they find more stable demand for money parameters (for narrow and broad money) than those obtained when money is taken as the dependent variable, and there is little or no implied overshooting in current period interest rates in response to a change in the current period money supply. It is not necessary that the money supply is taken to be weakly exogenous (in the econometric sense) in such single equation studies, but in practice this is usually the case. (Naturally any endogeneity would render Ordinary Least Squares (OLS) estimates inconsistent). A major problem with this single equation disequilibrium money approach is that only one argument may be chosen as the dependent variable, whereas on *a priori* grounds one might expect all the arguments of the demand function to adjust simultaneously.

3.2 Complete disequilibrium monetary models

The second type of buffer-stock model remedies the above defect and 'disequilibrium' money holdings are allowed to influence a wide range of real and nominal variables. In this complete model approach the following type of equations frequently appear:

$$\Delta X_t = f(Z_t) + \gamma(L) (M_t^s - M_t^d)$$

$$M_t^d = \alpha_0 P_t + \alpha_1 R_t + \alpha_2 Y_t$$

X_t may be a *set* of real and nominal variables (for example, output, prices, exchange rate), Z_t is a set of predetermined 'equilibrium' variables, M_t^d is the *long-run* demand for money and $\gamma(L)$ is a lag polynomial. As the money disequilibrium term appears in more than one equation, the model yields cross-equation restrictions on the parameters of the long-run demand-for-money function. This type of model has performed reasonably well for the US (Laidler and Bentley, 1983), UK (Davidson, 1984; Hilliard, 1980; Laidler and O'Shea, 1980), Australia (Jonson and Trevor, 1979), Canada (Laidler *et al.*, 1983) and Italy (Spinelli, 1979). In some of these models the money supply is taken to be exogenous (for example, Laidler and Bentley (1983) for the US, and Laidler *et al.* (1983) for Canada) and hence is not explicitly modelled, whereas for the UK (Davidson, 1984) and Australia (Jonson and Trevor, 1979) the money supply is determined by the financing requirement of the public sector borrowing requirement. By and large, these models have been estimated by 'systems methods' (for example, Three Stages Least Squares (3SLS) and Full Information Maximum Likelihood (FIML)) and have perhaps not proved as successful in explaining flexible exchange rate open economies as they have in the modelling of closed economies (such as the US).

If the coefficients of long-run money demand are the investigator's parameters of interest, then the approach has the drawback that any estimates of the latter are conditional on the correct specification of the whole model. For example, if one should want to test whether the co-efficients in the long-run demand for money remained stable over time, the need to estimate the whole model to obtain estimates of these parameters complicates the exercise to say the least. On the other hand, the complete model approach has the considerable advantage of showing the various routes whereby monetary growth affects the economy, whereas this second stage has yet to be attempted in the shock-absorber and forward-looking approaches to which we now turn.

3.3 Shock-absorber approaches

The third type of buffer-stock model directly estimates the demand-for-money function, but it is assumed that 'shocks' to the money supply are initially voluntarily held in transactions balances. The Carr–Darby (1981) (CD) version of this approach invokes the rational expectations hypothesis in that the monetary 'shock' is the difference between actual money in circulation and the expected money supply. Some of these unanticipated balances are voluntarily held in money balances. On the other hand, anticipated changes in the money supply are immediately reflected in price expectations, and if prices are perfectly flexible, real money balances remain unchanged.

CD test for the influence of unanticipated money on money demand using the following two equation model:

$$(m - p)_t = \beta' x_t + \alpha (m - m^a)_t + u_t \qquad (1)$$

$$m_t = \gamma' z_{t-1} + v_t \qquad (2)$$

where α is expected to lie in the closed interval $[0, 1]$. The first equation is a conventional demand-for-money function with the addition of an unanticipated money term. m_t is the logarithm of the nominal money stock at time t, p_t is the logarithm of the price level, x_t is a vector of determining exogenous variables observed at time t, β is a suitably dimensioned coefficient vector, and u_t is a random disturbance. m_t^a is the anticipated component of money supply and is determined as the predictions from equation (2). z_{t-1} is a vector of variables known to agents at $t-1$ which are considered to have a systematic influence on money supply, γ is a stable coefficient vector and v_t is the non-systematic component of the money supply process. The first two terms on the right hand side of (1) can be taken as representing planned and unplanned components of money demand respectively.

CD use a two-step estimation procedure: OLS on equation (2) yields predictions m_t^a which are then used in equation (1). CD report OLS estimates of equation (1) which appear to support the buffer-stock or shock-absorber hypothesis for a number of industrialised countries. However, MacKinnon and Milbourne (1984) (MM) formally demonstrate the intuitively obvious point that $(M - M^a)_t$ and u_t are correlated, and infer that OLS estimates of α are biased towards unity.[5] CD recognise this possibility and attempt to correct for the bias by using instrumental variables estimation, but MM argue that their use of a large number of principal components as instruments is likely to be dogged by very poor small sample performance (see Klein (1969)). However, a simple reparameterisation of (1) allows consistent estimates to be obtained by two-step OLS which are equivalent to the maximum likelihood estimates.

Equation (1) can be reparameterised:

$$(m - p)_t = \beta^{*\prime} x_t + \lambda (m^a - p)_t + u_t^* \tag{3}$$

where $\lambda = -\alpha/(1 - \alpha)$, $\beta^* = (1/(1 - \alpha))\beta$ and $u_t^* = (1/(1 - \alpha))u_t$.

If the buffer-stock hypothesis is correct, then the OLS estimate of λ (using predictions for m_t^a from (2)) should be significantly different from zero, and yield a consistent estimate of α significantly within the unit interval $[0, 1]$.[6]

MM point out that the second part of the buffer-stock hypothesis, namely that anticipated money does not influence real balances, may be tested by adding a term ϕm_t^a to equation (1), which after transformation yields:

$$(m - p)_t = \beta^{*\prime} x_t + \lambda (m^a - p)_t + \phi^* m_t^a + u_t^* \tag{4}$$

Under the null hypothesis we expect $\phi^* = \phi/(1 - \alpha)$ to be zero and λ to be negative.

Tests of the shock-absorber hypothesis are, of course, dependent on the form of the 'conventional' demand-for-money function assumed, and the model used to generate the anticipated (and unanticipated) money supply series.

CD, using US data on M1, include permanent and transitory income (as well as interest rates) in the demand function, and assume that only lagged values of money determine m_t^a via an ARIMA process. MM also use US data on M1 and assume an AR(4) model for m_t^a but include current income as the (only) transactions variable. MM find that OLS estimates of equation (4) yield a statistically significant, but *negative*, value of α (of around 4) and a statistically significant value for ϕ, thus rejecting the CD shock-absorber hypothesis.

Cuthbertson (1986b) using UK data on M1, an AR(4) model for m_t^a, and an autoregressive distributed lag (or error feedback) demand for money equation, finds that, for the MM formulation, the shock-absorber hypothesis is rejected. A representative equation is[7]

$$(m - p)_t = 2.4 + 0.01 (m - p)_{t-1} + 0.19 (m - p)_{t-2} \qquad (5)$$
$$\qquad\quad (0.7) \quad (1.4) \qquad\qquad (1.5)$$

$$+ 0.37 \Delta y_t + 0.24 y_{t-1} - 0.075 \Delta r_t - 0.037 r_{t-1}$$
$$\quad (1.5) \qquad (2.7) \qquad\quad (1.8) \qquad\quad (1.7)$$

$$- 0.86 \Delta p_t + 0.04 \Delta p_{t-1} + 0.67 (m^a - p)_t - 0.042 m_t^a$$
$$\quad (1.1) \qquad\quad (0.1) \qquad\qquad (0.9) \qquad\qquad (1.9)$$

IV, 64(i) – 81(iv), SE (%) = 1.67, LM(4) = 3.7, SARG = 3.7

All of the above-mentioned studies, when determining m_t^a, assume agents use univariate ARIMA fixed-coefficient models, estimated using the whole sample. Such models implicitly assume that the agent uses (unknown) future information when generating his expectations at an earlier date: the 'future information' is embodied in the estimate of γ. Friedman (1979) argues that this is implausible since, although $\hat{\gamma}$ approaches the 'true' γ asymptotically, agents never discover the true γ since they have only a finite information set and their 'optimal strategy' is to update their estimate of γ as new data becomes available. Using the Kalman filter (Duncan and Horn, 1972; Harvey, 1981) to generate expectations results in a form of generalised adaptive expectations (Lawson, 1984) where the partial adjustment parameter itself (the 'Kalman gain') evolves as agents learn about the data generation process. The Kalman filter therefore mimics Friedman's learning process, but is also optimal in the sense that agents are assumed to generate unbiased and minimum mean square error forecasts for time t based on information up to time $t-1$, the date that expectations are formed.[8] However, the particular model assumed to generate expectations is bound to be somewhat arbitrary. Cuthbertson and Taylor (1985) assume that agents are likely to use a fairly simple model, and suggest that expectations of the money supply are based on a stochastic time trend (Harvey and Todd, 1983). Using UK data, they take an error feedback (Hendry, 1979; Hendry, Pagan and Sargan, 1984) equation for M1 as their conventional demand-for-money function, and use a Kalman filter to generate the m_t^a series. Assuming money is endogenous, they utilise the MM formulation of the shock-absorber hypothesis (equation (3)) and estimate $\alpha = 0.12$, which is statistically highly significant, whilst anticipated money has no significant effect on real money balances. Hence, these results support the CD shock-absorber hypothesis even when the MM critique is accepted, but demonstrate the sensitivity of the results to the expectations scheme assumed (although we would wish to argue that the Kalman filter has intuitively desirable properties).

In a rejoinder to MM, Carr, Darby and Thornton (1985), (CDT) assert that the money supply is exogenous and that equation (1) must logically be considered as a price equation, thus precluding the problem of simultaneity. We feel that the former is a somewhat extreme view in the context of 'narrow money', given that the money supply is unlikely to be subject to perfect control by the authorities within the quarter, even when monetary targets are operating. However, we agree that it would be irrational for agents to use equation (2) to generate forecasts of the money supply (m_t^a) and then choose a value for endogenous money demand and hence the money supply using equation (1) (which incorporates these expectations). One can avoid this inconsistent behaviour either by abandoning 'rationality' or interpreting equation (1) as a price equation. Suppose we accept both of the CDT key assumptions in their rejoinder, do we then logically have to accept their 'consistent' estimates of 'α' which support the shock-absorber hypothesis? We would argue (Cuthbertson and Taylor, 1986a) that by using two-step methods, previous studies have neglected to test for the cross-equation rationality restrictions implicit in the CD shock-absorber hypothesis, and only if these are data acceptable can we accept the CDT estimates.

Since m_t^a is determined as the predictions from (2), we can consider joint estimation of the system formed from (2) and an equation derived from (1) after substituting for m_t^a:

$$m_t = \gamma' z_{t-1} + v_t \tag{6}$$

$$(m - p)_t = \beta' x_t + \alpha(m_t - \gamma^{*'} z_{t-1}) + u_t \tag{7}$$

By substituting the predictions from (2) into (1), two-step methods implicitly impose the rationality restriction $\gamma = \gamma^*$ in (7). However, a correct test of the buffer-stock hypothesis should test these cross-equation restrictions together with the significance of the estimated α. For example, using US data on M1B, Cuthbertson and Taylor (1986a) are largely able to replicate the CD and CDT results (assuming the exogeneity of the money supply in (1)). That is, unanticipated money is found to be a significant explanatory variable for real money holdings whilst anticipated money is insignificant, using a standard real partial adjustment 'demand' equation and a variety of forecasting equations. The latter included an ARIMA process, a pure autoregression and a money growth equation similar to those used by Mishkin (1983), containing lagged values of short-interest rates and the high employment budget surplus as well as lagged money. However, jointly estimating the system (2) and (7), they were able to reject strongly the cross-equation rationality restrictions. This undermines the results of CD and CDT since it suggests the imposition of invalid restrictions in these studies.

Cuthbertson and Taylor (1986b) test the implicit cross-equation rationality restrictions on UK data (identical to that used in Cuthbertson, 1986a). Specifically, they first generate a number of monetary anticipations series (using a pure autoregression, a seasonal ARIMA process, a Kalman filter and a stationary money growth equation containing lagged interest rates and lagged money) which are then used to test the buffer-stock hypothesis in a two-step fashion, using a real partial adjustment money demand function. A typical result is [9]

$$(m - p)_t = 0.178 + 0.058 y_t - 0.048 r_t + 0.937 (m - p)_{t-1}$$
$$ (0.48) \quad (3.1) \quad\quad (6.9) \quad\quad (37.5)$$

$$+ 0.757 (m - m^a)_t$$
$$ (8.3)$$

$$\text{OLS, } 64(\text{ii}) - 81(\text{iv}), \text{ R}^2 = 0.98, \text{ SE} = 1.2\%, \text{ h} = 0.87 \qquad (8)$$

where, for example, m_t^q are the predictions from a Mishkin-type stationary money growth equation containing four lags on interest rates and money growth. The coefficient on unanticipated money is within the unit interval [0, 1] and is strongly significant. Adding monetary anticipations as a separate explanatory variable in equation (8) yielded an insignificant coefficient. Taken at face value these results look as if they support the shock-absorber hypothesis. However, Cuthbertson and Taylor then go on to estimate jointly the system

$$m_t = \gamma' z_{t-1} + v_t \qquad (2)$$

$$(m - p)_t = \beta' x_t + \alpha(m_t - \gamma^{*'} z_{t-1}) + \delta \gamma^* z_{t-1} + u_t \qquad (9)$$

Imposition of both rationality ($\gamma = \gamma^*$) and neutrality ($\delta = 0$) yields the constrained system implicitly considered in the usual two-step set-up. Comparing this with a system in which we allow $\gamma \neq \gamma^*$ and $\delta \neq 0$ then allows a joint test of rationality and neutrality. In addition, comparing the fully constrained system ($\gamma = \gamma^*$ and $\delta = 0$) to a system in which we set $\gamma = \gamma^*$ but allow $\delta \neq 0$ then allows us to test neutrality ($\delta = 0$) subject to a maintained hypothesis of rationality ($\gamma = \gamma^*$) (which is implicitly what the two-step method does when anticipations are added into the design matrix). Finally comparing the fully constrained system ($\gamma = \gamma^*$, $\delta = 0$) to a system in which we impose neutrality ($\delta = 0$) but allow $\gamma \neq \gamma^*$ then allows a test of rationality subject to a maintained hypothesis of neutrality. If the joint hypothesis is rejected, careful examination of the other test statistics may then suggest which part of the joint null (neutrality plus rationality) is causing over-all rejection.[10] Cuthbertson and Taylor (1986b) do strongly reject this joint null for UK data and, in common with their US study (1986a), find that it is the cross-equation rationality restrictions which appear to be contributing most to over-all rejection.

Overall, our work therefore suggests that the CD model of buffer-stock money is not supported by the data, and it is the assumption of rational expectations which appears to be the main source of empirical failure.

3.4 A forward-looking buffer-stock model

On intuitive grounds it might appear somewhat bold to assume that agents who hold M1 (predominantly the personal sector in the UK, at least until very recently) form expectations of the *aggregate* money supply as posited by CD. However, in determining their *planned* money holdings, agents may be influenced by their *expected* level of transactions, and in addition may temporarily hold unanticipated increases in 'money' which they will perceive as innovations in nominal income (rather than in the aggregate money supply). These intuitively plausible ideas may be formalised in a tractable way by assuming that agents determine their planned money balances by minimising a multi-period quadratic cost function. The familiar one-period cost minimisation problem which has inspired so much money demand literature imputes myopic behaviour to the agents whose behaviour it describes, in the sense that these agents are depicted as computing their optimal current period money holding without regard for the condition into which this decision puts next period's minimisation problem. To overcome this, the quadratic cost function may be generalised to many periods. D is the discount factor, E is the expectations operator, m_t^*, is the long-run demand-for-money function and, with information available at $t-1$, the agent chooses m_t to minimise total cost C:

$$C = E_{t-1} \sum_{s=0}^{\infty} D^s \left[a_0 \left(m_{t+s} - m_{t+s}^* \right)^2 + a_1 \left(m_{t+s} - m_{t+s-1} \right)^2 \right] \quad (10)$$

The solution to this problem is an exercise in the discrete time calculus of variations (see, for example, Sargent, 1979) and results in a forward-looking model of the form.

$$m_t = \lambda_1 m_{t-1} + (1 - \lambda_1)(1 - \lambda_1 D) \sum_0^\infty (\lambda_1 D)^s E_{t-1} \, m_{t+s}^* \qquad (11)$$

where $E_{t-1} \, m_{t+s}^*$ are the expected values of future long-run money balances and λ_1 depends on the adjustment cost parameters a_i and the discount factor, D. The buffer-stock element arises because agents make decisions concerning m_t based on information in period $t-1$ and hence 'surprise' increases in nominal income are partly held as 'buffer money'. Hence if the long-run demand function is given by

$$m_t^* = c_0 \, p_t + c_1 \, y_t - c_2 \, r_t = c' x_t \qquad (12)$$

the estimating equation is (see Cuthbertson, 1984)

$$m_t = \lambda_1 m_{t-1} + \gamma (p - p^e)_t + \beta (y - y^e)_t - \delta (r - r^e)_t \qquad (13)$$
$$+ (1 - \lambda_1)(1 - \lambda_1 D) \, c' \, E_{t-1} \sum_0^\infty (\lambda_1 D)^s x_{t+s}^* + u_t$$

where we assume that monetary innovations are a linear combination of innovations in prices, income and interest rates, plus a 'catch-all' disturbance u_t.

To make the model operational we need to generate the expectations variables x_{t+s}^e and the surprise terms $(x - x^e)_t$: in the results reported below (see Cuthbertson, 1984) we use univariate autoregressive models. Predictions from the latter using the chain-rule of forecasting (based on information at $t-1$) are used in (13) to give 'two-step' estimates of the parameters of the buffer-stock demand-for-money function. The testable predictions of the demand-for-money function are that the weights on the expected future variables, x_{t+s}^e decline geometrically as the time horizon is extended, an intuitively plausible restriction, and that these 'weights' are related to the coefficients on the lagged dependent variable: the latter we refer to as the *backward-forward* restrictions.

The dynamic behaviour underlying equation (13) clearly differentiates between anticipated and unanticipated events. For example, an anticipated unit change in the level of income leads to a change in *current* period money holdings of $(1 - \lambda_1)c_1$ and money balances then rise monotonically to their long-run value c_1. Adjustment is not instantaneous because costs of adjustment are non zero (and finite). On the other hand, an unanticipated ('one shot') increase in income leads to a current period change in money holdings of β which then decline monotonically to their former level. The latter seems an intuitively acceptable buffer-stock response and is consistent with a slow real-balance effect. The model subsumes (Hendry, 1983; Mizon, 1984) 'conventional' demand-for-money functions. If the arguments of the demand-for-money function are generated by a random walk, equation (13) is of the autoregressive distributed lag (ADL) or error feedback form (Hendry, Pagan and Sargan, 1984). If, in addition, the 'surprise terms' are assumed to be zero, our model reduces to the partial adjustment or adaptive expectations approach. Cuthbertson (1984) reports that low-order autoregressive models provide a data coherent description of the evolution of the 'forcing variables' y_t, p_t, r_t, over the data period 64(i)-82(iv). The forward-looking demand-for-money function is estimated by OLS using predictions of the 'forcing variables' y^e_{t+s}, p^e_{t+s}, r^e_{t+s} obtained by the chain rule of forecasting. A representative equation for M1 for the UK reported in Cuthbertson (1984) which imposes the data acceptable unit price (expectations) elasticity and backward-forward restrictions[11] is

$$m_t = -0.2 + 0.88\, m_{t-1} + 0.024 \sum_0^8 (\lambda_1 D)^i\, y^e_{t+i} \qquad (14)$$
$$(0.5) \quad (26.1) \qquad (4.1)$$

$$-0.012 \sum_0^8 (\lambda D)^i\, r_{t-1} + 0.59\, (p - p^e) + 0.23\, (y - y^e)_t$$
$$(4.6) \qquad\qquad (2.5) \qquad\qquad (2.5)$$

$$-0.068\, \Delta r_t$$
$$(4.4)$$

64(i)-82(iv), SE (%) = 1.45, dw = 2.4

The current period impact of a one per cent increase in the expectations variables has a much smaller effect on current money holdings than their unanticipated counterparts. For example, an unanticipated change in real income has more than three times the *impact effect* of an anticipated increase in income. This emphasises the buffer-stock role of money. In the long run, anticipated changes have a more powerful effect as one might expect and, for example, the long-run effect of a permanent change in Y^e_{t+j} (for all *j*) yields an elasticity of 0.84. The long-run interest rate elasticity is −0.43 (a semi-elasticity of 4.3 for interest rates at 10 per cent).

The forward-looking buffer-stock model throws some light on possible deficiencies in 'conventional' backward-looking formulations of the demand-for-money function. Conventional models omit potentially important variables, namely *future* values of the arguments of the demand for money. It would be paradoxical for the demand for transactions balances to depend on the *past* level of transactions, unless these are a proxy variable for future transactions (as in the adaptive expectations formulation of conventional functions). Our proposed autoregressive equations, unlike the adaptive expectations hypothesis, provide minimum mean square error predictions of the relevant variables, conditional on the information set assumed. Also, by explicitly modelling the expectations process, we go some way towards meeting the Lucas critique. Conventional demand functions that estimate a convolution of expectations and adjustment lags (for example, certain error feedback equations, Coghlan, 1978; Hendry, 1979) may exhibit instability because of instability in the expectations generating process. Also, long-run (dynamic) equilibrium solutions from such models are, generally, invalid under rational expectations (Cuthbertson, 1986a).

A policy implication that is immediately apparent from the model is that 'overshooting' after an unanticipated independent change in the money supply is mitigated in our forward-looking model. If the increase in the money supply is accompanied by an unanticipated increase in nominal income this leads to a temporary increase in holdings of buffer money. Also to the extent that an increase in the money supply leads to a reappraisal of the *expected* future path of the price level and real income, the demand for money increases *today*, and this reduces any disequilibrium in the money market, at given interest rates.

In conclusion, it appears that the forward-looking buffer-stock model of the demand for M1 performs reasonably well on UK data, has intuitively plausible features, and partly reconciles some troublesome issues in empirical monetary economics.

4   POLICY IMPLICATIONS AND FURTHER RESEARCH

An important condition for the successful conduct of monetary policy is a stable demand for money function. The empirical approaches examined here to modelling buffer-stock money have all attempted to provide stable parameter estimates of the demand-for-money function and have undoubtedly improved the empirical performance of such equations. The 'disequilibrium money' approaches have also provided evidence on the real balance effect and on the 'long and variable lags' of the monetary transmission mechanism. The CD shock absorber and our forward-looking buffer-stock model combine elements of *voluntary* short-run holdings of buffer-stock money and their dissipation in a slow real balance effect (although the latter is not explicitly modelled). The former mitigates the possibility of interest rate overshooting under monetary targets. In addition, the forward-looking model highlights the distinction between anticipated and unanticipated events in the money markets and suggests that 'causality studies' (Sims, 1972; Goodhart, Gowland and Williams, 1976) are unlikely to reveal an invariant, or indeed informative, causal sequence: if events are anticipated and money is endogenous then 'money' supply may move prior to the actual change in the arguments of the demand-for-money function. Finally, the forward-looking model, because it explicitly models the expectations process (admittedly rather crudely), may provide some evidence on the empirical importance of the Lucas (1976) critique.

We believe that we have demonstrated considerable empirical support for certain versions of the buffer-stock approach, at least on UK data for narrow money. Much however remains to be done.

First, we should like to apply the above approaches to broader financial aggregates where one might expect buffer holdings to be somewhat larger than for M1. It may be that, particularly for the company sector, net rather than gross liquidity acts as the buffer stock. It may then be possible to begin exploring the link between buffer holdings of assets and real expenditure decisions (for example, liquidity problems and the subsequent collapse of stockbuilding in 1980-82).

Secondly, alternative expectations schemes such as the vector autoregressive approach of Hansen and Sargent (1980) and the Kalman filter need to be used in order to test the robustness of the forward-looking model. On a more technical level, the correct treatment for autocorrelation in RE models with forward-looking variables (Hayashi and Sims, 1983) must be applied to the forward-looking model. Finally, uncertainty needs to be introduced into the forward model and tractable methods would appear to involve use of the conditional variances of forecast error which are generated as by-products of the Kalman filter, or the use of the Autoregressive Conditional Heteroscedasticity (ARCH) model of Engle (1982). These two approaches provide practical methods of generating data on the variability of expectations about prices, income and interest rates that may be used in asset demand functions.

SUMMARY

Our understanding of monetary phenomena is in part a consequence of improved 'elegant' micro-theoretic models, and partly a consequence of testing more eclectic models (cf Duhem-Quine thesis – Cross, 1982) against the data and other competing models (for example, non-nested tests). On all fronts we believe the approach whereby money is treated as a buffer stock has reasonable theoretical appeal and enough empirical support to warrant further research. We are only too well aware of past failures to reach the monetary economist's nirvana to state our claim more boldly.

Notes

1. Cooley and Leroy (1981) provide an interesting discussion of the econometrics of this research programme in the context of extreme bounds analysis.
2. Only when the variable in question is an ARIMA (0, 1, 1) process is the adaptive expectations hypothesis 'optimal' – see Muth (1960).
3. Laidler (1983) appears to consider the buffer-stock approach in a very special way. He does not emphasise the Miller–Orr return point model but rather considers money as exogenous and consisting only of fiat currency. Since the economy in aggregate cannot get rid of fiat currency, such holdings are involuntary and are dissipated in a real balance effect. Thus Laidler's exposition embodies a more restrictive interpretation of 'buffer stock money' than that elaborated here.
4. An exception here is provided by Milbourne, Buckholtz and Wason (1983) who develop a micro-theoretic model in which net receipts follow a diffusion process and agents trade off brokerage costs, and the opportunity cost of holding money balances. The novelty of this target-threshold model lies in the explicit modelling of the adjustment process. A form of first order partial adjustment, with an adjustment parameter depending on the variance in receipts, and the level of interest rates, ensues.
5. Since u_t determines m_t and m_t^a is predetermined then u_t and $(m - m^a)_t$ are correlated.
6. It may seem in the MM formulation (equation (3)) that we merely replace the 'CD problem' of m_t appearing on both sides of the equation with p_t performing the same role. However, the crucial point for consistent OLS estimates is the (econometric) exogeneity of p_t. If p_t is exogenous and hence equation (3) is *interpreted as a demand-for-money function*, OLS estimates are consistent. We consider the alternative, whereby equation (3) is interpreted as a price equation later in the text. A valid criticism of equation (3) interpreted as a partial adjustment demand for money function is that it imposes an untested *instantaneous* unit price level elasticity. If we assume nominal partial adjustment and impose *only* long-run homogeneity and test for short-run homogeneity, the MM unrestricted regression using M1 (data as in Cuthbertson, 1986b) for equation (3) is:

$$m_t = -0.51 + 0.43m_{t-1} + 0.18y_t - 0.48r_t + 0.53p_t + 0.37\,(m^a - p)_t$$
$$\quad\;\;(1.3)\quad\;(1.7)\qquad\quad(4.2)\qquad(5.6)\qquad(2.1)\qquad\;(1.5)$$

OLS, 64(i) − 81(iv), SE (%) = 1.5, dw = 2.2

The Wald test against the restricted regression with instantaneous homogeneity gives a *t*-statistic of 2.7, rejecting the latter assumption at a 5 per cent significance level. Equation (5) below provides a more general autoregressive distributed lag (ADL) equation which imposes only long-run price level homogeneity.

7. All variables are in logarithms: p_t is the consumer price index, y_t is real personal disposable income, r_t is the 3-month local authority rate: all data are seasonally unadjusted and quarterly dummies are suppressed in results quoted. Because of the potential endogeneity of y_t, p_t, r_t and $(m^a - p)_t$ the equation is estimated using instrumental variables, IV. SARG is Sargan's (1964) test of the independence of instruments and errors which is asymptotically distributed as chi-squared (with, in this case, 8 degrees of freedom) under the null of 'independence'. The critical value at 5 per cent significance level is 15.5. LM(4) is the Breusch-Godfrey (1981) Lagrange multiplier statistic for serial correlation in the residuals of up to order 4 when the equation is estimated using IV. Under the null of no serial correlation the LM statistic is asymptotically distributed as chi-squared and here the critical value at a 5 per cent significance level is 9.5. SE is the percentage standard error of the equation, *t*-statistics are in parentheses.

8. Friedman (1979) suggests the use of recursive least squares to avoid this problem. However, recursive least squares is just a very special case of the Kalman filter.

9. *h* is Durbin's (1970) statistic for the first order serial correlation distributed as $N(0, 1)$ under the null of no serial correlation.

10. The system composed of (2) and (9) is formally similar to the 'efficient markets' models considered in Mishkin (1983). In particular, this implies that the test statistic associated with the joint test of rationality and neutrality is identical to the test statistic for the test of rationality subject to the maintained hypothesis of neutrality – see Mishkin (1983) ch. 2.

11. The data and definitions are those reported by Cuthbertson (1986b) and discussed in note 7. dw is the Durbin–Watson statistic. r_t is taken to be a random walk and hence future values depend only on r_{t-1}: unanticipated changes in the interest rate then become Δr_t. D is constrained to be unity in this equation.

References

Akerlof, G. and Milbourne, R. D. (1980) 'The short run demand for money', *Economic Journal*, 90: 885–900.

Artis, M. J. and Lewis, M. K. (1976) 'The demand for money in the United Kingdom 1963–1973', *Manchester School*, 44: 147–81.

Brunner, K. and Meltzer, A. (1976) 'An aggregative theory for a closed economy', in Stein, J. L. (ed.) *Monetarism* (Amsterdam: North Holland).

Carr, J. and Darby, M. R. (1981) 'The role of money supply shocks in the short run demand for money', *Journal of Monetary Economics*, 8: 183–200.

Carr, J., Darby, M. R. and Thornton, D. (1985) 'Monetary anticipations and the demand for money: reply to MacKinnon and Milbourne', *Journal of Monetary Economics*, 16: 251–7.

Coghlan, R. T. (1978) 'A transactions demand for money', *Bank of England Quarterly Bulletin*, 18(1): 48–60.

Cooley, T. F. and Leroy, S. F. (1981) 'Identification and estimation of money demand', *American Economic Review*, 71: 825–44.

Cross, R. (1982) 'The Duhem-Quine thesis, Lakatos and the appraisal of theories in macroeconomics', *Economic Journal*, 92: 320–40.

Cuthbertson, K. (1984) 'The demand for M1: A forward looking buffer stock model', *National Institute of Economic and Social Research*, Discussion Paper.

Cuthbertson, K. (1986a) 'Price expectations and lags in the demand for money', *Scottish Journal of Political Economy*, 33, forthcoming.

Cuthbertson, K. (1986b) 'Monetary anticipations and the demand for money: some UK evidence', *Bulletin of Economic Research*, forthcoming.

Cuthbertson, K. and Taylor, M. P. (1985) 'Monetary anticipations and the demand for money: results for the UK using the Kalman filter', *National Institute of Economic and Social Research*, Discussion Paper No. 90.

Cuthbertson, K. and Taylor, M. P. (1986a) 'Monetary anticipations and the demand for money in the US: further tests', University of Newcastle upon Tyne, mimeo.

Cuthbertson, K. and Taylor, M. P. (1986b) 'Monetary anticipations and the demand for money in the UK: testing the rationality of buffer stock money', *Journal of Applied Econometrics*, forthcoming.

Davidson, J. (1984) 'Money Disequilibrium: An Approach to Modelling Monetary Phenomena in the UK', London School of Economics.

Duncan, D. B. and Horn, S. D. (1972) 'Linear dynamic regression from the viewpoint of regression analysis', *Journal of the American Statistical Association*, 67: 815–21.

Engle, R. F. (1982) 'Autoregressive conditional heteroscedasticity with estimates of the variance of United Kingdom inflation', *Econometrica*, 50: 987–1007.

Friedman, B. M. (1979) 'Optimal expectations and the extreme information assumptions of rational expectations macroeconomics', *Journal of Monetary Economics*, 5: 23–41.

Goodhart, C. A. E. (1984) *Monetary Theory and Practice: The UK Experience* (London: Macmillan Press).

Goodhart, C. A. E., Gowland, D. and Williams, D. (1976) 'Money, income and causality', *American Economic Review*, 66: 417–23.

Grice, J. and Bennett, A. (1984) 'Wealth and the demand for £M3 in the United Kingdom, 1963–78', *Manchester School*, 52: 239–71.

Hansen, L. P. and Sargent, T. J. (1980) 'Formulating and estimating dynamic linear rational expectations models', *Journal of Economic Dynamics and Control*, 2: 7–46.

Harvey, A. C. (1981) 'The Kalman Filter and its applications in econometrics and time series analysis' *Methods of Operational Research*, 44: 3–4.

Harvey, A. C. and Todd, P. H. J. (1983) 'Forecasting economic time series with structural and Box-Jenkins models', *Journal of Business and Economic Statistics*, 1: 299–315.

Hayashi, F. and Sims, C. (1983) 'Nearly efficient estimation of time series models with predetermined but not exogenous instruments', *Econometrica*, 51: 783–98.

Hendry, D. F. (1979) 'Predictive failure and econometric modelling in macroeconomics: the transactions demand for money', in Ormerod, P. (ed.) *Economic Modelling* (London: Heinemann).

Hendry, D. F. (1983) 'Econometric modelling, the consumption function in retrospect', *Scottish Journal of Political Economy*, 30: 193–220.

Hendry, D. F., Pagan, A. R. and Sargan, J. D. (1984) 'Dynamic specification', in Griliches, Z. and Intrilligator, M. D. (eds) *Handbook of Econometrics* (Amsterdam: North Holland).

Hilliard, B. C. (1980) 'The Bank of England small monetary model: recent developments and simulation properties', *Bank of England*, Discussion Paper 13.

Jonson, P. D. and Trevor, R. (1979) 'Monetary rules: a preliminary analysis', *Reserve Bank of Australia,* Discussion Paper, 7903.

Judd, J. and Scadding, T. (1982) 'The search for a stable money demand function', *Journal of Economic Literature*, 20: 993–1023.

Klein, L. R. (1969) 'Estimation of interdependent systems in macroeconomics', *Econometrica*, 37: 171–92.

Laidler, D. E. W. (1980) 'The demand for money in the United States – yet again', in Brunner, K. and Meltzer, A. (eds) *On the State of Macroeconomics*, Carnegie-Rochester Conference Series on Public Policy, 12 (Amsterdam: North Holland).

Laidler, D. E. W. (1982) *Monetarist Perspectives* (Oxford: Philip Allan).

Laidler, D. E. W. (1983) 'The buffer stock notion in monetary economics', *Economic Journal*, 94: 17–34.

Laidler, D. E. W. and Bentley, B. (1983) 'A small macro-model of the post-war United States', *Manchester School*, 51.

Laidler, D. E. W., Bentley, B., Johnson, D. and Johnson, S. T. (1983) 'A small macroeconomic model of an open economy: the case of Canada', in Claassen, E. and Salin, A. *Recent Issues in the Theory of Flexible Exchange Rates* (Amsterdam: North Holland).

Laidler, D. E. W. and O'Shea, P. (1980) 'An empirical macro-model of an open economy under fixed exchange rates: the United Kingdom, 1954–1970', *Economica*, 47: 141–58.

Lawson, T. (1984) 'Generalized adaptive expectations', in van der Ploeg, F. (ed.) *Mathematical Methods in Economics* (New York: Wiley).

Lucas, R. E. (1976) 'Econometric policy evaluation: a critique', in Brunner, K. and Meltzer, A. (eds) *The Phillips Curve and Labor Markets*, Carnegie-Rochester Conference Series on Public Policy, 1 (Amsterdam: North Holland).

MacKinnon, J. G. and Milbourne, R. D. (1984) 'Monetary anticipations and the demand for money', *Journal of Monetary Economics*, 13: 263-74.

Milbourne, R. D. (1985) 'Re-examining the buffer stock model of money', London School of Economics, mimeo.

Milbourne, R. D., Buckholtz, P. and Wason, T. (1983) 'A theoretical derivation of the functional form of short run money holdings', *Review of Economic Studies*, 1: 531-41.

Miller, M. and Orr, D. (1966) 'A model of the demand for money by firms', *Quarterly Journal of Economics*, 80: 414-35.

Mishkin, F. S. (1983) *A Rational Expectations Approach to Macroeconomics*, Chicago: University of Chicago Press for the National Bureau for Economic Research).

Mizon, G. F. (1984) 'The Encompassing Approach in Econometrics', in D. F. Hanatry and K. F. Wallis (eds), *Econometrics and Qualitative Economics* (Oxford: Basil Blackwell).

Muth, J. F. (1960) 'Optimal properties of exponentially weighted forecasts', *Journal of the American Statistical Association*, 55: 299-306.

Sargent, T. J. (1979) *Macroeconomic Theory* (London: Academic Press).

Sims, C. A. (1972) 'Money, income and causality', *American Economic Review*, 62: 540-52.

Spinelli, F. (1979) 'Fixed exchange rates and monetarism; the Italian case', Research Report 7915, University of Western Ontario, mimeo.

Wren-Lewis, S. (1984) 'The company sector in disequilibrium: some preliminary results', *National Institute of Economic and Social Research*, Discussion Paper, 69.

6 Disequilibrium Money: Some Further Results with a Monetary Model of the UK*

James Davidson

The idea of modelling money as a buffer stock has recently attracted new interest, as papers such as Laidler (1984) and Goodhart (1984) testify, and a number of recent empirical studies are based on the concept. The approach, in some variation, is to embed a term measuring the difference between money held and money desired in one or more equations explaining real or financial adjustments in the economy, and possibly to estimate the parameters of the long-run money demand relation by this indirect route. An early instance was Johnson's monetary approach to the balance of payments (see Frenkel and Johnson, 1976). Other examples, in addition to the present author's work (Davidson and Keil, 1982; Davidson, 1984) include Howitt and Laidler (1979), Laidler and O'Shea (1980), Coghlan (1981), Jonson and Trevor (1981), Laidler and Bentley (1983), and Knoester and van Sinderen (1985).

Another approach to buffer-stock modelling, which is closer to the 'traditional' one of formulating a dynamic regression to explain the evolution of real balances, using either the partial adjustment or error correction principles to model the dynamics, is to include terms measuring money supply shocks in the equation, as in Carr and Darby (1981) and Artis and Cuthbertson (1985). By contrast, the embedding approach is cumbersome to implement and requires some justification. The aim of Section I of the paper is to argue the case that this is the 'correct' approach to the struc-

*This paper was prepared for presentation to the Money Study Group, 28 June 1985. I must thank David Vines, Charles Goodhart, Charlie Bean, Martin Weale and Peter Jonson for their comments on earlier versions of the model, though no responsibility attaches to them for the present one. I am also very grateful to Orazio Attanasio for research assistance, and to the Economic and Social Research Council Macroeconomic Modelling and Forecasting Consortium for support of this research.

125

tural modelling of money demand. In the following sections, some further developments with the system described in Davidson (1984) are reported.

I

Recent debates about the dynamics of money stock determination have brought a number of key problems into focus. One is the extent to which money is 'endogenous', by which we really mean, the extent to which the holders of money can control their nominal holdings in the aggregate and have the power to neutralise monetary shocks by 'countervailing' adjustments in the short or long run. More generally, the question raised is whether the variables which are important for restoring equilibrium in the money market are interest rates, prices, output, foreign flows, the money stock itself, or perhaps all of these to a significant extent. The 'traditional' money demand equation in which real balances are regressed onto the vector of arguments of money demand and lagged real balances is seen as an increasingly inadequate vehicle for the resolution of these questions (see Judd and Scadding, 1982, for a recent survey). The account of money-market dynamics given by this type of equation is typically rather implausible, with a lagged dependent variable coefficient sufficiently close to unity to cast doubt on the existence of a long-run solution. Cooley and LeRoy (1981) argue that the long-run elasticities of demand are not identifiable from such an equation.

An alternative model which avoids invoking the buffer stock concept, explored by Artis and Lewis (1976), inverts the money demand equation and treats it as a short-run interest rate equation exhibiting overshooting. This theory appears to be rejected empirically, and in any case seems incompatible with alternative explanations of interest rates in the short run (international parity, pegging by the authorities etc) (see also Goodhart, 1984).

It is a characteristic of buffer stock models that the relative speeds of adjustment to monetary shocks of interest rates and nominal income can be the reverse of those in the standard Keynesian model. Akerlof (1973) presents an 'inventory-theoretic' model of buffer stock money in which agents do not have a single-valued demand for money, but merely a band of acceptable holdings whose upper and lower limits depend on the usual arguments, and whose width is a function of information and transaction costs. In this model monetary receipts are absorbed without provoking a response (that is, a trip to the securities market) up to the point at which one or other of the boundaries is crossed. As Akerlof points out, an excess supply of money need not provoke an overshooting response in its price since the money may be *given* by the suppliers (the government, say) to the holders in exchange for goods and services, who therefore acquire it passively without any incentive being required to induce them to do so.

The concept of monetary 'shocks' is always a central one in this type of analysis, and Akerlof reminds us that money has the special characteristic (as the medium of exchange) that people can be induced to acquire additional quantities without demand conditions appearing to have altered. To adapt his quaint illustration, we cannot so easily conceive of an 'onion shock', since people do not acquire onions in the course of their other activities. Sources of monetary shocks, apart from deficit spending by the government, may include trade surpluses and, notably in the case of the UK, the removal of rationing constraints on bank credit issue. In principle open market operations are not shocks in this sense, since a price change is needed to induce a voluntary net sale of bonds by the non-bank private sector (NBPS) – but they can act as shocks if the interest elasticity of bond-holders is different from that of other agents to whom the extra money then passes.

The speed and character of the adjustment to shocks is a central issue here. We would not expect money-bond portfolios to be adjusted instantaneously. But for many small businesses and households towards the lower end of the income scale, transactions costs set the bounds on their permissible money holdings sufficiently wide that they effectively hold all their savings in liquid form, and adjust their holdings only through trades in labour and commodities. The effects of excess balances are transmitted by such trading like ripples through the economy and either dissipate through real balance effects on prices and output, or give rise sooner or later to an inter-sectoral transaction which tends to restore the volume of the nominal stock itself – for example, a purchase of government or foreign securities or an import of commodities. Rather than having a picture of each money-holder in the NBPS adjusting his/her money holdings by direct interaction with the other sectors, so that the rate of aggregate adjustment coincides with the average rate of individual adjustment, it ·may be more helpful to think of the markets through which money enters or leaves the system as *bottlenecks*.

Consider the money supply identity (which defines M3 if the conventional definition of the banking sector is adopted) showing how the money stock is defined as the sum of the net liabilities of the NBPS to the other main sectors of the economy (see Table 6.1 for variable definitions):

$$A^p + A^{po} + G - B^p + C + S^p - N = M + M^o$$

Setting aside the balancing item N, (the banks' non-deposit liabilities) and the foreign currency components $(A^{po} - M^o)$, £M3 is obtained for our purposes as the sum of bank loans to the NBPS (A^p), the public sector debt net of bond-holdings by the NBPS $(G - B^p)$, and the net liabilities to foreigners of the NBPS on current and capital account $(C + S^p)$.

The usefulness of this identity is to remind us of the routes by which money can enter or leave the system. In a simple model, the domestic items of credit are usually taken to be outside the control of the private sector. In the monetary approach to the balance of payments, the short-run demand for money becomes the equivalent of the demand for foreign credit. Since instantaneous adjustment of supply to demand implies un-realistically large imbalances in foreign payments flows, some unwanted money must be held in Johnson's model, and the balance of payments depends upon the supply-demand gap.

More realistically, we recognise that the control over the items of domestic credit has never been solely in the government's hands. The arguments for treating both bonds and bank loans as demand determined are made in Artis and Lewis (1976) for example. The NBPS has a measure of control over each of the components of money supply, in addition to which the path of prices and output can be influenced by a real balance effect associated with being off the money-demand curve.

An argument for very rapid countervailing adjustment of supply to demand is that this can take place through changes in bank credit holdings, particularly because the use of overdraft facilities do not have to be re-negotiated every time they are changed. This route of adjustment may of course be curtailed when bank lending is subject to regulation (and such regulations are effective), but what ensures that such adjustments are less than instantaneous is that overdraft facilities are neither freely available to bank customers, nor are they marketable. While the aggregate national overdraft may appear big enough to absorb the requisite degree of aggregate excess money, in practice the holders of the overdrafts and of the excess balances can be different people, who are able to join forces only if they can make mutually advantageous trades in goods and services. Neverthe-less, we would expect bank lending to be the most important single source of countervailing adjustments.

Countervailing purchases of government securities are the primary 'Keynesian' adjustment route, although we do not have to believe that prices take up all or any of the adjustment, given that for much of the pre-1979 period interest rates have been a more important target for governments than the money supply. One important characteristic of this particular bottleneck is that most investment decisions are taken by institutional managers with an eye to short-term capital gains, and these decisions are influenced by monetary conditions in the economy as a whole by several removes. Excess money may eventually show up in the form of additional funds available for investment in gilt-edged, but it seems unlikely that these same funds are also the site of the initial injection. The same sort of argument applies to leakages through the international money markets. We conclude that *complete* monetary adjustment must as a rule proceed at the pace of the most sluggish market.

A further conclusion of the foregoing analysis is that we should attempt to model the demand for the assets identified in equation (1), subject to the adding-up constraint. As Brainard and Tobin (1968) have pointed out, such a system of equations, especially if dynamic, embodies a complicated set of cross-equation parameter dependencies (see Green, 1984, for a recent effort at this type of modelling for the UK). Fortunately, the concept of buffer-stock money cuts through the difficulties of this approach by asserting that *money is the residual* in the system. In each period agents trade in goods and assets in a manner which satisfies their ex post wealth constraint. But the existence of a buffer stock allows these decisions to be made in a relatively independent manner. The equation for the buffer variable is, of course, defined by equation (1) together with a set of specifications for the left-hand side components, but there are no grounds to suppose it will have the same functional form as other asset demand equations (for example, elasticities depending on the variables in the same manner, and so on). To do so would almost certainly be to impose a misspecification. One should expect to predict the change in money holdings best as the sum of the net trades in all inter-sectoral markets, and for it to be determined in the short-run *in no other way*.

On this interpretation the traditional money demand equation has to be viewed as the sum of a set of equations explaining the net flows of sectoral liabilities. Whether such an equation should be called a demand or a supply function is really a semantic question. We have argued that the flows are basically demand determined, but supply arguments (shocks) will also appear in it, an aspect of the model captured by the Carr-Darby approach. But each of the constituent equations contributes a set of explanatory variables, and some will be subject to policy switches. It is perhaps not surprising that the dynamics of such a relationship should be hard to capture in a simple and stable specification (Gordon, 1984, argues similarly). As well as resolving this difficulty, the embedding approach has two other distinct advantages. First, it can distinguish between supply shocks and unanticipated changes, whereas Carr and Darby, for example, must use the latter to proxy for the former; secondly, it can make use of information about monetary disequilibrium contained in other economic adjustment relationships, which the simple dynamic money equation cannot capture.

Little has been said so far about the definition of money, but in general the above considerations must apply with greater force, as money is defined more broadly. The underlying assumption is that there are non-negligible transactions costs and/or capital risk involved in switching between money and non-money assets. One of the problems of this area is that the distinction between broad and narrow money as stores of value become increasingly ill-defined as competition increases the liquidity of interest-bearing deposits, and building society deposits become very close substitutes for checking deposits, for example. This is an issue taken up in the empirical work below.

II

The scheme used to model money and related variables is an *error correction system*. Briefly, a relation of the general form

$$M/PY = F(Y, r^l, r^s, \dot{p}) \tag{2}$$

is assumed to represent a target, towards which (the inverse velocity of) money would tend in a steady state. The deviation of the right-hand from the left-hand side of (2), denoted $\hat{V}$, is embedded in a system of dynamic adjustment equations describing the evolution of money-stock components, income, and commodity and security prices. The complete error correction system is written schematically as

$$A_1(L)\Delta y_t + A_2(L)\Delta z_t + C(L)f(y_{t-1}, z_{t-1}) = u_t \tag{3}$$

where $A_1(L)$, $A_2(L)$ and $C(L)$ are matrix polynomials in the lag operator, y_t and z_t are the vectors of endogenous and exogenous variables and u_t is a disturbance vector. $f(y, z) = 0$ is the system of *target relations* corresponding to the long run of the system, and assuming the system to be stable they will be satisfied on a constant steady-state path on which $\Delta y_t = u_t = 0$ and $\Delta z_t = 0$. More generally, the $f(y, z)$ for a given realisation of the variables are called the *target deviations*.

The vector of target relations assumed in the present model is given in Table 6.2, the various symbols being defined in Table 6.1. These relations are simplified and not intended to constitute a complete comparative static model of equilibrium. Their role here is to provide a minimal dynamic

Table 6.1 Variable definitions   131

In general, current values of domestic variables are treated as endogenous, in the sense that they are not available for use as instrumental variables. Variables whose current values have been used as instruments are labelled EXOG below, and note in particular that the exchange rate changes its exogeneity status when the exchange rate regime changes.

A^p = Sterling bank loans to NBPS
A^f = Sterling bank loans to overseas sector
B^{pm} = Market value of public sector debt of NBPS
P^g = *Financial Times Index* of gilt-edge prices
Y = GDP at constant 1975 prices
P = GDP deflator
C = Cumulated current account surplus
S^p = NBPS's net capital liabilities to overseas
ϵ = Exchange Rate ($/£ rate (EXOG) until 1971 (iv); 2.4x 'sterling effective' index thereafter)
M = Sterling money balances (M3 or PSL2)
B^b = Banks' holdings of public sector debt
B^p = Book value of public sector debt held by NBPS
D = Bank deposits
R = Cumulated transactions in official reserves
R^* = value of official reserves
r^l = yield on UK government stock over 20 years
r^s = rate on three months' Local Authority deposits
W = Average earnings
G = Cumulated PSBR
Cl = Dummy for bank lending restrictions
B^f = book value of public sector debt held by overseas sector
N = Banking sector's non-deposit liabilities
Pr = Output per man employed
r^f = 3-month eurodollar rate (EXOG)
r^{lf} = yield on US government stock over 20 years (EXOG)
r^{lf*} = MERM-weighted index of foreign long rates (available from 1972(i) only) (EXOG)
P^f = Foreign price level (UK imports price index)
D^* = SD/D, where SD = Banking sector's special deposits with the Bank of England
X = real exports (EXOG)
ΔO = balance of trade in petroleum-related products
FP = 3 months' forward premium on US dollars
$D79$ = Dummy for switch to monetary targets (= 0 to 1979(ii), = 1 thereafter)
Cc = Dummy for competition and credit control (= 1 in 1971(iii), = 0 otherwise) (EXOG)
EC = Dummy for removal of exchange controls (= 1 in 1979(iii), = 0 otherwise)
Y^f = index of world real income
$A(x)_i$ = polynomial distributed lag of x of length 13 quarters and order i
LT = $1 - 1/(1 + exp\{0.1t-7.7\})$

Table 6.2   The target relations

(a) $M/PY = \gamma_1 exp\{\delta_1 (r^s - 200.\Delta_2 lnP) + \delta_2 (r^l - r^s) + \delta_3 LT\}$
(b) $B^{pm}/M = \gamma_2 exp\{\delta_4 (r^l - r^s)\}$
(c) $(A^p + A^f)/D = \gamma_3$
(d) $r^l = r^s + ln\{\gamma_4 [(B^p + B^f)/(G + R)]^{\delta 5}\}$
(e) $r^s = r^f$
(f) $r^l = r^{lf}$
(g) $P = \gamma_5 P^f/\epsilon$
(h) $W/P = \gamma_6 Pr^{\delta 6}$
(i) $Y = \delta_7 Y^f$
(j) $S^p = \gamma_8$

framework within which to test theories of money demand. It's important to be clear about this aspect of the modelling methodology, and the following digression will summarise the issues. The stability analysis of models of this kind is discussed more fully in Davidson (1983).

The 'steady state', like any other equilibrium concept, is an imaginary construct. Steady state relationships are defined as the concomitants of an absence of change in the model, and are *not* expected to prevail either in any observed period, nor even 'on average', unless the changes average to zero over the period. In a state of non-zero steady growth of the exogenous variables, they are generally attained only up to a (logarithmically) additive constant (see also Currie, 1981).

A non-stationary time series variable is defined to be an *integrated process of order d* if differencing d times reduces it to a stationary process. If a linear function of d-integrated variables is an integrated process of order less than d, the variables are said to be *co-integrated* (see Granger, 1981; Granger and Weiss, 1984). In a system such as (3), it cannot be legitimate to assume that the disturbances on the system are white noise if the target deviations and the differences of the variables are not integrated to the same order. For simplicity we would take d as one, and in that case, we require the target deviations to form a vector of stationary processes. But clearly, the target deviations need not even be stationary provided the changes in the variables are not stationary either.

The economic theory underlying this kind of model must therefore assert, minimally, that the target deviations must be integrated to the same order as the differences of the variables, and be stationary when the latter are stationary. The model would be rejected if the coefficients of the targets (the relevant elements of $C(L)$) were not significantly different from zero – although note that the problems of inference in this type of model are not yet well understood (see, for example, Stock, 1984). The special case of target deviations being themselves white noise, so that the target is a stochastic equation in its own right, is subsumed under the general case of co-integration. But it is assumed here that the much weaker requirement that sets of variables are co-integrated is the appropriate method of incorporating stylised equilibrium relations into the model. The money demand function, in particular, is being characterised in just this way.

To take another somewhat controversial case, inclusion of the purchasing power and uncovered interest parity conditions in the model implies a theory that when these conditions do not hold, some variables in the system (exchange rates, relative price levels, and so on) must be changing, or expected to change, and hence that deviations from the targets are correlated with, and help to predict, subsequent changes in the variables. Equations (e) and (f) in Table 6.2 do not contradict covered interest parity, but the cover must be zero when the exchange rate is on a constant path, and it is *un*covered differentials which appear in the exchange rate equation. Note that it is innocuous to include rates of change as arguments of the targets, as may be done to aid interpretation, since such terms can be redeployed into the first two terms of (3); the rate of inflation *is* included in (a) in Table 6.2 since we are interested in the coefficient δ_3. A term for expected capital gains could similarly be added to (b) without altering its status as a steady-state relation one way or the other.

III

In Davidson (1984) estimates of the model are reported for the period 1964(ii) – 1978(iv) with a structural break in 1972(i) corresponding to the switch to floating exchange rates. A non-linear three-stage least squares estimation procedure allows the switch of exogeneity of the exchange rate at this date, also allowing the parameters of the foreign balance equations to shift while keeping the rest of the model fixed, apart from intercepts and error covariances. The aim is to estimate the key behavioural parameters with maximum efficiency while permitting structural flexibility in the model.

The specification nonetheless was found not to be stable beyond 1979, a few added observations proving notably influential and producing implausible switches of sign and magnitude. Some revisions are now incorporated which, while not yet entirely satisfactory, allow the model to give a consistent account of the data up to 1982(iv). First, there are some changes of specification, mainly to the advances and exchange rate equations. Dummy variables are introduced to allow for the policy effects of the removal of exchange controls and concentration on monetary targets post-1979. Secondly, the specification of the money-demand relation is also revised. A unit income elasticity is now imposed – this coefficient had earlier been found to be poorly determined and unstable – and the other arguments are transformed, so that they now comprise the interest spread – the difference of a representative long and short rate – and the *real short interest rate* measured as the difference between the short rate and a moving two-quarter average of inflation.

Another possibility considered is of a shift in the money-demand relationship, because of the technological and institutional innovations of recent years. We assume that credit cards and other improvements in the efficiency of making payments may increasingly enable people to economise on money holdings. (Be careful to note though that, as opposed to *technical* change, changes in banking institutions and competitive practices such as CCC (Competition and Credit Control) should not affect money *demand*, although they will affect supply through changes in credit rationing and so on.)

This is a difficult modelling problem, since we are bound to fall back on some sort of dummy variable to represent the change. There are objections, of different kinds, to the use of both intervention dummies ('zero-one' shifts) and linear or polynomial trends as devices to capture such changes, and a compromise which overcomes these to some extent is the *logistic trend*, a variable with the general form $LT_t = exp\{\alpha + \beta t\}/(1 + exp\{\alpha + \beta t\})$. This permits a smooth transition from one intercept value to another at a rate and date depending on the parameters α and β, which can in principle be fitted to the data, and hence allows us to model the transitional effects of a period of (say) technological innovation. Imposing the constraint that LT_t should be close to zero prior to 1970, experiments with values of β between 0.1 and 0.5 were performed, resulting in the former value being chosen (on the basis of the general characteristics of the equations, rather than a simple 'goodness of fit' criterion). This yields a trend curve which attains the value of 0.57, somewhat above its point of inflection, by the end of the sample.

The other increasingly serious consideration in modelling the recent period is the definition of money. The previous work used £M3, but this series now contains a very large break (about 10 per cent in 1981(iv), corresponding to the redefinition of the banking sector (now called the 'monetary sector'). One of the ways considered to deal with this problem was to distribute the effects of the step change over earlier periods, once again using a logistic trend which is zero before 1970, and attains unity by 1981 (iv). This variable multiplied by the difference between the post- and pre-revision figures for 1981(iv) is added to the series in each period prior to that date. The assumption which underlies this scheme is that the appropriate definition of money has been changing progressively, with the published definition being revised belatedly.

The second approach, with the recent availability of a series for PSL2 extending back to 1963, is to estimate the model with the variable 'M' given this broader definition. In view of the arguments of Section I, this ought to be the more appropriate stock, at least in the later part of the sample, if not necessarily in the earlier period before 1970. However, it ought to be emphasised that the model has not been respecified for each case, and the version of the model reported has, for the most part (except where noted in Section IV), been developed with the £M3 definition of money, and using the data to 1978 (iv).

Of the four cases examined – two definitions of the money stock, with and without a trend term included in $\hat{V}$ – the full estimates are given only for one (M = £M3 adjusted for break, trend in $\hat{V}$ included) in Table 6.3, while the main results, the coefficients of money-demand and the coefficients of $\hat{V}$ from each equation, are presented for each version in Table 6.4.

IV

This section of the paper provides a commentary on some of the equation specifications. One can jump to Section V without loss of continuity, and return here to aid interpretation of the results, as required. Additional details can be found in Davidson (1984).

Bank loans (equation (i), Table 6.3) are assumed to be demand-determined subject to rationing constraints (see Wills, 1982, for an analysis of bank behaviour). We have consistently failed to find a significant, appropriately signed role for interest rates other than through the $\hat{V}$ term. The ratio of non-public sector loans to total deposits is assumed to have a ceiling at which the banks themselves would ration customers – a term of this type is necessary to ensure the model has a long-run solution. Coghlan's (1981) equation is similar.

Equations (ii) and (iii) describe transactions and prices in the gilt-edged market. To interpret the left-hand side variable in (ii), note that the market value and nominal value of debt holdings are related by

$$B_t^{pm} = \Delta B_t^p + (P_t^g/P_{t-1}^g)\, B_{t-1}^{pm} \tag{4}$$

Table 6.3 Adjustment equations (M = £M3)

These estimates embody the cross-equation restrictions implicit in embedding the deviations from equation (a) (Table 6.2) in log form, denoted $\hat{V}$, in each equation. The estimates of (a) are given in (ix) below. The (incomplete) system is estimated by a variant of non-linear Three Stage Least Squares (3SLS) (a member of the class defined in Amemiya, 1977) in which each equation has its own set of instrumental variables. Each set of instruments is defined as the lagged or exogenous variables included in the equation, plus the first four principal components of the set of all such variables in the system but not in the equation.

The fixed and floating exchange rate regimes define two versions of the system, only the second containing equation (viii). The estimator minimises the sum of the 3SLS criterion functions for the two regimes, but with equality of the slope coefficients (not constants and seasonals, or residual variances and covariances) imposed across regimes in all equations except (vi) and (vii). The covariance matrices used to define the criteria were evaluated from the residuals in a first run of the search algorithm, and the reported parameter estimates obtained in the second run. All computations were performed on the Cray II computer at the University of London Computer Centre.

(i) $\Delta \ln(A^P/P)_t = \underset{(0.192)}{0.505} \ \Delta \ln Y_t - \underset{(0.051)}{0.287} \ \ln((A^P + A^f)/D)_{t-4}$

$\quad - \underset{(0.028)}{0.162} \ \ln \hat{V}_{t-3} - \underset{(0.204)}{0.430} \ \Delta D^*_{t-1} - \underset{(0.0034)}{0.0087} \ Cl_t$

$\quad + \underset{(0.0025)}{0.0174} \ A(Cc)_{1t} - \underset{(0.00022)}{0.0011} \ A(Cc)_{2t} + \underset{(0.028)}{0.157} \ LT_t$

$\quad + \begin{Bmatrix} -0.056 \\ -0.092 \end{Bmatrix} + \begin{Bmatrix} -0.081 \\ -0.030 \end{Bmatrix} Q1_t + \begin{Bmatrix} -0.014 \\ -0.030 \end{Bmatrix} Q2_t + \begin{Bmatrix} 0.007 \\ 0.017 \end{Bmatrix} Q3_t$

$\quad s = \begin{Bmatrix} 0.0186 \\ 0.0133 \end{Bmatrix}$: *Correlogram:* $\begin{Bmatrix} 0.145, & 0.241, 0.347, -0.167 \\ 0.090, & -0.156, 0.034, -0.334 \end{Bmatrix}$

(ii) $\Delta \ln(B^{pm}/P^g)_t = \underset{(0.070)}{0.502} \ \Delta \ln P^g_t + \underset{(0.173)}{0.074} \ \Delta \ln M_t$

$\quad - \underset{(0.013)}{0.033} \ (B^{pm}/M)_{t-4} + \underset{(0.001)}{0.0031} \ (r^l - r^f - FP)_{t-4}$

$\quad - \underset{(0.055)}{0.044} \ (\Delta G/PY)_{t-2} + \underset{(0.036)}{0.054} \ \hat{V}_{t-3}$

$\quad + \begin{Bmatrix} -0.002 \\ -0.026 \end{Bmatrix} + \begin{Bmatrix} 0.012 \\ 0.003 \end{Bmatrix} Q1_t + \begin{Bmatrix} -0.007 \\ -0.006 \end{Bmatrix} Q2_t + \begin{Bmatrix} 0.013 \\ 0.013 \end{Bmatrix} Q3_t$

$\quad s = \begin{Bmatrix} 0.0124 \\ 0.0275 \end{Bmatrix}$: *Correlogram:* $\begin{Bmatrix} -0.020, & -0.258, -0.201, -0.271 \\ 0.429, & 0.077, -0.048, -0.161 \end{Bmatrix}$

(iii) $\Delta \ln P_t^g = -0.0060\ \Delta r_t^s - 0.0058\ \Delta r_t^f + 0.787\ \Delta \ln(B^p + B^f)_t$
$$\ (0.004)\qquad\ (0.0020)\qquad\quad (0.152)$$

$$-\ 0.031\ \hat{V}_{t-1} + 0.005\ [(r^l - r^s) + 38.7\ \ln((B^p + B^f)/(G + R))]_{t-2}$$
$$(0.043)\qquad\ (0.001)\qquad\qquad\qquad (16.0)$$

$$+ \begin{Bmatrix} -0.057 \\ -0.030 \end{Bmatrix} + \begin{Bmatrix} -0.026 \\ -0.011 \end{Bmatrix} Q1_t + \begin{Bmatrix} 0.007 \\ 0.0 \end{Bmatrix} Q2_t + \begin{Bmatrix} -0.012 \\ -0.030 \end{Bmatrix} Q3_t$$

$$s = \begin{Bmatrix} 0.021 \\ 0.034 \end{Bmatrix};\ Correlogram:\ \begin{Bmatrix} 0.368,\ 0.177,\ -0.080,\ 0.057 \\ -0.199,\ 0.031,\ -0.032,\ -0.223 \end{Bmatrix}$$

(iv) $\Delta \ln Y_t = -0.287\ \Delta Y_{t-1} + 0.174\ \Delta(\Delta G/PY)_t + 0.096\ \Delta(\Delta G/PY)_{t-3}$
$$\ (0.079)\qquad\ (0.062)\qquad\qquad\quad (0.049)$$

$$+\ 0.192\ \Delta \ln X_t + 0.068\ \Delta \ln X_{t-1} + 0.090\ \Delta \ln(M_t/P_{t-1})$$
$$(0.026)\qquad\quad (0.026)\qquad\qquad (0.109)$$

$$-\ 0.088\ \Delta\Delta_2 \ln P_{t-1} + 0.030\ \hat{V}_{t-3}$$
$$(0.135)\qquad\qquad\quad (0.026)$$

$$+ \begin{Bmatrix} -0.042 \\ -0.040 \end{Bmatrix} + \begin{Bmatrix} 0.081 \\ 0.091 \end{Bmatrix} Q1_t + \begin{Bmatrix} 0.046 \\ 0.069 \end{Bmatrix} Q2_t + \begin{Bmatrix} 0.027 \\ 0.011 \end{Bmatrix} Q3_t$$

$$s = \begin{Bmatrix} 0.0099 \\ 0.015 \end{Bmatrix};\ Correlogram:\ \begin{Bmatrix} -0.291,\ -0.382,\ -0.006,\ 0.400 \\ -0.033,\ -0.290,\ 0.074,\ -0.061 \end{Bmatrix}$$

(v) $\Delta \ln P_t = -0.219\ \Delta \ln P_{t-1} + 0.323\ \Delta \ln(M/Y)_t + 0.424\ \Delta \ln W_t$
$$\ (0.087)\qquad\qquad (0.059)\qquad\qquad (0.084)$$

$$+\ 0.090\ \Delta \ln Pr_{t-2} - 0.095\ \ln(\epsilon P/P^f)_{t-1} + 0.051\ \hat{V}_{t-1}$$
$$(0.076)\qquad\qquad (0.012)\qquad\qquad\quad (0.019)$$

$$+\ 0.151\ [\ln(W/P)_{t-1} - 1.029\ \ln Pr_{t-4}]$$
$$(0.034)\qquad\qquad\quad (0.251)$$

$$+ \begin{Bmatrix} -0.034 \\ -0.028 \end{Bmatrix} + \begin{Bmatrix} 0.016 \\ 0.008 \end{Bmatrix} Q1_t + \begin{Bmatrix} -0.005 \\ 0.006 \end{Bmatrix} Q2_t + \begin{Bmatrix} 0.001 \\ -0.002 \end{Bmatrix} Q3_t$$

$$s = \begin{Bmatrix} 0.0071 \\ 0.012 \end{Bmatrix};\ Correlogram:\ \begin{Bmatrix} 0.083,\ -0.039,\ 0.215,\ -0.062 \\ -0.154,\ 0.006,\ 0.168,\ -0.444 \end{Bmatrix}$$

(vi) $(\Delta C/PY)_t = (\Delta O/PY)_t + \begin{Bmatrix} 0.051\,(0.103) \\ 0.040\,(0.119) \end{Bmatrix} (\Delta C/PY)_{t-1}$

$$+ \begin{Bmatrix} 0.185\,(0.064) \\ 0.253\,(0.072) \end{Bmatrix} \Delta \ln \epsilon_t + \begin{Bmatrix} 0.294\,(0.107) \\ 0.418\,(0.112) \end{Bmatrix} \Delta_2 \ln P_{t-2}$$

$$+ \begin{Bmatrix} -0.095\,(0.062) \\ 0.029\,(0.064) \end{Bmatrix} \Delta \ln Y_{t-1} + \begin{Bmatrix} 0.301\,(0.138) \\ 0.217\,(0.101) \end{Bmatrix} \Delta \ln Y_{t-1}^f$$

$$+ \begin{Bmatrix} -0.009\,(0.034) \\ -0.006\,(0.018) \end{Bmatrix} \ln(\epsilon P/P^f)_{t-4} + \begin{Bmatrix} -0.118\,(0.024) \\ 0.144\,(0.070) \end{Bmatrix} \ln(Y/Y^f)_{t-3}$$

$$+ \begin{Bmatrix} -0.005\,(0.033) \\ -0.033\,(0.026) \end{Bmatrix} \hat{V}_{t-3} - 0.0006\ A(EC)_{1t} + 0.0070\ A(EC)_{2t}$$
$$\phantom{+ \begin{Bmatrix} -0.005 \end{Bmatrix} \hat{V}_{t-3}\ }(0.0002)\qquad\qquad (0.003)$$

138

Table 6.3 continued

$$+ \begin{Bmatrix} -0.018 \\ -0.006 \end{Bmatrix} + \begin{Bmatrix} 0.0 \\ 0.014 \end{Bmatrix} Q1_t + \begin{Bmatrix} 0.006 \\ 0.008 \end{Bmatrix} Q2_t + \begin{Bmatrix} 0.0 \\ 0.015 \end{Bmatrix} Q3_t$$

$$s = \begin{Bmatrix} 0.0074 \\ 0.0128 \end{Bmatrix}; \quad Correlogram: \quad \begin{Bmatrix} -0.195, & -0.159, & -0.025, & -0.243 \\ -0.033, & -0.031, & -0.276, & -0.267 \end{Bmatrix}$$

(vii) $\quad \Delta S_t^p = \begin{Bmatrix} 1433 & (935) \\ -24624 (6416) \end{Bmatrix} \Delta \ln \epsilon_t + \begin{Bmatrix} -52.9 (11.4) \\ 267 \ (66.4) \end{Bmatrix} \Delta \ln r_t^{lf}$

$$+ \begin{Bmatrix} -0.038 (0.037) \\ 0.071 (0.044) \end{Bmatrix} S_{t-2}^p + \begin{Bmatrix} 1.87 & (11.2) \\ 155.5 (68.8) \end{Bmatrix} (r^l - r^f - FP)_{t-1}$$

$$+ \begin{Bmatrix} -0.37 & (470) \\ -1105 (1150) \end{Bmatrix} \ln(\epsilon P/P^f)_{t-4} + \begin{Bmatrix} -650 & (523) \\ -6991 (1785) \end{Bmatrix} \hat{V}_{t-1}$$

$$- \underset{(208)}{995} \ A(EC)_{1t} + \underset{(18.3)}{87.8} \ A(EC)_{\frac{1}{2}t}$$

$$+ \begin{Bmatrix} 286 \\ -1370 \end{Bmatrix} + \begin{Bmatrix} -223 \\ 13.2 \end{Bmatrix} Q1_t + \begin{Bmatrix} 27 \\ 899 \end{Bmatrix} Q2_t + \begin{Bmatrix} 16 \\ 352 \end{Bmatrix} Q3_t$$

$$s = \begin{Bmatrix} 126 \\ 1005 \end{Bmatrix}; \quad Correlogram: \quad \begin{Bmatrix} -0.241, & -0.135, & -0.026, & 0.011 \\ 0.018, & 0.087, & -0.116, & -0.057 \end{Bmatrix}$$

(viii) For 1972(i) - 1982(iv):

$$\Delta \ln \epsilon_t = \underset{(0.0046)}{-0.0053} \ \Delta(r^f - r^s)_t + \underset{(0.0048)}{0.0010} \ \Delta(r^f - r^s).D79_t$$

$$\underset{(0.0103)}{-0.0043} \ \Delta(r^{lf*} - r^l)_t + \underset{(0.012)}{0.0054} \ \Delta(r^{lf*} - r^l).D79_t$$

$$\underset{(0.0029)}{-0.0024} \ (r^f - r^s)_{t-1} - \underset{(0.0037)}{0.0013} \ [(r^{lf*} - r^l) - (r^f - r^s)]_{t-1}$$

$$+ \underset{(0.013)}{0.033} \ \ln(R^*/\epsilon P)_{t-1} - \underset{(0.061)}{0.081} \ \hat{V}_{t-3}$$

$$+ 0.245 + 0.0094 \ Q1_t + 0.034 \ Q2_t + 0.028 \ Q3_t$$

$$s = 0.0315; \ Correlogram: \ -0.116, 0.0133, 0.0276, -0.219$$

(ix) $\quad \hat{V}_t = \ln(M/PY)_t - \underset{(0.0026)}{0.0128} \ (r^s - 200.\Delta_2 \ln P)_t - \underset{(0.0048)}{0.0020} \ (r^l - r^s)_t$

$$+ \underset{(0.178)}{0.401} \ LT_t$$

Notes: Standard errors are in parentheses below or following parameter estimates.
Braces enclose estimates for 1964(ii) – 1971(iv) and 1972(i) – 1982(iv) subperiods.

Standard errors are not available for constant and seasonal dummies.
For a variable x_t, $\Delta_i x_t = x_t - x_{t-i}$, and $i = 1$ implicitly when omitted.

System Test Statistics:
W denotes a Wald test, constructed from the estimates under the alternative. ALR (analogue likelihood ratio) denotes a test based on the difference between the 3SLS criterion functions under null and alternative, equivalent to the T^0 test of Gallant and Jorgenson (1979). Each statistic is asymptotically χ^2 with the degrees of freedom shown in parentheses, though a small-sample correction could shrink them somewhat (see Davidson, 1984).

1. Test of overidentifying restrictions and cross-regime equality of parameters, where imposed: $ALR(117) = 157$
2. Test of cross-regime parameter equality, where not imposed.
   Equation (vi) only: $W(6) = 38$
   Equation (vii) only: $W(8) = 20.8$
   Equations (vi) and (vii): $W(14) = 69$
3. Test of joint significance of $\hat{V}$ coefficients in all equations: $W(10) = 50$
4. Test of the model against linear alternative, arguments of $\hat{V}$ appearing unrestricted in each equation: $ALR(24) = 36.5$

which implies, equating logarithmic and proportionate changes,

$$\Delta \ln(B^{pm}/P^g)_t \approx \Delta B_t^p / B_{t-1}^{pm} \tag{5}$$

Target relation (b), together with (a) and also (j), represents the desired 'outside asset' portfolio of the NPBS. The empirical form of the target deviation combines targets (b) and (e), simply because this relatively parsimonious form is suggested by the data. The right-hand side term in $\Delta \ln P_t^g$ is assumed to act as a proxy for price expectations. Here and elsewhere in the model (for example (a) of Table 6.2) the current or smoothed current changes in a variable have been taken as the best simple measure of short-run expectations. The bond price equation contains policy reaction terms, with (d) representing the trade-off between the government's desires for low interest rates relative to the money rate and for minimum monetisation of the debt. Note that $G + R - B^p - B^f$ corresponds to the monetary base, and we assume that the government has an implicit target ratio of monetary base to total debt which it will intervene in the bond market to maintain, eventually. Of course, if we are to solve (d), (e) and (f) simultaneously and assume that foreign rates are totally exogenous, the implication is that the public sector debt aggregates must move into line under a full steady state – although we should emphasise once again that such scenarios do not need to be entertained very seriously, and the model could be elaborated with a fuller account of the term structure.

Equation (iv) is no more than a minimal reduced form equation for real income, while the inflation equation (v) contains three targets; money disequilibrium, purchasing power parity (g) and a neoclassical labour demand schedule (h). Note that earnings are thought of as jointly determined, though the earnings equation is not specified here.

The two foreign balance equations, (vi) and (vii), are problematic because the available data are for net transactions, which may be of either sign in principle, so that data-admissability enforces a rather awkward semi-logarithmic specification. It appears reasonable to express the current account surplus in a ratio with nominal income, in expectation of a scale effect in trade flows, but there does not appear to be any such basis for scaling net capital flows – hence some parameters of equation (vii) have units of millions of pounds sterling. Equations (i) and (j) in Table 6.2 are stylised steady-state conditions reflecting a deficiency of useful theory in this area. It appears reasonable that different growth rates at home and abroad should lead to current account imbalance *ceteris paribus*, that is, unless other adjustments such as in relative secular inflation rates, are also taking place. On the other hand, the most plausible steady-state value of S^P is probably zero.

The exchange rate equation (viii) is based on the monthly model of Davidson (1985). There is a problem in such equations that the current interest rate coefficients are subject to structural shifts associated with changes of policy. Shift dummies for 1979(ii) are an attempt to allow for this.

V

The main feature of these specifications of the money-demand equation (see Table 6.4) is that the coefficient of the real short interest rate (regarded as the real return on money holdings) is significant and correctly signed, and implies a long-run elasticity with respect to inflation of around −1.5. This is about half the value obtained with the earlier specification, which speaks in favour of the modification. The coefficient of the interest spread is wrongly signed to be interpreted as the current net return on competing assets, although it could evidently be acting as a proxy for the same omitted effect that the trend is intended to capture. There is also the pos-

Table 6.4 Alternative money demand specifications

	M = £M3		M = PSL2	
	1	2	3	4

Coefficients of money demand (equation (a), Table 6.2):

	1	2	3	4
δ_1	0.014	0.013	0.011	0.012
	(0.003)	(0.003)	(0.003)	(0.002)
δ_2	0.014	0.002	0.011	0.002
	(0.007)	(0.005)	(0.006)	(0.005)
δ_3	–	−0.401	–	0.857
		(0.178)		(0.225)

Coefficients of $\hat{V}$ in adjustment equations:

		1	2	3	4
(i)	(A^P)	−0.148	−0.162	−0.174	−0.174
		(0.029)	(0.028)	(0.031)	(0.028)
(ii)	(B^{pm})	0.075	0.055	0.081	0.023
		(0.034)	(0.036)	(0.041)	(0.038)
(iii)	(P^g)	−0.044	−0.031	−0.041	0.001
		(0.039)	(0.043)	(0.040)	(0.042)
(iv)	(Y)	0.0066	0.029	0.0044	0.013
		(0.021)	(0.026)	(0.017)	(0.026)
(v)	(P)	0.049	0.051	0.040	0.039
		(0.018)	(0.019)	(0.015)	(0.019)
(vi)	(S^P) to 1971 (iv)	−0.804	−0.650	−1.254	−0.757
		(0.607)	(0.523)	(0.741)	(0.532)
(vi)	(S^P) from 1972 (i)	−2.829	−6.99	−1.739	−8.010
		(1.399)	(1.78)	(1.38)	(1.867)
(vii)	(C) to 1971 (iv)	0.0028	−0.0048	0.015	0.0075
		(0.036)	(0.033)	(0.048)	(0.039)
(vii)	(C) from 1972 (i)	−0.011	−0.033	0.0035	−0.031
		(0.029)	(0.026)	(0.035)	(0.031)
(viii)	(ϵ) from 1972 (i)	−0.058	−0.081	0.049	−0.071
		(0.066)	(0.061)	(0.061)	(0.066)

sibility, which could account for the sign obtained, that this variable is used as a predictor of future inflation.

The money-disequilibrium term itself is not nominally significant in all the equations, although most of the adjustment coefficients and all the significant ones are correctly signed. Note, none the less, if an attempt is made to exclude those equations where the adjustment coefficients are small or not well-determined, the model collapses. Anything resembling the reported estimates cannot be obtained from the advances and price equations alone, even though the advances equation is a relatively close relation of the conventional money-demand equation. All the equations appear to play some sort of role. The one really surprising result is the consistent absence of any big real balance effect on income. These findings support a decidedly monetarist view of the inflationary process.

Figure 6.1 to 6.4 give the plots of actual and 'desired' $\ln(M/PY)$, deseasonalised and in mean deviation form, for each of the four alternatives reported in Table 6.4. The vertical distance between the two plots is itself plotted at the base of each figure. In Figures 6.5 and 6.6, $\ln M$ (each definition) and $\ln PY$ are plotted together in seasonal mean-deviation form. It is the vertical distance between these two plots which appears as $\ln(M/PY)$ in Figures 6.1 and 6.2, and 6.3 and 6.4 respectively. Figure 6.7 reproduces the movements over time of the two variables in the demand function, so that the pattern of the broken lines in Figures 6.1 to 6.4 can be interpreted. Be careful to note that the true mean distance between the plots in the latter figures is an unidentifiable parameter, and has been arbitrarily set at zero. It is only their *relative* positions which are significant. Moreover, all equations incorporate an intercept shift at the exchange rate regime switch point (see Table 6.3) which implies that a step shift in $\hat{V}$ is 'permitted' by the estimation. This implies some loss of efficiency but no bias in the estimates. In other words, there is implicitly both an intercept term and a shift dummy present in equation (ix), Table 6.3, but their coefficients are both unidentified, since to compute them from the fitted intercepts of the adjustment equations would require us to assume that the latter are uncontaminated by the means of omitted terms in the regression, which is scarcely justifiable. However, the estimated relations between money supply and demand *assuming* stability of the demand function can be compared in the plots, as long as we remember that the observed gap is not imposed in the estimation.

In the period up to 1971, the supply and demand plots can be fitted together quite well, and it is no surprise that ordinary regressions for money are quite stable over this period. Apart from the 1972–5 episode itself, the most notable feature of the data is that the ratio of PSL2 to nominal income appears to fall permanently after that period, while for the 'adjusted' £M3 it does not. In Figure 6.5 we can see rather nicely how in the 1972–6 episode, £M3 and PY moved apart and together again, as the monetary shock was followed by the countervailing inflationary adjust-

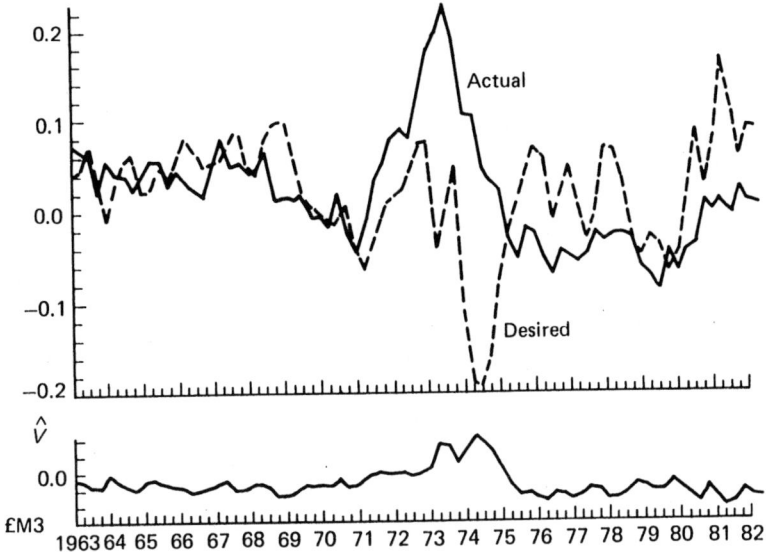

Figure 6.1 $M = £M3, \delta_3 = 0$

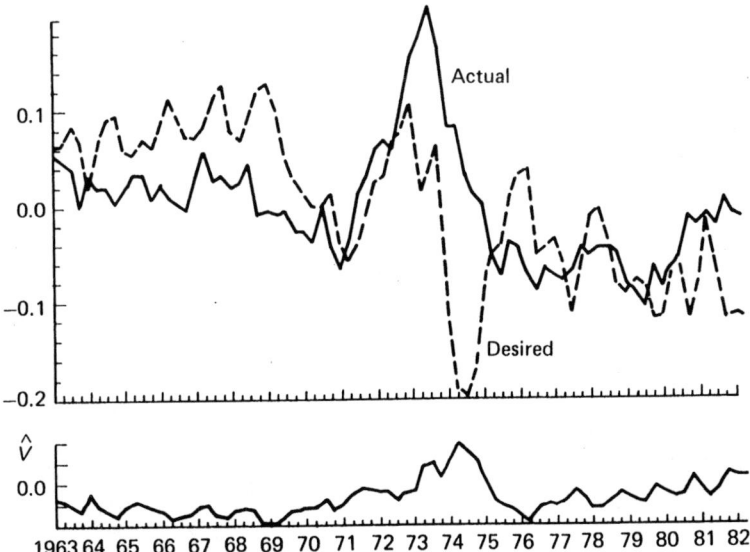

Figure 6.2 $M = £M3, \delta_3 \neq 0$

144

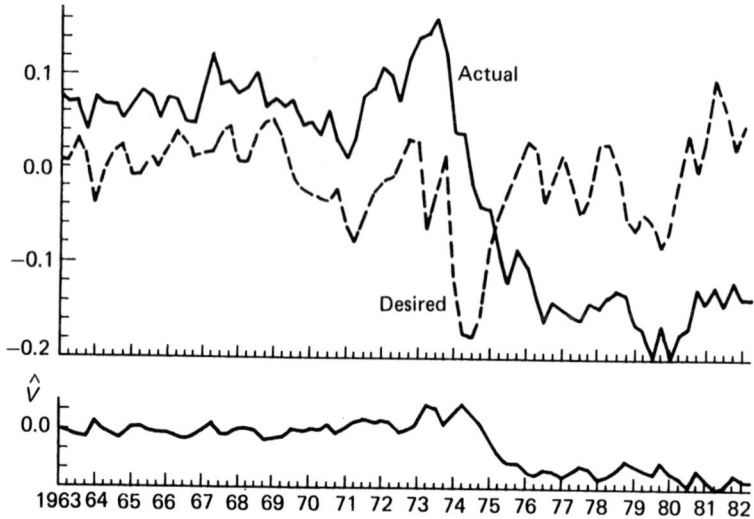

Figure 6.3 M = PSL2, $\delta_3 = 0$

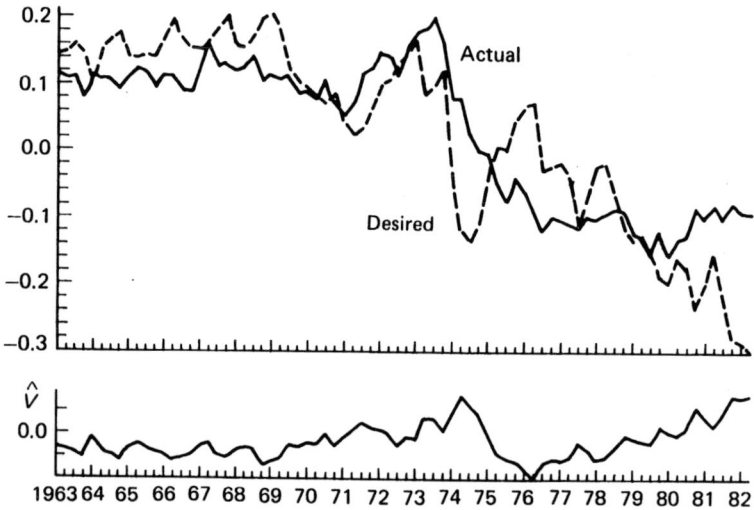

Figure 6.4 M = PSL2, $\delta_3 \neq 0$

145

Note: Figures 6.1 to 6.4 show the time plots of actual (————) and 'desired' (– – – –) $\ln(M/PY)$, where the latter is estimated from the coefficients in Table 6.4, columns 1–4. The lower part of each figure shows $\hat{V}$, the difference of the 2 upper plots. All data in the plots are residuals from regressions on a constant and seasonals, hence all plots are centred on zero and the relative vertical positions (and the absolute values of $\hat{V}$) have no significance. Also, in assessing the track of $\hat{V}$, note that an intercept shift at 1972(i) is permitted in the estimation. The mean and mean shift of $\hat{V}$ are not identified.

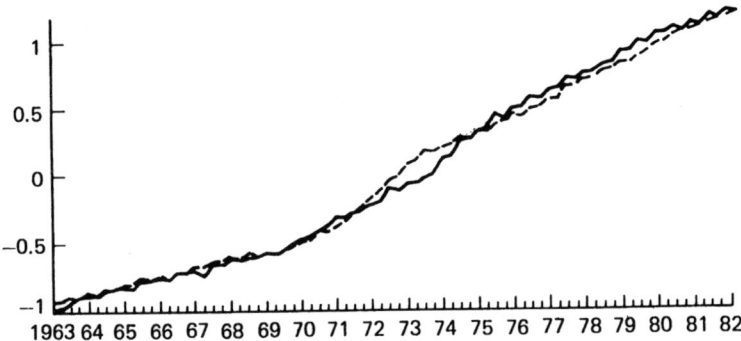

Figure 6.5　$\ln(PY) = ($————$)$, $\ln M = ($– – – –$)$, $M = £M3$

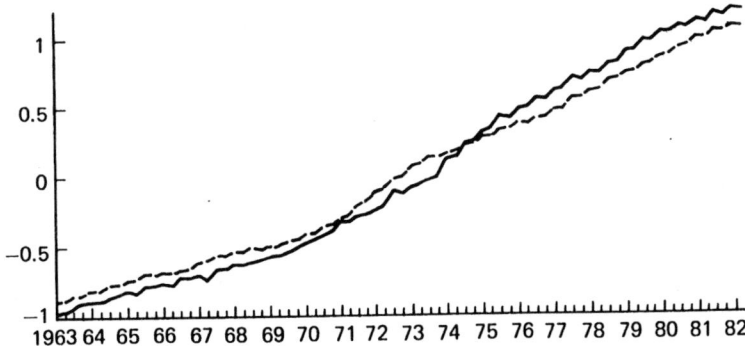

Figure 6.6　$\ln(PY) = ($————$)$, $\ln M = ($– – – –$)$, $M = $ PSL2

Note: The data in Figures 6.5 and 6.6 are residuals from regressions on a constant and seasonals. The relative vertical positions of the series have no significance.

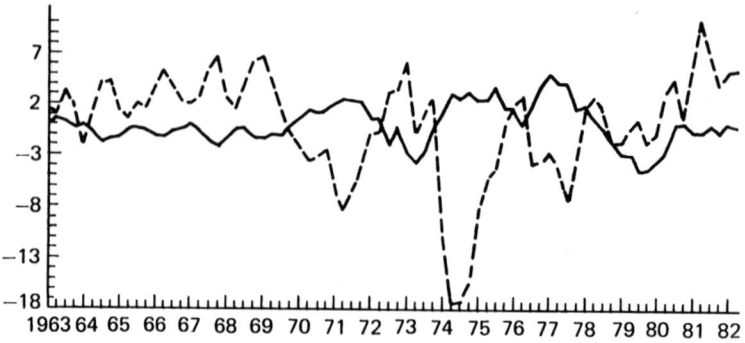

Figure 6.7 $r^l - r^s = ($————$),\ r^s - 200.D_2 \ln P = ($— — — —$)$

ment. While the two series often grew at different rates over several periods, they have 'tracked' each other over the long span of time and, in the terminology of Section II, they appear cointegrated, that is, their difference might be explained by stationary variables. On the other hand, the tracks of PSL2 and *PY* in Figure 6.6 cannot be superimposed both before 1971 *and* after it, and some secular shift or trend would be required to explain their relationship over the period.

It appears (consider Figures 6.3 and 6.4, and Figure 6.7) that the money-demand equation with or without the trend variable cannot supply the explanation for this, and to stick with the preference for a broad money definition we would be forced to conclude, either that the appropriate definition of money actually changed, or that the model remains inadequate. Probably both of these is true, but it is not clear that relaxing the most obvious limitations of the present demand equation - the imposition of a unit income elasticity, or perhaps the omission of a wealth variable - will explain a fairly large and permanent *rise* in velocity, measured with respect to a fixed definition of money, since the mid-1970s. Financial innovation and the changing role of certain kinds of deposits might be more likely to provide the explanation.

All the models present a similar picture of the 1972–5 episode. The rise in the money stock in 1972 is seen to coincide with a constant or rising excess supply, identifying this event (if we did not know already) as a supply shock. Subsequently, inflation helps to raise velocity, but at the same time reduces the attractiveness of money still further. The rise in velocity after mid-1973 is seen as a corrective response to the shock, through inflation and a slowdown in monetary growth. While the latter will be due in part to the reimposition of credit control, the model predicts quite rapid countervailing adjustments too. Assuming the adjustment of deposits by the running down of bank loans is at a proportionate rate of 0.16 for each percentage point of excess money (from equation (i) of Table 6.3, also Table 6.4, column 2), linearising the equation assuming $A^P/M \approx 0.75$ (the 1975 value) yields a median lag of only $7\frac{1}{2}$ quarters, including the deadstart of three-quarters – rather faster than the estimate of Davidson (1984). By contrast, we still obtain for the same model a median lag in the inflation adjustment of about 13 quarters, and for income of about 25 quarters. Because of the semi-log specification, rates of adjustment are not fixed in the capital account equation, but assuming $M = £60\,000m$. in the floating exchange rate period, we also obtain the surprisingly low median lag of $7\frac{1}{2}$ quarters for monetary adjustment via the capital account of the balance of payments. By comparison this is negligible in the pre-1972 period, and is also a much larger effect than that estimated with the data to 1978(iv).

To conclude, these results still have to be considered provisional since the issues raised in Section III remain unresolved, but they appear to represent a considerable advance over those obtained with the previous versions of the model. The difficulties of this type of modelling are pretty formidable, although this is partly because problems of model specification which are manifest in this approach are merely implicit in single-equation models. However, I believe the results continue to support the basic contention that the money-demand function is not a regression equation; it is a valid operational concept only within the kind of modelling framework employed here.

References

Akerlof, G. (1973) 'The demand for money: a general-equilibrium inventory-theoretic approach', *Review of Economic Studies*, 40: 115–30.

Amemiya, T. (1977) 'The maximum likelihood estimator and the nonlinear three-stage least squares estimator in the general nonlinear simultaneous equations model', *Econometrica*, 45: 955–78.

Artis, M. J. and Cuthbertson, K. (1985) 'The demand for M1: a forward-looking buffer stock model', *National Institute of Economic and Social Research*, Discussion Paper, 87.

Artis, M. J. and Lewis, M. K. (1976) 'The demand for money in the United Kingdom: 1963–73', *Manchester School*, 44: 147–82.

Brainard, W. C. and Tobin, J. (1968) 'Pitfalls in financial model building', *American Economic Review*, 58: 99–122.

Carr, J. and Darby, M. J. (1981) 'The role of money supply shocks in the short run demand for money', *Journal of Monetary Economics*, Vol. 8: 183–200.

Coghlan, R. (1981) *Money, Credit and the Economy* (London: Allen & Unwin).

Cooley, T. F. and LeRoy, S. F. (1981) 'Identification and estimation of money demand', *American Economic Review*, 71: 825–44.

Currie, D. (1981) 'Some long run features of dynamic time series models', *Economic Journal*, 91: 704–15.

Davidson, J. (1983) 'Error correction systems', ICERD Econometrics Discussion Paper 83/79, London School of Economics.

Davidson, J. (1984) 'Money disequilibrium: an approach to modelling monetary phenomena in the U.K.', ICERD Econometrics Discussion paper 84/96, London School of Economics.

Davidson, J. (1985) 'Econometric Modelling of the Sterling Effective Exchange Rate', *Review of Economic Studies*, 52: 231–50.

Davidson, J. and Keil, M. (1982) 'Modelling monetary disequilibrium and the balance of payments in the U.K.', ICERD, London School of Economics, mimeo.

Frenkel, J. A. and Johnson, H. (eds) (1976) *The Monetary Approach to the Balance of Payments* (London: Allen & Unwin).

Gallant, A. R. and Jorgenson, D. W. (1979) 'Statistical inference for a system of simultaneous, nonlinear implicit equations in the context of instrumental variable estimation', *Journal of Econometrics*, 11: 275–302.

Goodhart, C. A. E. (1984) 'Disequilibrium money – a note', in *Monetary Theory and Practice, the UK Experience* (London: Macmillan Press).

Gordon, R. J. (1984) 'The short-run demand for money: a reconsideration', *Journal of Money, Credit and Banking*, 16: 403–34.

Granger, C. W. J. (1981) 'Some properties of time series data and their use in econometric model specification', *Journal of Econometrics*, 16: 121–30.

Granger, C. W. J. and Weiss, A. (1983) 'Time series analysis of error correction models', Paper presented to Econometric Society European Meeting, Pisa, September 1983, University of California at San Diego.

Green, C. J. (1984) 'Preliminary results from a five-sector flow of funds model of the United Kingdom, 1972–1977', *Economic Modelling*, 1: 304–26.

Howitt, P. and Laidler, D. (1979) 'Recent Canadian monetary policy – a critique', in D. Purvis and R. Wirick (eds), *Proceedings of Queens University Conference on Economic Policy* (Queens University).

Jonson, P. D. and Trevor, R. D. (1981) 'Monetary rules: a preliminary analysis', *The Economic Record*, 57: 150–67.

Judd, J. and Scadding, T. (1982) 'The search for a stable money demand function', *Journal of Economic Literature* 20: 993–1023.

Knoester, A. and van Sinderen, J. (1985) 'Money, the balance of payments and economic policy', *Applied Economics*, 17: 215–40.

Laidler, D. (1984) 'The "buffer stock" notion in monetary economics', *Economic Journal Supplement*, 94 – Selected Papers from the RES/AUTE Annual Conference, 1983: 17–34.

Laidler, D. and Bentley, B. (1983) 'A small macro-model of the post-war United States', *Manchester School*, 51: 317–40.

Laidler, D. and O'Shea, P. (1980) 'An empirical macro-model of an open economy under fixed exchange rates: the United Kingdom, 1954–1970', *Economica*, 47: 141–58.

Stock, J. (1984) 'Asymptotic properties of least squares estimators of cointegrating vectors" Harvard University, mimeo.

Wills, H. R. (1982) 'The simple economics of bank regulation', *Economica*, 49: 249–59.

7 In What Sense Do Compulsory Ratios Reduce the Volume of Deposits?*

Anthony S. Courakis

INTRODUCTION

Except for possible positive 'psychological effects' stemming from increased confidence by depositors in the solvency of controlled institutions, the general view in the literature is that compulsory cash/securities/or other ratios reduce the equilibrium volume of deposits. Often this outcome is conceived in terms of settings where compulsory ratios are assumed to be combined with control (rationing) by the authorities of the supply of assets that the intermediaries are compelled to hold in fixed proportion to their deposits, in order to impose a limit on deposits below the level that could otherwise materialise.[1] But even those writers on this subject who assume no such 'compulsory asset availability constraint' reach the same verdict, since they see compulsory ratios as reducing the return per unit of deposits accruing to controlled intermediaries, and hence the rate that these inter- mediaries are willing to pay on deposits.[2] In the latter vein, furthermore, it has become increasingly fashionable to think of compulsory ratios as a tax;[3] and, whether in the context of highly-developed, or in the context of less-developed, economic systems, also to proclaim the undesirability of such devices.[4]

Recently, however, this consensus has been upset by the appearance of analytical findings (Courakis, 1984a, 1984b) that reveal that (i) compul- sory zero-interest-bearing cash ratios can cause deposit rates and deposit volumes to be higher than they would otherwise have been, while (ii) the sense in which they constitute a tax on intermediation is more particular than has often been envisaged. The present study builds on the same

*I am grateful to Charles Goodhart for his comments on a previous draft of this paper.

theme, aiming partly to stress the rather special assumptions on which the conventional wisdom rests, partly to trace alternative premises that can sustain outcomes consistent with the conventional wisdom, and more generally to provide a clearer perspective on the nexus between the scale of intermediation and resource allocation that compulsory ratios define.

1 SOME UNORTHODOX RESULTS FROM A SIMPLE BANKING MODEL

Limiting the analysis in the first instance to the minimum degree of complexity possible, consider the case depicted in Figure 7.1. Here *Ld* and *Dd* denote respectively the demand for loans from the banking system and supply of deposits to the banking system by deficit and surplus economic units. In general, neither the loan rates, r_L, nor the deposit rates, r_D, on which these functions depend, will suffice to describe the returns and costs per unit of funds entrusted to financial intermediaries. But for the time being, in the interests of clarity (and as is often the practice in formal treatments of the effects of constraints on bank choices)[5] I shall abstract from default risks, from holdings of other assets, and from real resource

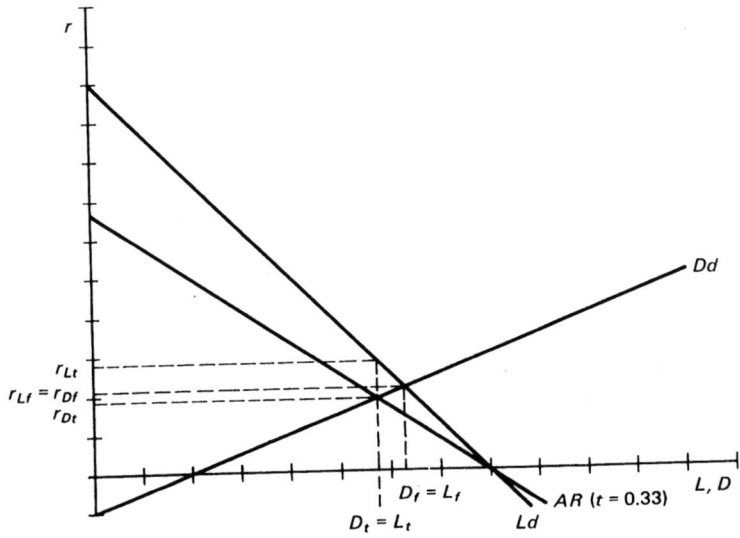

Figure 7.1   Competitive banking equilibrium before and after the imposition of a direct tax on deposit returns

costs (inputs of labour and physical capital).[6] Then in the absence of government intervention Ld and Dd describe also the average revenue and average cost curves of the banking industry.

Assuming a perfectly competitive banking system,[7] the equilibrium of the industry is defined by the intersection of these average revenue and average cost curves; and thus at the competitive equilibrium in the absence of constraints the volume of loans is $L_f = D_f$, while the loan rate is equal to the deposit rate at $r_{Lf} = r_{Df}$.

Suppose now that in this setting the government levies 'a direct tax on deposit returns. . .'[8] such as the cash ratio is often said to comprise. With the tax rate, t, set at, say, one-third (33.33 per cent), the average revenue curve of the banking industry is that described in Figure 7.1 by AR ($t = 0.33$). Consequently, the equilibrium volume of loans and deposits declines to $L_t = D_t$ as the loan rate rises to r_{Lt} and the deposit rate falls to $r_{Dt} = (1 - t)r_{Lt}$.

The story can be told in other ways; in terms, for instance, of a per-unit tax on deposits, or an income tax levied on deposit interest income. But (except for the detail that, analytically, the exercise then entails a shift in the average cost curve of the banking industry, rather than in the average revenue curve) the conclusion of a negative effect of the tax on the equilibrium volume of deposits is *inescapable*.

In contrast to this, consider the case where, instead of t, the government imposes a 33.33 per cent, $k = 0.33$, *zero-interest-bearing cash ratio* on deposits. This implies that only two-thirds of any given volume of deposits can be granted as loans, which is to say that, for any given volume of loans, deposits must be one and a half times that volume. The corollary of this inequality between loans and deposits is that the cost of funds to the intermediaries per unit of loans is not equal to the cost per unit of deposits, and, similarly, the revenue per unit of loans is not equal to the revenue per unit of deposits.

In Figure 7.2 quadrant (i) depicts the effect of the cash ratio in terms of loans, and quadrant (ii) its effect in terms of deposits, while quadrant (iii) depicts the relationship between loans and deposits that the cash ratio defines, and quadrant (iv) is an identity used for presentational convenience. Seen in terms of loans the cash ratio leaves the average revenue curve, $ARL = Ld$, unchanged, but twists the average cost curve from $ACL = Dd$ to $ACL(k = 0.33)$, making it steeper. On the other hand, although exactly equivalent, seen in terms of deposits, the effect of the cash ratio is to twist the average revenue curve to $ARD(k = 0.33)$, making it flatter, while leaving the average cost curve, $ACD = Dd$, unchanged. The nature of the displacement of the average revenue curve in quadrant (ii) reflects the fact

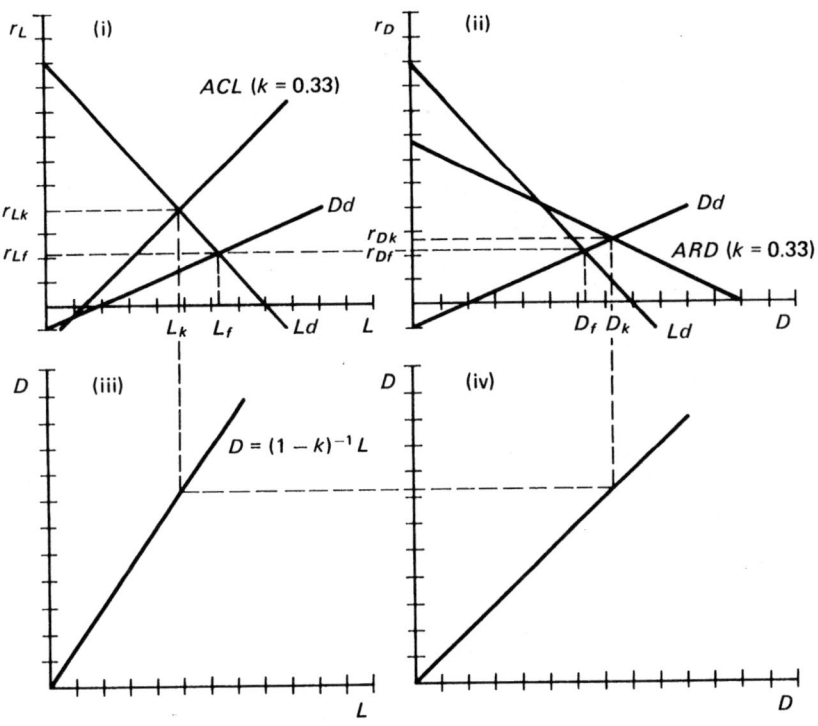

Figure 7.2 The effect of a zero-interest-bearing compulsory cash ratio

that, with any downward-sloping demand for loans, the introduction of a cash ratio k implies that the average revenue at any particular volume of deposits, D_x, does not depend on the rate on loans that can be charged were the whole of D_x free to be granted as loans, but on the higher market clearing loan rate that $L_x = (1 - k)D_x$ implies.

Evidently, the effect of the quantity constraint is to reduce the volume of loans, from L_f to L_k, and increase the loan rate from, r_{Lf} to r_{Lk}. This reduction in the volume of loans accords well with the intuitive perception of the cash ratio as an instrument that reduces the supply of funds available for bank loans. Granted, however, that loans are not equal to deposits, it does not also follow that the volume of funds channelled to deposit-taking intermediaries declines. Indeed, in Figure 7.2 the effect of the compulsory zero-interest-bearing cash ratio is to increase the deposit rate from r_{Df} to $r_{Dk} = (1 - k)r_{Lk}$, and thus the volume of deposits from D_f to D_k.

This example suffices to convey the fact that a compulsory cash ratio may have a positive effect on the equilibrium volume of deposits,[9] and to signify that the treatment of the cash ratio as a direct tax on deposit returns is misplaced. However, the result implies neither that the effect of a compulsory zero-interest-bearing cash ratio on the volume of bank deposits is always positive, nor that, starting from any given cash ratio, increases (decreases) in the compulsory ratio result in higher (lower) volumes of deposits.

Specifically, casting the analysis in algebra, we have:

$$Ld = a + br_L \qquad a > 0, b < 0 \qquad\qquad \text{(Loan demand)} \quad (1)$$

$$Dd = c + hr_D \qquad c > 0, h > 0 \qquad\qquad \text{(Deposit demand)} \quad (2)$$

$$L \equiv (1 - k)D \qquad\qquad\qquad\qquad \text{(Balance sheet constraint)} \quad (3)$$

$$AR = AC \qquad\qquad\qquad\qquad\qquad \text{(Competitive equilibrium condition)} \quad (4)$$

From (1), (2) and (3) the total revenue and total cost functions expressed in terms of deposits, are, respectively defined as

$$TR = [(1 - k)^2 D^2 - a(1 - k)D]b^{-1} \tag{5}$$

$$TC = (D^2 - cD)h^{-1} \tag{6}$$

whence, average revenue and average costs, are[10]

$$AR = [(1 - k)^2 D - a(1 - k)] b^{-1} \qquad (7)$$

$$AC = (D - c)h^{-1} \qquad (8)$$

so that, substituting into (4) and rearranging terms, the equilibrium volume of deposits is given by [11]

$$D = [a(1 - k)h - bc] \, [h(1 - k)^2 - b]^{-1} \qquad (9)$$

As equation (9) reveals, the relationship of deposits to cash ratio is not monotonic. For example, for the particular numerical values of the intercepts and slope coefficients used in the construction of Figure 7.2 (notably $a = 40$, $b = -2$, $c = 10$, and $h = 5$, with interest rates expressed in per cent) the relationship of deposits to cash ratio is shown in Figure 7.3. In this case, as the cash ratio rises from zero to 46 per cent, the equilibrium volume of deposits increases continuously; only thereafter does the volume of deposits decline.

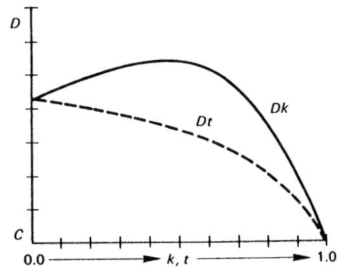

Figure 7.3 The relationship of deposits to cash ratios and to taxes on deposit returns

More generally, differentiating (9) with respect to k, yields the first order condition

$$dD/dk = [a(1 - k)^2 h^2 - 2cbh(1 - k) + abh] \, [h(1 - k)^2 - b]^{-2} = 0 \qquad (10)$$

whence the value of the cash ratio at which deposits are maximised is given by

$$k_D^* = [(ha - bc) - (b^2 c^2 - a^2 hb)^{\frac{1}{2}}] \, (ah)^{-1} \qquad (11)$$

From equation (11) it transpires that the deposit-maximising cash ratio will (other things being equal) be higher (lower) the lower (higher) the elasticity of demand for loans, and the higher (lower) the elasticity of demand for deposits. In turn this implies that in circumstances where borrowers have ready access to 'not similarly controlled' sources of funds (such as, for instance, to other intermediaries, be it at home or abroad) the effect of any particular compulsory ratio on the volume of deposits is more likely to be negative, whereas the opposite will be true where access to alternative sources of borrowing is (whether by law or otherwise) limited. On the other hand, in the context of the model described, where by appeal to equation (11) we find that $k_D^* = 0$ if $bh^{-1} = -a(a - 2c)^{-1}$, the deposit maximising cash ratio will be positive at least so long as the response of the demand for loans to a unit change in the loan rate is, in absolute magnitude, less than the response of the demand for deposits to a unit change in the deposit rate. Thus, unless we are prepared to assume *a priori* that the demand for loans is infinitely elastic, we are not entitled to assume *a priori* that the deposit-maximising cash ratio is zero.[12]

2   VARIATIONS ON THE THEME (ALLOWING FOR OTHER FEATURES OF REALITY)

Much of the flavour of these results remains when, in contrast to the analysis so far, we allow for loan defaults, for real resource costs, and for different types of assets and/or liabilities in bank portfolios, and also when other financial intermediaries are taken explicitly into account.

Clearly this is trivially true when allowance for loan default is taken to warrant some fixed (percentage or absolute) deduction from the loan rate, when with regard to resource costs we assume constant returns to scale in terms of the volume of deposits, and when other assets take the form of prudential reserves that comprise some given proportion of the banks' total assets/liabilities.[13] But it also holds when other assumptions about these features of banking reality are applied.

2.1   Real resource costs

To the best of my knowledge, the literature on compulsory cash ratios has nothing of consequence to offer on the interaction between this constraint and the real resource costs of intermediation. On the other hand, in the literature on the banking firm there is now a considerable body of theoretical work that 'views real resource costs as a crucial aspect of any attempt to understanding the role and behaviour of banks. . .'[14] and also a number of empirical studies on these 'production function' aspects of banking.[15]

In tracing the effects of cash ratios, the varying emphasis on deposits as opposed to loans, or vice versa,[16] as the 'primary' product of the banking firm is, as we shall see later, of considerable significance. For the present, leaving aside these issues stemming from questions on 'the role of banks', I shall treat loans and deposits at par, while assuming for simplicity, 'that the production functions and thus cost functions associated with servicing loans and deposits are separable'[17] and (as our perfect competition assumption compels) relative to market size subject to decreasing returns to scale.[18]

In the latter vein let

$$ARCD = \delta + \epsilon D_i + \zeta D_i^2 \quad \delta, \zeta > 0, \epsilon < 0 \tag{12}$$

and

$$ARCL = \eta + \theta L_i + \mu L_i^2 \quad \eta, \mu > 0, \theta < 0 \tag{13}$$

be the perfectly competitive ith firm's average resource cost functions for, respectively, deposits and loans. From these, granted the budget constraint $L_i \equiv (1 - k)D_i$, the 'combined average resource cost function' of the individual firm in deposit space is given by

$$ARCC = [\delta + \eta(1 - k)] + [\epsilon + (1 - k)^2 \theta]D_i + [\zeta + \mu(1 - k)^3]D_i^2 \tag{14}$$

whence the firm's optimal scale of operations $D_i^* = (1 - k)^{-1}L_i^*$ defined by the minimum of equation (14) is given by

$$D_i^* = -[\epsilon + (1 - k)^2 \theta]\{2[\zeta + \mu(1 - k)^3]\}^{-1} \tag{15}$$

Substituting for D_i in equation (14) yields the expression for the minimum 'combined real resource costs'

$$ARCC^* = [\delta + \eta(1 - k)] - [\epsilon + \theta(1 - k)^2]^2 [4\zeta + 4\mu(1 - k)^3]^{-1} \tag{16}$$

which together with equation (2) defines the average resource plus deposit interest costs of the industry

$$ATC^* = (D - c)h^{-1} + ARCC^* \tag{17}$$

and hence, given average revenue as in equation (7), and the zero profit equilibrium condition described by equation (4), the equilibrium volume of deposits of the banking industry

$$D_R = [a(1 - k)h - bc] \, [h(1 - k)^2 - b]^{-1} +$$
$$+ \, bh \, \{ARCC^*\} \, [h(1 - k)^2 - b]^{-1} \tag{18}$$

Since the first term on the right hand side of equation (18) is that already traced in our example of Section 1, while the second term is unambiguously negative, the equilibrium volume of deposits described by (18) is certainly lower than that described by (9) above. However, of itself, that tells us nothing about the relationship of deposits to cash ratios. On the other hand, since the identity of the first term of equation (18) to equation (9) means that part of the effect of the cash ratio implied by (18) is (for some range of values of k) positive, it follows that in the context of (18) a throughout negative relationship of deposits to cash ratio cannot be assumed *a priori*. Indeed, in the absence of any additional assumptions regarding the parameter values of the real resource cost functions for loans and deposits, we cannot even presume that the deposit maximising cash ratio is lower than that traced when real resource costs were disregarded. Neither, for that matter, can we say anything *a priori* about the effect of the compulsory cash ratio on the optimal size of the banking firm.

Consider Figure 7.4. Here, for two particular sets of assumptions (*A* and *B*) regarding real resource costs, the two left-hand side quadrants present the equilibria of the competitive firm, and the two right-hand side quadrants present the equilibria of the industry. It will be noticed that – since, by design, in the absence of a compulsory ratio the 'combined average cost functions' shown in quadrants (*A*1) and (*B*1) by *ARCC* are identical – the free market equilibria for the firm, and for the industry, are in both cases the same. However, whereas in the case depicted in quadrant (*A*1) the average resource costs of deposits, *ARCD*, is convex, and the average cost of loans, *ARCL*, is constant, in the case depicted in quadrant (*B*1), the converse is true. The corollary of this difference (a difference of a kind totally unnoticed in discussions of the effects of compulsory ratios) is that while, given the slope of *ARCD* in quadrant (*A*1) and of *ARCL* in quadrant (*B*1), in both cases a cash ratio $k = 0.33$ results in a lower minimum combined average resource cost, each case implies a different displacement of *ARCC*. Thus, although in both cases the equilibrium volume of deposits of the industry, depicted in quadrants (*A*2) and

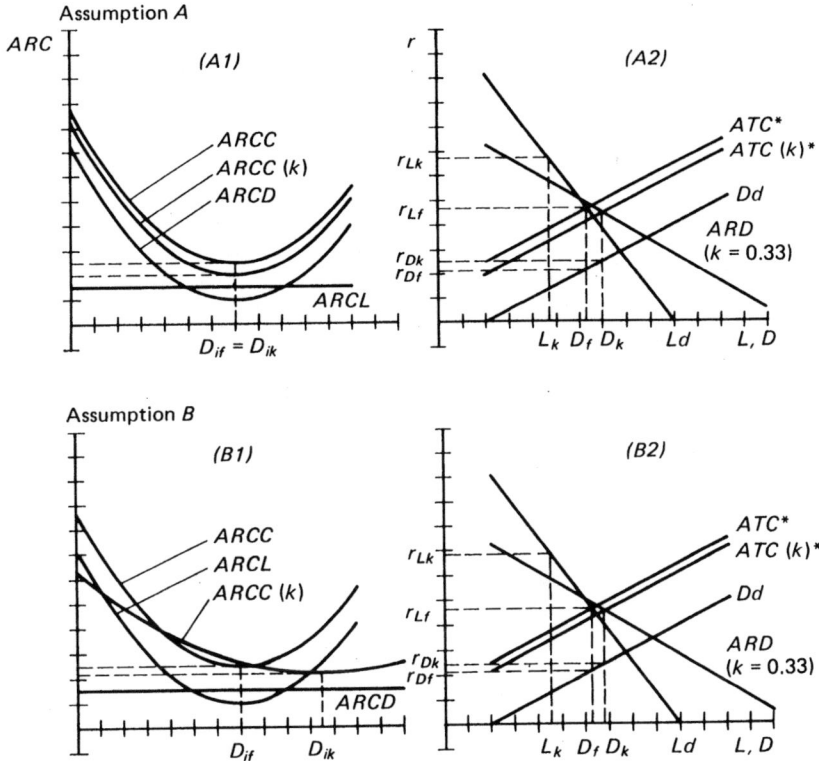

Figure 7.4   Some implications of real resource costs for the effect of
compulsory cash ratios

(B2), is higher than before the imposition of the compulsory cash ratio, the equilibrium of the industry and the optimal size of the firm differs between A and B.

Other examples can be easily constructed where the resource cost component of the effect of any given compulsory ratio on the equilibrium of the industry, or on the optimal size of the firm, is negative. Generally, however, for any given combined average resource cost function, it transpires that the deposit maximising cash ratio is positively related to the relative contribution of resource costs directed to servicing loans.

Simplifying, while maintaining a distinction between resource costs of loans and resource costs of deposits, let us assume constant returns to scale for *both* loans and deposits. Let ϕ be the average resource costs of providing loans, and ψ be the average resource costs of providing deposits. Thinking of ϕ as a deduction from the loan rate, and of ψ as an additional outlay per unit of deposits, we have, in place of equations (7) and (8) above,

$$AR_\phi = [(1-k)^2 D - a(1-k)]b^{-1} - \phi(1-k) \tag{19}$$

$$AC_\psi = (D-c)h^{-1} + \psi \tag{20}$$

The equilibrium volume of deposits, therefore, is

$$D_{\phi\psi} = \{[a(1-k)h - bc) + bh[\phi(1-k) + \psi]\}[(1-k)^2 - b]^{-1} \tag{21}$$

With respect to k, equation (18) has a maximum at

$$k^*_{\phi\psi} = \{[h(a+b\phi) - b(c-h\psi)] - [b^2(c-h\psi)^2_-$$
$$- hb(a-b\phi)^2]^{\frac{1}{2}}\}[(a+b\phi)h]^{-1} \tag{22}$$

from which

$$\left.\begin{array}{l} \dfrac{dk^*_{D\phi\psi}}{d\phi} > 0 \\[3ex] \dfrac{dk^*_{D\phi\psi}}{d\psi} < 0 \end{array}\right\} \tag{23}$$

This contrast between resource costs of producing loans and resource costs of producing deposits can be understood with reference to our finding of Section 1 that the deposit maximising cash ratio is higher (lower) the lower (higher) the elasticity of demand for loans and the higher (lower) the elasticity of demand for deposits. For, except at the limit of infinite elasticity of demand for loans, a rise in ϕ is equivalent to a reduction in the elasticity of demand for loans; and except at the limit of infinite elasticity of demand for deposits, a rise in ψ is equivalent to a reduction in the elasticity of demand for deposits.

2.2 Loan default

In part at least, the real resource costs of loans reflect expenditures involved in acquiring information relevant to assessing the repayment prospects of competing loan applications, and in drafting and enforcing loan agreements that enhance the likelihood of repayment. Granted, however, decreasing returns to such expenditures, in general, information costs (regarding customer quality and the prospects of the project for which any given loan is to be used) imply not only the possibility of loan default, and hence that (resource costs apart) the expected return per unit of loans granted, $E(r_L)$, falls short of the rate charged to customers, r_L, but also that the relationship between these two variables is likely to be non-linear and that beyond a certain point a higher loan rate results in a lower expected return per unit of loans granted.[19]

Suppose then that, in a manner analogous to that of $E(r_L) = f(r_L)$ in the leftwards facing quadrant of Figure 7.5,

$$E(r_L) = \alpha + \beta r_L + \gamma r_L^2 \qquad \beta > 0 \quad \alpha, \gamma < 0 \qquad (24)$$

describes, for some given level of information, the banks perceptions of the relationship between expected return and rate charged to customers.[20]

From equation (24) it follows that, irrespective of the levels of demand for loans and of the demand for deposits, the banking system (whether competitive or monopolistic) will not charge a loan rate higher than that at which $E(r_L)$ is at a maximum, that is, $r_L^* = -\beta(2\gamma)^{-1}$. Thus, given the demand for loans described in equation (1) above, the expected average revenue is defined by

$$E(AR) = \begin{cases} (4\alpha\gamma - \beta^2)(4\gamma)^{-1} & \text{for } r_L = r_L^* \\ \overline{[\alpha b + \beta(L-a) + \gamma(L-a)^2 b^{-1}]b^{-1}} & \text{for } r_L < r_L^* \end{cases} \qquad (25)$$

as depicted in Figure 7.5, quadrant (i), by *abc*, or, equivalently, in deposit space

162

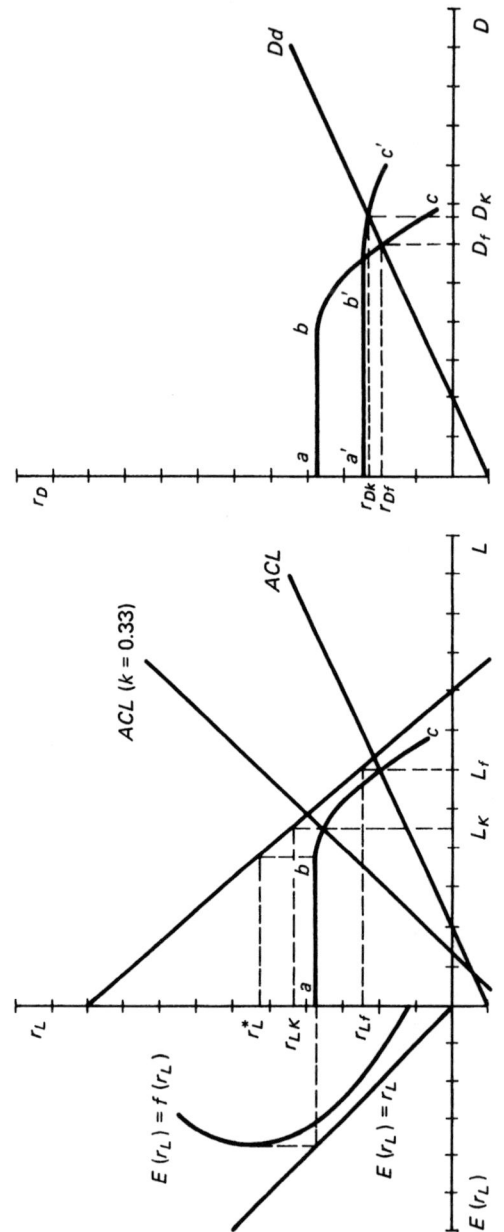

Figure 7.5 Loan default risks and the effects of compulsory cash ratios

$$E(AR) = \begin{cases} (1-k)(4\alpha\gamma - \beta^2)(4\gamma)^{-1} \\ (1-k)\{\alpha b + \beta[(1-k)D - a] + \\ \quad + \gamma[(1-k)D - a]^2 b^{-1}\}b^{-1} \end{cases} \tag{25'}$$

Assuming risk neutral banks,[21] equations (25') and (8) above yield the expression for the competitive equilibrium volume of deposits

$$D = \begin{cases} (1-k)[(4\alpha\gamma - \beta^2)h + 4\gamma c](4\gamma)^{-1} & \text{for } r_L = r_L^* \\ \{-[h(\beta b - 2a\gamma)(1-k)^2 - b^2] \pm \{[h(\beta b - & \text{for } r_L < r_L^* \\ \quad -2a\gamma)(1-k)^2 - b^2]^2 - 4h\gamma(1-k)^3[h(\alpha b^2 - \\ \quad -\gamma a^2 - ab\beta)(1-k) - b^2 c]\}^{\frac{1}{2}}\}[2h\gamma(1-k)^3]^{-1} \end{cases} \tag{26}$$

Accordingly, if in the absence of quantity constraints the equilibrium loan rate is at the maximum that (given Ld and Dd and perceptions of default risks) the banking system will contemplate, then the imposition of any compulsory zero-interest-bearing cash ratio will reduce the volume of deposits, causing loans to be rationed (or, if already rationed prior to the imposition of the compulsory ratio, to be rationed even more). On the other hand, when, as in Figure 7.5, in the absence of constraints $r_{Lf} < r_L^*$, then for some range of values ($0 < k_D^e < k_D^*$, where k_D^* is the deposit-maximising cash ratio obtained in equation (11) above, while k_D^e is the deposit-maximising cash ratio implied by equation (26)) the relationship of deposits to cash ratio is again positive. Thus, in the example of Figure 7.5 the 33.33 per cent compulsory cash ratio causes the loan rate to rise from r_{Lf} to r_{Lk} and the volume of loans to fall from L_f to L_k, but raises the deposit rate from $r_{Df} = E(r_{Lf})$ to $r_{Dk} = (1-k)E(r_{Lk})$ and hence the volume of deposits from D_f to $D_k = (1-k)^{-1}L_k$.

2.3 Other assets and other liabilities

All of the above abstracts from various non-homogeneities that even inspection of bank balance sheets reveals as characteristic of bank port-folios. In models of the banking firm the menu of freely-held assets and of liabilities is generally carefully accounted for, by appeal to stochastic demands for loans and deposits, stochastic returns on assets, real resource costs, and the like.[22] But in discussions of constraints the models utilised are generally more simple.

In the latter tradition, consider the model of Figure 7.6A.[23] This differs from the previous models in that banks are now assumed to deal also in some asset, bonds, the return on which is independent of the

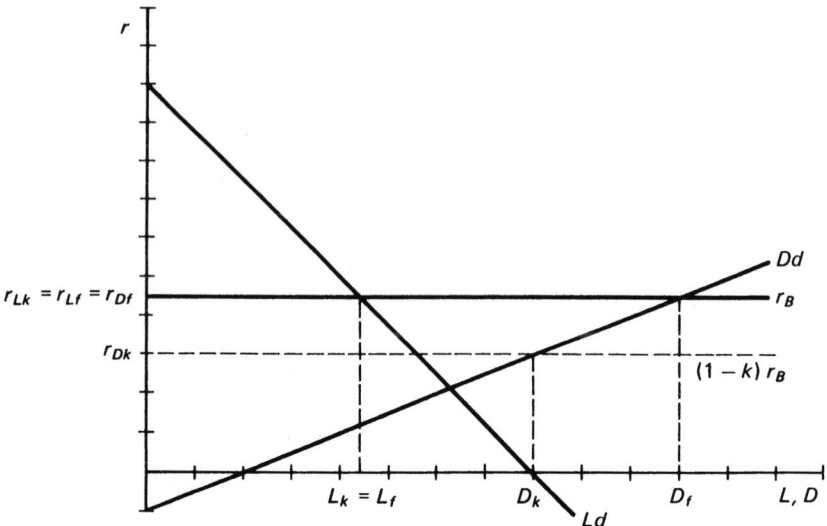

Figure 7.6A Cash ratio effects when the banking system is a rate-taker
with regard to some asset (bonds)

Note: the stock of bonds held by banks declines from $B_f = (D_f - L_f)$
to $B_k = [(1 - k) D_k - L_k]$

quantity of this asset that the banking system chooses to hold. In this
case, in the absence of constraints, the average revenue over the relevant
region is equal to the bond rate, r_B. A zero-interest-bearing compulsory
ratio (of a magnitude such as to imply that the banking system continues,
in the presence of this ratio, to hold bonds voluntarily) then leaves the
average revenue per unit of earning assets (loans and bonds) and the
volume of loans unchanged. But it reduces the average revenue per unit of
deposits to $(1 - k)r_B$, thus reducing the deposit rate and the volume of
deposits.

It is tempting to think of the case just described as suggesting that the
possible positive effect of cash ratios on deposits is in practice conditional
on the absence of a large market in government or private securities in
which the banking system is a participant but unable to influence security
prices (rates). This would then commend the postulate that cash ratios
bear negatively on deposit rates, as an appropriate operating guide when
looking at the UK and the US. Yet to draw such a conclusion is too hasty.
For the example of Figure 7.6A reveals only that the existence of a large
securities market allows us to entertain *the possibility* of a throughout
negative relationship of deposits to cash ratio. And with regard to the two

countries cited, the existence of a large securities market, entitles us no less readily to the opposite conclusion; namely, that, other things being equal, the likelihood that any particular cash ratio has a positive effect on the volume of bank liabilities is higher than in the absence of such a market.

Continuing to focus on non-homogeneities on the assets side of bank balance sheets, it is, of course, no less appropriate to conceive of bank holdings of bonds as comprising precautionary reserves, held to allow for random variations in demand for loans and/or deposits.[24] In the extreme, if (for simplicity) we assume that banks' desired holdings of this asset are rather unresponsive to movements in the loan rate, we have, as a first approximation,

$$B = \rho(1 - k)D \tag{27}$$

Accordingly, in the presence of a compulsory zero-interest-bearing cash ratio, the balance sheet constraint and the average revenue of the banking industry are, respectively,

$$L \equiv (1 - k)(1 - \rho)D \tag{28}$$

$$AR = [D(1 - k)^2(1 - \rho)^2 - a(1 - k)(1 - \rho) + b(1 - k)\rho r_B]b^{-1} \tag{29}$$

whence, given average costs as in equation (8) above, the equilibrium volume of deposits is described by

$$D_{Bk} = [h(1 - k)((1 - \rho)a - b\rho r_B) - bc] \, [h(1 - k)^2(1 - \rho)^2 - b]^{-1} \tag{30}$$

By manipulations analogous to those of Section 1, it can be shown that, for any given set of values of ρ and $r_B < r_L$, the deposit-maximising cash ratio k_{DB}^* entailed in equation (30) is lower than that traced by equation (11) above. Furthermore, the higher the value of ρ the more likely that $k_{DB}^* = 0$. Yet neither of these suffices to ensure that the relationship of deposits to cash ratio is throughout negative; and the conclusion still holds that the effect of any given compulsory cash ratio is more likely to be positive the lower the elasticity of demand for loans and the higher the elasticity of demand for deposits.[25]

Besides this, however, with regard to the two countries cited, the presence of banks in a market where the banking system is a participant, but unable to influence security prices, is (today) no less conspicuous when looking at the liabilities side of banks' balance sheets as when looking at the assets side. Accordingly, in Figure 7.6B a distinction is drawn between retail deposits, such as that on which our discussion has so far implicitly focused, and wholesale deposits, notably negotiable certificates of deposit (CDs) with regard to which the banking system is a rate taker.[26]

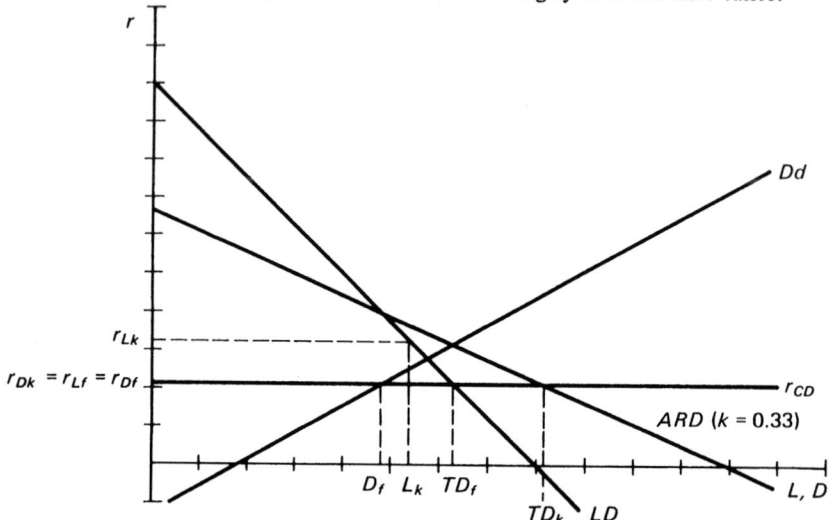

Figure 7.6B   Cash ratio effects when the banking system is a rate-taker with regard to some liability (CDs)

Note: $CD_f = (TD_f - D_f)$ and $CD_k = (TD_k - D_f) > CD_f$

Whether with or without constraints, the equilibrium of the industry is defined by the equality of average revenue from assets, and of average cost of retail deposits, to the average cost of wholesale deposits. Abstracting from default risks and resource costs, in the absence of constraints, the equilibrium volume of loans is $L_f = D_f + CD_f = TD_f$, as banks charge a rate on loans $r_{Lf} = r_{CD}$ and pay a rate on retail deposits of $r_{Df} = r_{CD}$. In sharp contrast to Figure 7.6A, the effect of the $k = 0.33$ compulsory ratio is to raise the loan rate to $r_{Lk} = (1 - k)^{-1} r_{CD}$, reducing the volume of loans to L_k, while leaving the rate on, and volume of, retail deposits unchanged, but increasing the volume of wholesale deposits[27] to CD_k.

In short, therefore, the presence of a large securities market in which the banking system is a participant but unable to influence security prices, does not automatically entitle us to assume the validity of a throughout negative relationship of deposits to cash ratio. Indeed, since the example of Figure 7.6B is but a limiting case of the model of Figure 7.2 - specifically, describing a circumstance where the elasticity of demand for deposits 'over the relevant region' is infinite – it transpires that the issue of CDs as an equilibrium phenomenon enhances the likelihood that the effect of any particular cash ratio on the volume of banks liabilities is positive, since, for any given downward-sloping average revenue curve, it increases the value of the bank liabilities maximising cash ratio.

2.4 Other intermediaries

Finally, let us examine the implications of non-bank financial intermediaries, ready, presumably, to respond to the differentials between loan rates and deposit rates that compulsory cash ratios imply.

Given substitution between bank deposits, D, and non-bank-financial-intermediary (NBFI) liabilities (shares), S, as well as on the assets side between bank loans, L, and NBFI credit, E, the demand/supplies of assets and liabilities are described by[28]

$$L = m + b_1 r_L + b_2 r_E \quad m, b_2 > 0, \quad b_1 < 0, \quad (b_1 + b_2) < 0 \quad (31)$$

$$D = n + h_1 r_D + h_2 r_S \quad n, h_1 > 0, \quad h_2 < 0, \quad (h_1 + h_2) > 0 \quad (32)$$

$$E = e + f_1 r_L + f_2 r_E \quad e, f_1 > 0, \quad f_2 < 0, \quad (f_1 + f_2) < 0 \quad (33)$$

$$S = g + q_1 r_D + q_2 r_S \quad g, q_2 > 0, \quad q_1 < 0, \quad (q_1 + q_2) > 0 \quad (34)$$

where r_E and r_S denote respectively the rates on NBFI credit and shares.

Assuming that NBFIs are not subject to any compulsory ratio, and again, abstracting from other assets, the balance sheet constraint of NBFIs is described by

$$E \equiv S \quad (35)$$

while for a competitive system of NBFIs at equilibrium

$$AC_N = AR_N \quad \text{implying } r_E = r_S \quad (36)$$

For banks the corresponding conditions are those of equations (3) and (4) above.

Substituting (3) and (35) into, respectively, (31) and (33) and deriving, by manipulations analogous to those leading to (7) and (8) above, the average cost and average revenue expressions for banks and for NBFIs, yields the simultaneous solution for the equilibrium volume of bank deposits

$$D = \{Q\,[m(1-k)h_1 - b_1 n] - n\,[b_1 h_2 - b_2 h_1(1-k)]\,Z\}\,V^{-1}$$

$$Q = (f_2 - q_2)\,(h_1 q_2 - h_2 q_1) - h_2\,(f_1 q_2 - f_2 q_1) \qquad (37)$$

$$Z = q_1(f_2 - q_2) + (f_1 q_1 - f_2 q_2)$$

$$V = \{Q\,[h(1-k)^2 - b_2] - [b_1 h_2 - b_2 h_1(1-k)]\,Z\}$$

Clearly, as before, the relationship of deposits to cash ratio is not monotonic.[29] From equation (37) the expression for the deposit-maximising cash ratio is so convoluted as to indicate little directly. On the other hand, examination of various special cases (combinations of parameters) is revealing. Specifically, for any given set of values of the intercepts and own rate coefficients of the demands for bank loans and bank deposits, the deposit-maximising cash ratio will generally be lower than that implied by the same relationships in a world in which non-bank financial intermediaries either do not exist or do not compete with banks. Furthermore, other things being equal, the deposit-maximising cash ratio is lower the higher the response of bank loans to a unit change in the NBFI credit rate and the higher the response of bank deposits to a unit change in the NBFI share rate. However (abstracting from resource costs and default risks), the deposit-maximising cash ratio is still in general positive, so long as the last column of inequalities featuring in equations (31) to (34) hold and the response of deposits to a unit change in the deposit rate exceeds the response of bank loans to a unit change in the loan rate.[30]

3   COMPULSORY CASH RATIOS IN A WORLD OF MUTUAL FUNDS AND 'DO IT YOURSELF' BANKING

Although the results presented so far allow us to imagine various circumstances in which the conventional wisdom will still hold true, they can hardly be said to provide support to an axiom of an inverse relationship between compulsory ratios and the volume of deposits. But how then is it that such a belief has survived?

Part of the answer, I believe, lies in willingness to presume from the outset of any enquiry the universal validity of the conclusion. This is encouraged by a tendency to think in the first instance in a 'money stock control' context, where familiarity with, and willy-nilly acceptance of, the qualitative validity of exercises that examine the relationship between deposits, reserve ratios and reserve asset availability, carry strong powers of suggestion – even when we may feel uneasy about the lack of any mention, not only of loans and loan rates, but even of deposit rates.

More substantially, however, at least with regard to writings that focus, explicitly or implicitly, on developed financial systems, the answer is to be found in willingness to assume *a priori* that under perfect competition the average revenue of the banking industry is indeed perfectly elastic; in that not only each firm in the industry but the industry itself is a rate taker with regard to all assets comprised in bank portfolios.

Perplexing though such a position may seem to the *ingénu* not versed in the theory of money and banking, and likely to think of banks as loan suppliers, to the specialist the position is not incompatible with his view of banking as an industry, qualitatively/behaviourally like any other industry. For in the dominant tradition the output of the banking industry is deposits; and on the asset side of the banks' operations nothing, in this tradition, entitles us to distinguish between them and the man in the street, let alone between banks and other financial intermediaries.

More specifically, the reasoning involves four elements:[31]

1. The main function of banks is the provision of a payments mechanism, that is, the maintenance of a system of accounts in which transfers of wealth are made.
2. In competition with other borrowers, banks issue claims on themselves, that is, deposits.
3. In competition with other investors, including their depositors, in respect to whom they possess no informational advantage, they use the proceeds to purchase securities.
4. Loans and securities are indistinguishable.

The first of these appeals easily to trained intuition, whether of the 'old' or 'new view' variety.[32] And though the second, being the pinnacle on which the 'new view' rests, is anathema to those of the 'old view', and no less obnoxious to those of strong monetarist persuasion, the banking specialist's milieu is certainly that of the 'new view' and there seems to be no reason to oppose it. The third and fourth seem no less easily digestible. For at the macroeconomic level (except very recently), for many years loans hardly ever received a mention – indeed the whole of the earning assets of bank balance sheets often remained out of sight. And at the micro level (again, except recently) the view of loans as simply purchases of securities has, under the influence of the Yale school, been ingrained in studies of bank behaviour – the vast majority of which do indeed treat banks as Tobinesque rate-taking quantity-setting portfolio holders, acting on given endowments of information (about returns and risks) not obviously different from those of other intermediaries or of their depositors, and some at least explicitly define a setting where this is true independently of the scale of the banking industry itself.[33]

Yet, apparently compatible with bits of familiar reasoning though the propositions seem, one must - upon reflection - feel uneasy to rely on the package too strictly. For in the extreme - where also, as Fama (1980) argues, the Modigliani–Miller theorem applies to the financial intermediaries themselves - we are encouraged to think of perfect capital markets, where, alas, surplus economic units, being perfectly capable of duplicating any efficient portfolio, have no need of banks (distinct from book-keepers), or indeed of other financial intermediaries.

On the other hand, if we bypass this - as we may by emphasising the provision of transactions (payment) services and economies of scale in transactions in securities/portfolio management - we should also recognise that it does not then directly follow that:

> in an unregulated environment there is unlikely to be a clear distinction between banks and other portfolio managers. Although banks may be more interested in supplying transactions services, competition will induce them to provide different types of portfolios against which their depositors can hold claims. Although other financial intermediaries, like mutual funds, may be more interested in managing portfolios, competition will induce them to provide the transactions services associated with banks. In the end one will observe financial institutions all of which can be called banks that provide accounts with different degrees of risk and allow individuals to make transfers of wealth through their accounts.
>
> (Fama, 1980, p. 41).[34]

At least it does not follow without some assumption of jointness in production of portfolio management and transactions services - which strictly neither Fama's (1980) nor Black's (1970) earlier account of such a position permit.[35] Neither does it follow that in a circumstance where jointness in production does indeed cause banks and mutual funds to be indistinguishable:

> the reserve requirement causes *some* intermediaries to choose not to provide access to the accounting system of exchange, so the reserve requirement has the effect of differentiating banks from other intermediaries.
>
> (Fama, 1980, p. 47, emphasis added).

Anthony S. Courakis 171

What does follow, is that the (continued) existence of banks - explicable
by appeal to some widening of the opportunity set of surplus economic
units - does not (in the presence of mutual funds at least) widen the
opportunity set of deficit economic units. The banking industry, therefore, is delimited from the mutual funds industry in terms of its liabilities
but not in terms of its assets with regard to all of which it is a rate-taker
(thus facing what, in the context of the model of the preceding sections I
have described as a perfectly elastic average revenue curve). Consequently,
a compulsory zero interest-bearing cash ratio levied against the liabilities
of the banking industry will reduce the equilibrium volume of these
liabilities, just as a similar ratio levied on the liabilities of mutual funds
will reduce their volume, and exactly like an equal rate tax on returns from
assets held against the liabilities in question.

In the last ten years, however, the characterisation of *all* financial intermediaries as merely managers of portfolios that are drawn, in Tobinesque
manner, from a set of securities the characteristics of which are defined
independently of the presence or absence of the intermediaries themselves,
and of banks as distinct from mutual funds only in terms of the range of
liabilities that they respectively issue, has been strongly qualified. More in
the spirit (though strictly not always the letter) of Gurley and Shaw (1960),
Shaw (1973), and more generally the broad tenor of the literature on
financial intermediaries and economic development, the existence of
financial intermediaries is now thought to reflect in the main informational
asymmetries in the capital market,[36] and thus (also) to imply as a *sine qua
non* a widening of the opportunity set of deficit units. With regard to
banks in particular, furthermore, considerable attention is now placed in
accounting for the differences in the functioning of loan markets distinct
from private or government 'efficient' securities markets.

Specifically, in the framework first proposed by Leland and Pyle, it is
suggested that

informational asymmetries [between borrowers and lenders] may be a
primary reason that intermediaries exist. For certain classes of asset . . .
information which is not publicly available can be obtained with an
expenditure of resources. This information can benefit potential lenders;
[and] if there are some economies of scale, one might expect organisations to exist which gather and sell information about particular classes
of assets. Two problems, however, hamper firms which might try to sell
information directly to investors. The first is the appropriability of
returns by the firm - the well-known 'public good' aspect of information . . . The second problem in selling information is related to the
credibility of that information.

Both these problems in capturing a return to information can be overcome if the firm gathering the information becomes an intermediary, buying and holding assets on the basis of its specialised information.

(Leland and Pyle, 1977, pp. 382-3).

Clearly, such reasoning undermines element (3) above, to provide an alternative, to economies of scale in transactions costs, *raison d'être* for financial intermediaries. But it does not directly provide for (i) distinctions between loans and securities, or for (ii) differences among intermediaries that reflect such distinctions. Yet, as Goodhart notes:

One of the major differences between banks and unit trusts, in their roles as financial intermediaries relates to the nature of the valuation of their assets. The assets held by unit trusts are, for the most part, marketable; in the case of banks, the assets held by them are, for the most part, non marketable (or, at least, are not marketed) and there is no market mechanism for establishing in a competitive and open fashion their true expected value. One of the more interesting questions about banking . . . is why any sizeable (secondary) market in bank loans, or at least loans of certain specific kinds, has not already developed.

(Goodhart, 1985, pp. 16-17).[37]

With regard to (i), the answer probably lies in that informational asymmetries are not only sufficient (as explained by Leland and Pyle) to ensure that the Modigliani–Miller theorem does not hold, but also imply that honest borrower behaviour will generally be such as to communicate to prospective lenders inside information conducive to the lenders' confidence in the borrowers' credit-worthiness. Granted this, then following Diamond (1984), and Fama in a different incarnation (Fama, 1985), we can reason that some borrowers find it cheaper to concentrate their quality signals on one prospective lender than to incur the (higher) costs of a wider dissemination of information that borrowing through floating of security issues requires. As Diamond explains, in this case we shall observe contracts between intermediaries and their borrowers that (like bank loans) are fixed in nominal terms and non marketable ('illiquid'). An increase in the rate charged on such contracts – such as the discussion of the previous sections traces as a consequence of a non-interest bearing cash ratio – will, of course, tend to induce some borrowers to incur the additional cost of wider dissemination of information that access to the securities market entails. But this in no way implies that the two markets can be regarded as one, or that the elasticity of demand with respect to the loan rate is infinite. Furthermore, when (with an eye to (ii)), this is combined with the fact that for a wide range of borrowers the history of the borrower as a depositor enhances the informational level available to the bank, or with any other reasoning that implies that intermediaries prepared to issue loan contracts will also issue liabilities that are fixed in nominal terms, we begin to have a glimpse of banks as an industry distinct from mutual funds, but so too a reason for the average revenue curve on loans to be downward sloping.

4 IMPLICIT TAXES AND THE FINANCE OF GOVERNMENT

Besides querying the general validity of the inverse relationship between a compulsory non-interest-bearing cash ratio and the volume of deposits, the analysis so far reveals that the interpretation of this quantity constraint as a tax on deposit returns, an *ad valorem* tax, is generally invalid. Yet, common though this interpretation is in discussions of compulsory non-interest-bearing cash ratios, it is by no means the only one. For with regard to compulsory ratios on liabilities – be they cash, securities or other – the *tax on intermediation* element of such arrangements is sometimes taken to be that 'implied by the difference between the rates paid on these compulsory holdings and the rates at which these assets would be *voluntarily* held by the banks in the volumes secured by these compulsory ratios'.[38] Something of the same, furthermore, seems to be implied in recommendations that government be made to pay 'some competitive interest on compulsory reserves'.

From this standpoint, however, the analysis of the effects of compulsory cash ratios warrants comparisons of a different kind to those entered into so far. Specifically, the comparisons in this case must reflect the fact that the choice facing the authorities is between, on the one hand, imposing a cash ratio and, on the other hand, resorting to borrowing in the market (through loans or security sales) the same sum as can be transferred to the government through the cash ratio.

In the latter vein, consider a decision by the government to increase its (permanent) borrowing by an amount G and suppose (in line with widespread reality) that this amount must be raised through the banking system. At one extreme, the government can transfer to itself the sum G in perpetuity through the imposition of a compulsory non-interest-bearing cash ratio, k, such that at equilibrium $kD_k = G$. At the other extreme, the government can resort to borrowing from the banks at whatever rate market conditions define. Clearly, the latter case implies that the government's outlays per unit time (per annum) are increased by a sum $T = r_G G$, where r_G is the rate at which the government can borrow G. This in turn begs the question of how T is to be raised.

For our purposes the range of possibilities for T is defined by, on the one hand, a circumstance where the taxes levied are not paid by the banks and do not impinge on demand for loans and deposits by other customers (what, for brevity, I will refer to in what follows as *financially neutral taxes*) and on the other hand by *taxes on intermediation* – such as taxes on interest income accruing to depositors, or commissions per unit of deposits or per unit of loans granted to other customers, or taxes on bank profits.[39] Figure 7.7 illustrates the effects of these alternatives to cash ratios on the equilibrium of the banking system when, as in the previous examples, a $k = 0.33$ cash ratio is taken as the reference point.

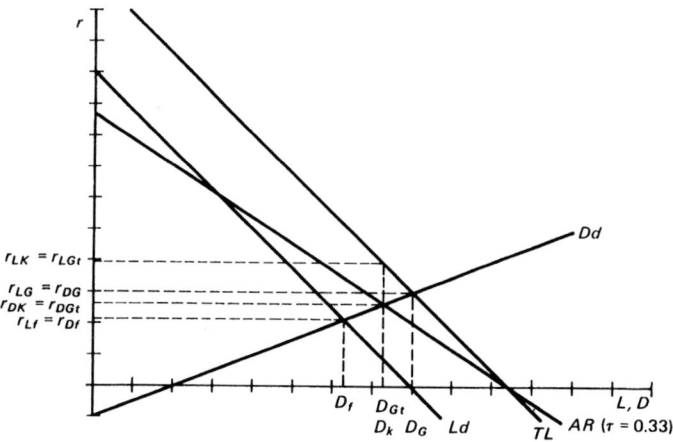

Figure 7.7   Government borrowing under alternative ways of servicing the loan, compared to raising the same sum through a zero interest-bearing cash ratio

In either case, the total demand for loans facing the banks is now

$$TL = a + br_L + G \tag{38}$$

whence, abstracting from default risks and resource costs (and thus also from differences in these as between loans to government and loans to other customers) the gross of tax average revenue can be straightforwardly derived.

With *financially neutral taxes* the equilibrium volume of deposits, defined as in the example of Figure 7.1 (and, equivalently, by manipulations analogous to those of pp. 154-5 above while setting $k = 0$), is thus

$$D_G = [(a + G)h - bc] \ (h - b)^{-1} \tag{39}$$

On the other hand with *taxes on intermediation*, such as, for instance, a tax on deposit returns of the kind examined in Section 1, levied (on the assumption that the rate of return on loans to government is equal to the average rate of return on the rest of bank assets), at a rate

$$\tau = G/D_{G\tau} \tag{40}$$

where $D_{G\tau}$ denotes the equilibrium volume of deposits that results from this arrangement, the net of tax average revenue function is

$$AR_\tau = (1 - \tau) [D_{G\tau} - (a + G)] \ b^{-1} \tag{41}$$

which, combined with the average interest cost of deposits defined by the public's demand for bank liabilities, yields the solution

$$D_{G\tau} = [(a + G) (1 - \tau)h - bc] \ [h(1 - \tau) - b]^{-1} \tag{42}$$

Comparing equation (42) to equation (39), it is immediately apparent that, as shown in Figure 7.7, $D_{G\tau}$ is less than D_G. However, compared to the case where, instead of direct borrowing cum intermediation taxes, the government transfers to itself the sum G through a compulsory non-interest-bearing cash ratio, it also transpires, by substituting $G = \tau D_{G\tau} = kD_k$ into equation (42), that

$$D_{G\tau} = [a(1 - k)h - bc] \ [h(1 - k)^2 - b]^{-1} = D_k \tag{43}$$

In this respect, under competitive banking,[40] a compulsory cash ratio is equivalent to a *tax on intermediation*, levied at a rate such as to ensure a revenue transfer to the government equal to the difference between the (in our example, zero) rate on compulsory holdings and the rate at which the banking system will voluntarily lend to the government the same volume of funds as the compulsory ratio secures. Obviously this means that, in the setting described, the authorities should be indifferent between pursuing 'share of government objectives' through compulsory ratios or through conventional taxes levied on the banks at the rate required to service the interest payments on the loans raised from these same taxes. Both these options imply a lower volume of deposits than if the government interacts with the banks and their customers only as a bank borrower. But then again both imply, up to a point, a larger volume of deposits than when the government neither borrows from the banks nor taxes them or their customers.[41]

Similar conclusions apply when, in the manner of Section 2, we allow for other features of banking reality and hence also for differences in default risks and real resource costs as between loans to government and loans to other customers. In the context of such refinements, however, what is particularly worthy of attention is the case where different types of bank liabilities are recognised. For with regard to cash ratios and to direct borrowing cum intermediation taxes, the government has then an option on the range of bank liabilities on which the cash ratio is to apply or the intermediation tax to be levied.

Utilising the equivalence between cash ratios and direct borrowing cum intermediation taxes traced above, let us contrast the case where the sum G is transferred to the government through a uniform cash ratio on both retail and wholesale deposits, to that in which the same interest-free loan is secured through a (higher) cash ratio on retail deposits only. In the former case, with $TD = D + CD$, and D and CD characterised as in Section 2, the average revenue of the banking industry is described by

$$AR_\tau = (1 - \tau)\,[TD - (a + G)]\,b^{-1} \tag{44}$$

whence, granted that at equilibrium the cost of supplying loans through wholesale and retail deposits must be equal, the equilibrium volumes of total deposits and of retail deposits are defined by

$$TD_\tau = (a + G) + b\,(1 - \tau)^{-1} r_{CD}$$
$$D_\tau = c + h r_{CD} \tag{45}$$

On the other hand, if the whole of the tax burden corresponding to the interest repayments on G is levied on retail deposits, through the imposition of tax rate τ_D on the average return on such deposits, the equilibrium of the industry is defined by

$$AR_{\tau D} = [TD - (a + G)]\,b^{-1}$$
$$AC = r_{CD} = (1 - \tau_D)^{-1} r_D \tag{46}$$

whence

$$TD_{TD} = (a + G) + br_{CD} > TD_\tau$$
$$D_{\tau D} = c + (1 - \tau_D)hr_{CD} < D_\tau$$

(47)

The difference, of course, reflects the difference in the elasticities of demands between retail deposits and wholesale deposits; and granted concern with the size of the banking industry commends the conclusion (reinforced when substitution elasticities between, on the one hand, retail and wholesale deposits and, on the other hand, currency are considered) that 'share of government objectives' are best pursued through differential compulsory ratios negatively related to the elasticities of demands for different types of bank liabilities.[42]

CONCLUDING REMARKS

That compulsory ratios reduce the equilibrium volume of deposits has long been a tenet that economists do not question. As shown in this paper, however, even with perfectly competitive banking this does not generally hold. Rather, the effect of such constraints on the volume of deposits depends on the characteristics of demand/supply for the assets and liabilities traded by the constrained intermediaries and what 'other things' we may strictly treat as 'being equal' when comparing constrained states to unconstrained ones.

For settings where under free market conditions it is appropriate to assume that the average revenue curve of the banking industry (over the relevant region) is downward sloping, there generally exists under competitive banking some compulsory zero-interest-bearing ratio that, other things being equal, implies a higher equilibrium volume of deposits than a zero compulsory ratio renders. The same is never true of 'a direct tax on deposit returns. . .' – such as the cash ratio is invariably said to comprise. This is not to say that cash ratios do not comprise 'a tax' on intermediation. Rather it is to stress that – except under assumptions that beg the question of the existence of banks – the tax on intermediation element of compulsory ratios, that has loosely comprised a rationalisation for the belief in an always inverse relationship between compulsory ratios and the volume of deposits, strictly involves a different process of reasoning and different *ceteris paribus* clauses than those which our mode of analysis of the effect of compulsory ratios has often involved.

178 *Do Compulsory Ratios Reduce the Volume of Deposits?*

Conceived as a tax, a compulsory ratio must be interpreted as *a specie tax*. And when so interpreted, then in a world where 'banking is just another industry whose equilibrium is subject to standard economic analysis',[43] the likelihood of a positive relationship between deposits and a compulsory ratio is much less formidable for intuition to grasp.

By way of illustration, let us take a trip to a future of Fama (1980, pp. 55-6) *spaceships* and *unregulated banks*. Suppose that in the interests of efficiency in Federal Galactic Government it is reasoned that government officials must be exposed to regular cultural exchanges. The question thus arises of how is government to service such space travel. One possibility suggested is to compel spaceship owners to reserve gratis for official use some fraction of the seats of every space flight. Whether 'the reserve requirement . . . has a depressing effect on the spaceship industry'[44] and its suppliers will depend on the elasticity of demand for space travel, on the elasticity of supply of space travel industry inputs, and on the level at which the reserve requirement is set.[45] This is not, of course, to deny that the spaceship industry is certainly smaller than it would be if the official cultural exchanges were to be financed through the levy of a general value added tax. Neither, however, can it be denied that 'the reserve requirement' described implies a larger spaceship industry (and suppliers) than the scale computed by some economist who, simply reading the headlines in the Galactic (video?) Press, chooses to interpret *k* as equivalent to a tax whose effects on the equilibrium of the industry can be inferred either on the assumption that the price of space travel is unchanged, or as if the tax proceeds were used to furnish and service a 'Teleporter'[46] capable of handling all official cultural exchanges and requiring in its use inputs quite different to those used by spaceships.

Come to think of it though, the Teleporter is a distinct possibility. And in the discussion in the Galactic Council it is suggested (at least by the lobby of spaceship owners) that one such is built, and in such a way as to require next-to-zero future outlays, save for the interest payments on the loan to be raised for its construction. All records of past forms of intervention in the banking industry having been destroyed since long ago – the year 1986, some say, but no one is sure – the novel idea is put forward that the funds could be had through a compulsory ratio on the banks who in this world (we discover) have still, in the absence of perfect information, a role to play.

As with spaceships, whether the banking system as a result issues more or less liabilities on itself depends on the elasticity of demand for the rest of the loans it provides, on the elasticity of demand for its liabilities and on the level at which the reserve requirement is to be set so as to generate the interest-free loan contemplated by the government. Again, however, as with spaceships, the banks' lobby is quick to point out at the Galactic Council that the arrangement implies a smaller volume of bank liabilities than would be had were the government to borrow from the banks and pay the interest on the loan through some value added tax. Yet on further discussion it transpires that the latter is administratively more costly, and that though the welfare losses of the former should not be overlooked neither should it be forgotten that the value added tax too (as indeed any other tax) implies a distortion in the presence of which *Pareto* criteria do not strictly apply.

Notes

1. Clearly, any of the plethora of bank deposit multiplier stories, from Philips (1923) and Crick (1927) onwards, can serve as the basis for such an exercise. What is perhaps more curious is that Tobin's (1963) discussion of the effect of reserve ratios is based on the implicit assumption that a 'compulsory asset availability constraint' applies (see note 9 below).
2. See Johnson (1968), Monti (1971), Shaw (1973) pp. 82–3, Fama (1980), Artis and Lewis (1981) pp. 111–13, Courakis (1981a), McKinnon (1981), McKinnon and Mathieson (1981) and Wills (1982), but note that careful reading reveals some subtle differences on this issue among authors.
3. Ibid. and also, for instance, Courakis (1973), Johnson (1974), Coats and Khatkhate (1980) and Goodhart (1984) p. 169.
4. See, for example, Johnson (1968), Shaw (1973), Fama (1980), McKinnon (1981) and McKinnon and Mathieson (1981), Greenbaum and Kellogg (1983) and IMF (1983). Alternatively, it is sometimes argued that the government/central bank should pay 'a competitive rate of interest on compulsory holdings of reserves', e.g. Johnson (1968), Coats and Khatkhate (1980) and Monti *et al.* (1983).
5. Exactly the same simplifying assumptions are employed, for instance, in McKinnon (1981) and McKinnon and Mathieson (1981), while for the average revenue curve the same applies, for instance, in the setting defined by Llewellyn *et al.* (1982) p. 69. Furthermore, as explained below, several other authors rely on models that allow for these features of reality only in a rather inconsequential way.
6. These simplifying assumptions are relaxed in Section 2.
7. For a discussion of the role and implications of quantity constraints also under monopoly banking see Courakis (1984a, 1984b).
8. Fama (1980) p. 47.
9. The example also highlights the fact that Tobin's (1963) remarks to the effect that 'In a world without reserve requirements the preferences of depositors, as well as those of borrowers, would be very relevant in determining the volume of bank deposits' (p. 7) while, by

implication, these preferences are not relevant in a world of reserve requirements; and further, that 'In a regime of reserve requirements the limit which they impose normally cuts the expansion [of credit and deposits] short of the competitive equilibrium' (p. 8) are valid only if we assume that there is some given (deficient) supply of reserve assets. Furthermore, to the extent that the second of these statements is to be understood as describing a disequilibrium situation, it should be stressed that, at least in circumstances where the non-bank public holds government debt, the validity of the statement requires that banks are also subject to ceilings on deposit rates.

10.   Equations (7) and (8) describe the relationship depicted in quadrant (ii) of Figure 7.2. The analogous expressions for quadrant (i) of that figure are as follows:

$$AR = (L - a)b^{-1} \tag{7'}$$

$$AC = [L(1 - k)^{-2} - c(1 - k)^{-1}]h^{-1} \tag{8'}$$

11.   In contrast, a tax on deposit returns implies, in place of (3), that $L \equiv D$. In turn, this means that while average cost is still as in equation (8), average revenue is in this case given by $AR = (1 - t)(D - a)b^{-1}$ which, combined with (8), yields the expression for the equilibrium volume of deposits

$$D(t) = [a(1 - t)h - bc][h(1 - t) - b]^{-1} \tag{9'}$$

Comparing equations (9) and (9') we find that for $0 < t = k$, $D(t) < D(k)$, which means that, in the context of the model described, the treatment of the cash ratio as a direct tax would generally lead us to expect a lower equilibrium volume of deposits than that which, other things being equal, the imposition of any particular cash ratio will produce.

12.   The same conclusion holds when monopoly, rather than perfect competition, is assumed – perhaps more appropriately for many countries – to comprise the relevant market structure (see Courakis, 1984a, 1984b).

13.   This is rather close to the set of assumptions made in Artis and Lewis (1981) p. 110. More generally, authors abstract from default risks and often assume real resource costs to be a constant, independent of the volume of bank assets or liabilities – see, for instance, Monti (1971) and Wills (1982).

14.   Baltensperger (1980) p. 30.

15.   See the survey papers of Baltensperger (1980), Santomero (1984) and Gilbert (1984).

16.   For example, whereas in Pesek (1970) and Towey (1974) the output of the banking industry relates to the provision of deposit services, more recent work – for example, Sealey and Lindley (1977), Mullineaux (1978), Sealey (1980) and Clark (1984) – stresses loans as the output, with a tendency to treat deposits as an input. In discussing the effects of constraints, Wills (1982) explicitly adopts the

Anthony S. Courakis 181

latter stance; but the majority of authors (see Section 3 of this paper) tend to proceed on the opposite premise.

17. Sealey (1980) p. 1142.

18. In passing, however, we should note that the general impression in the literature on real resource costs, and indeed on information costs, is that the optimal scale of the banking firm is considerably larger than even the largest establishments in the most advanced industrial countries. And in the literature on constraints on bank choices (where the scenario is generally one where, in the absence of bank regulation, perfect competition will reign supreme – for example, Black, 1970; Fama, 1980; McKinnon, 1981; McKinnon and Mathieson, 1981), it is sometimes recognised that 'unrestricted competition among banks tends to lead to concentration of the industry . . . presumably [because] there are significant economies of scale – both in the operation of the deposit payments mechanism, and in the operation of the lending and investment side of the banking business . . . In general, . . . [this] forces social policy concerned with efficiency to contemplate the familiar choice between (a) designing a regulatory system that will enable private competitive organisations to obtain economies of scale while preventing them from exercising monopoly power, and (b) replacing private enterprise by a public utility that will obtain the efficiency of a monopoly while operating in the public interest' (Johnson, 1968, p. 975). With regard to empirical evidence see Gilbert (1984).

19. The existence of information costs ensures that banks' perceptions (regarding customer quality and prospects of the project for which the loan is to be used) of loan default risks relate to classes of borrower and classes of project, to classes of loan such that *for each class,* though the loans granted are understood to involve the possibility of different degrees of default risk, it is also deemed that the costs of acquiring the information necessary for further subclassification exceeds the gains to be had from so doing. In such circumstances, the expected return to a bank per unit of loans granted to any given risk class will tend to rise less than proportionately to the rate charged, and beyond some point it may actually decline. This is so because, other things being equal, higher rates may: (i) induce firms to select projects that (though indistinguishable to the bank from the projects that will materialise at some lower rate) entail lower probabilities of success (and thus for the bank higher probabilities of default), but higher pay-offs to the borrower when successful; and (ii) result in a higher proportion of loans granted to higher than 'class average risk customers', in that the willingness of such customers to pay the higher rate reflects their lower intention to repay the loan. See Barro (1976), Jaffee and Russell (1976) and Stiglitz and Weiss (1981). Here information costs are assumed, for simplicity, to imply one class of loans.

20. Note that no intrinsic value attaches to the choice of a quadratic equation to describe the relationship between $E(r_L)$ and r_L. But at least with regard to the issue at hand, no gain is had from the use of more complicated functions.

21. Risk neutrality being what is generally assumed in discussions of loan default (see, for instance, Stiglitz and Weiss, 1981).

22. See, for instance, the survey papers of Baltensperger (1980) and Santomero (1984).

23. This is merely the perfect competition analogue of the monopoly banking model of Monti (1971) – disregarding the *fixed* total resource costs assumed by Monti.

24. See, for instance, Spencer (1982, 1984).

25. This conclusion is in no way undermined if we relax the assumption that the share of bonds held is unresponsive to changes in the loan rate. For since in that case ρ will be negatively related to the loan rate, ρ is inversely related to k, which implies that for any particular value of ρ observed in the absence of constraints, the deposit maximising cash ratio is higher when ρ is a function of r_L, than when ρ (as in our exercise) constant.

26. Such a distinction is drawn, for instance, in Spencer (1982) and Wills (1982).

27. Given the equilibrium condition $AR = AC_D = AC_{CD}$, the equilibrium volume of bank liabilities is defined by

$$(D + CD) = [a(1 - k) + br_{CD}] \, (1 - k)^{-2}$$

with retail deposits being equal to $D = c + hr_{CD}$.

28. Notice that the model defined implies, by virtue of the last column of inequalities, the holding, by surplus economic units, of other assets besides bank deposits and NBFI shares, and/or that the savings ratio is positively related to the rate of return on financial intermediary liabilities.

29. The increase in loan rates caused by the imposition of the compulsory zero-interest-bearing cash ratio on banks, we should note, definitely results in a larger volume of NBFI liabilities. Consequently, by appeal to the wealth constraint of surplus economic units (not explicitly modelled here), if the equilibrium volume of deposits is also to be larger, then either holdings of other assets (for example, currency and securities) by the public must have fallen or the savings ratio must have risen. For developing economies the latter is often stressed as a corollary of higher rates of return on deposits (see, for instance, Fry, 1978, and International Monetary Fund, 1983).

30. This is not to dispute the claim, made also in the context of studies concerned with financial innovation, namely that constraints encourage a process of attempts to circumvent the constraints. Rather it is to stress that, unless we assume that this process includes the possibility of bypassing the constraint by mere *re-labelling* of the product – so that institutions emerge who, although engaged in the very same activity as the banks, escape the required ratio simply by calling themselves, say, credit banks, their deposits credit-bank-liabilities and their loans credit-bank-loans – the process cannot be assumed *a priori* to imply a reduction in the volume of banks liabilities.

31. See Johnson (1968), Black (1970) and Fama (1980).
32. See Tobin (1963) and Brainard (1964).
33. See Pyle (1971), Hart and Jaffee (1974) and the survey of Santomero (1984). At the empirical level the use of this type of model has generally been more qualified as loans are often treated as distinct from securities, at least in the sense that for this asset quantity taking (in the short run at least) seems a more appropriate assumption to make (see, for instance, Courakis, 1980, and Spencer, 1984).
34. Fama attributes this position to Tobin (1963). But in fact Tobin's claim is simply that 'the commercial banking industry is not qualitatively different from any other financial intermediary . . . [in the sense that for both banks and other intermediaries] at some point the returns from additional loans or security holdings are not worth the cost of obtaining the funds from the public' (p. 7) and not that in the absence of constraints they will be indistinguishable in terms of the range of assets and liabilities comprised in their portfolios.
35. Any more than it follows that perfectly competitive unregulated fishmongers will diversify into being also butchers simply because both butchers and fishmongers use deep freezes.
36. Leland and Pyle (1977), Campbell and Kracaw (1980) and Santomero (1984).
37. Contrast this to Wills's (1982) premise that 'wholesale deposits and loans are broadly the same security' (p. 49).
38. Courakis (1981b) p. 218; also Courakis (1981a) p. 224.
39. Inflation and/or other constraints on banks' choices can serve the same ends – see Courakis (1984b) and, particularly, Courakis (1985) for analogues between cash ratios, inflation taxes and constraints on bank interest rates.
40. As explained in Courakis (1984a) pp. 355, 368, the equivalence between a compulsory cash ratio and a combination of direct borrowing plus intermediation taxes does not apply in the case of monopoly. With monopoly, however, a lump sum tax equal to the government's interest outlay on the loan can be combined with direct borrowing to deliver exactly the same outcome as the cash ratio delivers. The same outcome, furthermore, can be secured through a combination of a cash ratio with a ceiling on loan rates and a floor on deposit rates (see Courakis (1985)).
41. Note that in all cases discussed in this Section we have disregarded the effect on currency holdings of the public, which, however, in line with the spirit of the exercise should also be borne in mind.
42. See McKinnon (1982) p. 160.
43. Fama (1980) p. 47.
44. Ibid. p. 49.
45. The reader can easily convince himself that similar observations apply in the case where the government imposes such a reserve requirement on, shall we say, only *first class spaceships*.
46. I am grateful to my ten-year-old son and his friends for useful discussions on this subject.

References

Artis, M. J. and Lewis, M. K. (1981) *Monetary Control in the United Kingdom* (Oxford: Philip Allan).

Baltensperger, E. (1980) 'Alternative approaches to the theory of the banking firm', *Journal of Monetary Economics*, 6: 1–37.

Barro, R. J. (1976) 'The loan market, collateral, and rates of interest', *Journal of Money, Credit and Banking*, 8: 439–56.

Black, F. (1970) 'Banking and interest rates in a world without money', *Journal of Bank Research*, 1: 19–20.

Brainard, W. C. (1964) 'Financial intermediaries and a theory of monetary control', *Yale Economic Essays*, 4(1). Reprinted as Chapter 4 in Hester, D. and Tobin, J. (eds) (1967) *Financial Markets and Economic Activity* (London: Wiley) pp. 94–141.

Campbell, T. S. and Kracaw, W. A. (1980) 'Information production, market signalling and the theory of financial intermediation', *Journal of Finance*, 35: 863–82.

Clark, J. A. (1984) 'Estimation of economies of scale of banking using a generalised functional form', *Journal of Money, Credit and Banking*, 16: 53–68.

Coats, W. L. and Khatkhate, D. R. (1980) 'Money and monetary policy in less developed counries: survey of issues and evidence', in Coats, W. L. and Khatkhate, D. R. (eds) *Money and Monetary Policy in Less Developed Countries* (Oxford: Pergamon Press).

Courakis, A. S. (1973) 'Monetary policy: old wisdom behind a new facade', *Economica*, 40: 73–86.

Courakis, A. S. (1980) 'In search of an explanation of bank short-run portfolio selection', *Oxford Bulletin of Economics and Statistics*, 42: 305–35.

Courakis, A. S. (1981a) 'Banking policy and commercial bank behaviour in Greece', in Veirheirstraeten, A. (ed.) *Competition and Regulation in Financial Markets* (London: Macmillan Press) pp. 220–64.

Courakis, A. S. (1981b) 'Financial structure and policy in Greece: retrospect and prospect', *The Greek Economic Review*, 3: 205–44.

Courakis, A. S. (1984a) 'Constraints on banks' choices and financial repression in less developed countries, *Oxford Bulletin of Economics and Statistics*, 46: 341–70.

Courakis, A. S. (1984b) 'On the rationale and implications of constraints on the choices of deposit-taking financial intermediaries (with particular reference to seven European economies)', in Fair, D. E. and Leonard de Juvigny, F. (eds) *Government Policies and the Working of Financial Systems in Industrialized Countries* (Dordrecht: Martinus Nijhoff).

Courakis, A. S. (1985) 'The public finance dimension of bank regulation', Brasenose College, mimeo.

Crick, W. F. (1927) 'The genesis of bank deposits', *Economica*, 191–202.

Diamond, D. W. (1984) 'Financial intermediaries and delegated monitoring', *Review of Economic Studies*, 54: 339–414.

Fama, E. F. (1980) 'Banking in the theory of finance', *Journal of Monetary Economics*, 6: 39–58.

Fama, E. F. (1985) 'What's different about banks?' *Journal of Monetary Economics*, 15: 29–39.

Anthony S. Courakis   185

Fry, M. J. (1978) 'Money and capital or financial deepening in economic development', *Journal of Money, Credit and Banking*, 9: 464–75.
Gilbert, R. A. (1984) 'Bank market structure and competition: a survey', *Journal of Money, Credit and Banking*, 16: 617–44.
Goodhart, C. A. E. (1984) *Monetary Theory and Practice: the UK Experience* (London: Macmillan Press).
Goodhart, C. A. E. (1985) 'The implications of shifting frontiers in financial markets for monetary control', presented to the 1985 *Société Universitaire Européenne de Recherches Financières* (SUERF Colloquium) Cambridge, England, March 1985 (forthcoming in Fair, D. E. and Leonard de Juvigny, F. (eds) (1986) *Shifting Frontiers in Financial Markets* (Dordrecht: Martinus Nijhoff).
Greenbaum, S. I. and Kellogg, J. L. (1983) 'Legal reserve requirements: a case study in bank regulation', *Journal of Bank Research*, 13: 59–69.
Gurley, G. J. and Shaw, E. S. (1960) *Money in a Theory of Finance* (Washington, D.C.: Brookings).
Hart, O. D. and Jaffee, D. M. (1974) 'On the application of portfolio theory to depository financial intermediaries', *Review of Economic Studies*, 41: 129–47.
International Monetary Fund (1983) *Interest Rate Policies in Developing Countries*, IMF Occasional Paper, 22.
Jaffee, D. M. and Russell, T. (1976) 'Imperfect information, uncertainty and credit rationing', *Quarterly Journal of Economics*, 90: 651–66.
Johnson, H. G. (1968) 'Problems of efficiency in monetary management', *Journal of Political Economy*, 76: 971–90.
Johnson, O. E. G. (1974) 'Credit controls as instruments of development policy in the light of economic theory', *Journal of Money, Credit and Banking*, 5: 85–99.
Kane, E. J. and Buser, S. A. (1979) 'Portfolio diversification at commercial banks', *Journal of Finance*, 34: 19–34.
Leland, H. E. and Pyle, D. H. (1977) 'Informational asymmetries, financial structure and financial intermediation', *Journal of Finance*, 32: 371–87.
Llewellyn, D. T. *et al.* (1982) *The Framework of UK Monetary Policy* (London: Heinemann).
McKinnon, R. (1981) 'Financial repression and the liberalisation problem in less developed countries', in Grassman, S. and Lundberg, E. (eds) *The Past and Prospects for the World Economic Order* (London: Macmillan Press) pp. 365–86.
McKinnon, R. I. (1982) 'The order of economic liberalisation: lessons from Chile and Argentina', Carnegie Rochester Series on Public Policy, *Journal of Monetary Economics*, 17 (supplement): 159–86.
McKinnon, R. I. and Mathieson, D. J. (1981) 'How to manage a repressed economy', *Princeton Essays in International Finance*, 145.
Monti, M. (1971) 'A theoretical model of bank behaviour and its implications for monetary policy', *L'Industria*, No. 2.
Monti, M. *et al.* (1983) 'Report on the Italian credit and financial system', *Banca Nazionale del Lavoro Quarterly Review*, special issue, June.
Mullineaux, D. J. (1978) 'Economies of scale and organisational efficiency in banking: a profit function approach', *Journal of Finance*, 33: 259–80.

Pesek, B. (1970) 'Bank's supply function and the equilibrium quantity of money', *Canadian Journal of Economics*, 3: 357–85.

Philips, C. (1923) *Bank Credit* (London: Macmillan Press).

Pyle, D. H. (1971) 'On the theory of financial intermediation', *Journal of Finance*, 26: 737–47.

Santomero, A. M. (1984) 'Modelling the banking firm: a survey', *Journal of Money, Credit and Banking*, 15: 576–616.

Sealey, C. W. (1980) 'Deposit rate setting, risk aversion, and the theory of depository financial intermediaries', *Journal of Finance*, 35: 1139–54.

Sealey, C. W. and Lindley, T. (1977) 'Inputs, outputs and the theory of production and cost at depository financial institutions', *Journal of Finance*, 32: 1251–66.

Shaw, E. S. (1973) *Financial Deepening in Economic Development* (Oxford: Oxford University Press).

Spencer, P. D. (1982) 'Bank regulation, credit rationing and the determination of interest rates', *Manchester School*, 50: 41–60.

Spencer, P. D. (1984) 'Precautionary and speculative aspects of behaviour of banks in the UK under CCC', *Economic Journal*, 94: 554–68.

Stanhouse, B. and Sherman, L. (1979) 'A note on information in the loan evaluation process, *Journal of Finance*, 34: 1263–9.

Stiglitz, J. E. and Weiss, A. (1981) 'Credit rationing in markets with imperfect information', *American Economic Review*, 71: 393–410.

Tobin, J. (1963) 'Commercial banks as creators of "money" ', in Carson, D. (ed.) *Banking and Monetary Studies* (Irwin), pp. 408–19. Reprinted in Hester, D. and Tobin, J. (eds) *Financial Markets and Economic Activity* (London: Wiley) pp. 1–11.

Towey, R. E. (1974) 'Money creation and the theory of the banking firm', *Journal of Finance*, 29: 57–72.

Wills, H. R. (1982) 'The simple economics of bank regulation', *Economica*, 49: 249–59.

Part III
Modelling Financial
Markets

8 Rational Forecasts in Models of the Term Structure of Interest Rates

Richard T. Baillie and Patrick C. McMahon

INTRODUCTION

A large amount of contemporary macroeconomic and finance literature is dominated by the assumption of rational expectations – where the expectations of agents are considered not to be significantly different from optimal forecasts made from a set containing all available and relevant information. The concept of agents' expectations being equivalent to optimal forecasts dates back to Muth (1960, 1961) and it is now well known that when combined with the natural rate hypothesis, this idea leads to dramatic conclusions in macroeconomic models; such as the deterministic part of monetary policy having no effect on real output or employment in the economy, for example, Lucas (1972) and Sargent and Wallace (1975).

While many researchers have doubted the validity of rational expectations holding in all markets of the economy, it has frequently been considered to be a good approximation to reality in speculative auction markets, such as bonds, stocks and foreign exchange markets where prices are considered to reflect all available information. This has led to the so-called efficient markets hypothesis (EMH). In its weak form, the hypothesis implies that a current price incorporates all information in past prices, so that the difference between two successive prices is a random innovation reflecting new information. This form of the hypothesis led to the popularity of the so-called martingale random walk model (see Fama, 1970). Generally the EMH is considered to imply a semi-strong form where the current price of an asset incorporates all publicly-known information, including its own past prices. One important implication of the EMH is that no unexploited profit opportunities exist in an asset market.

The existence or otherwise of the EMH in asset markets is, of course, of considerable importance for the appropriateness of the many macro models that perceive monetary policy acting on aggregate demand by influencing long-term bond prices through a term structure of interest rates where expectations of future rates are formed rationally.

In this paper we consider some alternative models linking long- and short-term interest rates. These models make implicit assumptions concerning the generation of forecasts of the future short-term rate. We consider a simple distributed lag-type model where it is assumed that there is unidirectional causality from short- to long-term rates, and compare this with a bivariate autoregressive model which allows for joint determination of the short- and long-term rates series. We then discuss the Rational Expectations model of the Term Structure (RETS) where the short- and long-term interest rates series are assumed to be generated by an unrestricted bivariate autoregression. This standard version of the term structure model has recently been criticised by Begg (1984) for being a wrong characterisation of asset market equilibrium under certainty-equivalence. Thus empirical rejection of the RETS may be due to a failure of rational expectations or the inappropriate underlying model of equilibrium pricing, or both. In what follows we concentrate on the standard, largely North American, literature on the topic, which should be distinguished from that of Begg (1984).

The contribution of this paper is partly methodological and partly concerned with practical comparisons of alternative forecasts. Firstly, we derive asymptotically efficient econometric estimates of the models' parameters under the RETS and derive appropriate Wald and likelihood ratio (LR) tests of the RETS hypothesis. We then examine two well-known sets of data, one for the US and one for the UK, and show that, contrary to previous studies, the RETS theory is inappropriate. In particular, more efficient forecasts can be derived by basing predictions on information contained in the past short- and long-term interest rates series. One of these data sets was originally analysed by Sargent (1979) and has been extensively cited as being evidence in favour of the RETS. We find that careful specification of the alternative model leads to a rejection of the RETS hypothesis.

A further innovation in the paper is that when testing the RETS hypothesis we take data that is sampled more frequently than the shortest maturity rate. The statistical problems in doing this are found to be easily solved and the resulting technique allows for far more efficient econometric testing and generation of forecasts.

ALTERNATIVE MODELS RELATING INTEREST RATES

Most theories of interest rate behaviour typically view the long-term rate as being formed from a linear combination of unknown future short-term rates. We consider two interest rate series, r_t and R_t^n, which are one and n period rates respectively.

Assuming the standard approximation of $\ln(1 + r_t) \approx r_t$, then the general expectations hypothesis is of the form

$$R_t^n = \frac{1}{n} E_t \sum_{j=0}^{n-1} r_{t+j} \tag{1}$$

where E_t is the expectations operator conditioned on all relevant and available information at time t. Sometimes a constant representing a constant liquidity premium may be added to (1), for example, Fildes and Fitzgerald (1980). Many authors have proxied (1) with a distributed lag model on past short-term rates, so that (1) is replaced by

$$R_t^n = W(L) r_t \tag{2}$$

where $W(L) = W_0 + W_1 L + \ldots + W_m L^m$ and L is the lag operator. This model has been used by Modigliani and Sutch (1966), assumes unidirectional causality from short- to long-term bonds and has been found to give reasonable empirical fits to data. A further unidirectional causality technique is to assume a particular univariate time series model for r_t and to derive the implied time series representation for R_t^n. Various possible tests then exist to see if R_t^n and r_t conform with this theory. For example, let us assume that r_t follows the $AR(1)$ process:

$$r_t = \rho r_{t-1} + \epsilon_t \tag{3}$$

$$\epsilon_t \sim NID(0, \sigma^2) \text{ and } |\rho| < 1.$$

Then $E_t r_{t+j} = \rho^j r_t$ and substituting into (1) gives

$$R_t^n = \frac{1}{n} \sum_{j=0}^{n-1} \rho^j r_t = \frac{1 - \rho^n}{n(1 - \rho)} r_t \tag{4}$$

so that R_t^n is itself proportional to an $AR(1)$ process and hence follows the process

$$R_t^n = \rho R_{t-1}^n + v_t$$

where $v_t \sim NID \left(0, \left[\dfrac{1 - \rho^n}{n(1 - \rho)} \right]^2 \sigma^2 \right)$

Thus

$$\text{var}(r_t) = \sigma^2 (1 - \rho^2)^{-1}$$

and

$$\text{var}(R_t^n) = \sigma^2 n^2 (1 - \rho^2)/[n^2 (1 - \rho^2) - (1 - \rho^n)^2]$$

It can be shown that the variance of the long-term rate is always smaller than the variance of the short-term rate series. This result will usually depend upon the one-way causality assumption. Shiller (1979, 1981) and Le Roy and Porter (1981) have devised various tests of the model (1) by comparing point estimates of the variances and the asymptotic covariance matrix of the estimates to see if the empirical estimate of var (R_t^n) significantly exceeds that predicted from theory. Flavin (1983) has re-examined these test statistics in the light of small-sample theory.

Following Modigliani and Shiller (1973), the distributed lag model (2) can be justified in terms of forward-looking expectations variables being replaced by their optimal forecasts. For example, suppose r_t follows the commonly encountered exponentially weighted moving average process, that is, the ARIMA (0, 1, 1) model:

$$r_t = r_{t-1} + \epsilon_t - \theta \epsilon_{t-1} \tag{4}$$

which can alternatively be expressed as

$$r_{t+1} = (1 - \theta) \sum_{i=0}^{\infty} \theta^i r_{t-i} + \epsilon_{t+1}$$

Optimal predictions are then given by:

$$E_t r_{t+1} = (1 - \theta) \sum_{i=0}^{\infty} \theta^i r_{t-i}$$

and $E_t r_{t+j} = E_t r_{t+j-1}$ for $j \geqslant 2$

On substituting into (1) we obtain

$$R_t^n = \frac{1}{n} [r_t - (n - 1) E_t r_{t+1}]$$

so that the long-term bond rate R_t^n can be expressed as the infinite distributed lag on short-term rates r_t:

$$R_t^n = \left(1 - \theta \left(1 - \frac{1}{n}\right)\right) r_t + (1 - \theta) \sum_{i=1}^{\infty} \theta^i r_{t-i} \tag{5}$$

It should also be noted that another variant of (1) is to replace the expectation with the assumption of perfect foresight, so that (1) becomes

$$R_t^{n^*} = \frac{1}{n} \sum_{j=0}^{n-1} r_{t+j}$$

which Shiller (1981) has termed 'ex post rational' and which will have a greater variability than R_t^n defined in (1), since the perfect foresight version includes the stochastic component of r_{t+j} as well as its expectation.

Flavin (1983) has considered (3) in this context, and since

$$r_{t+j} = \rho^j r_t + \sum_{i=0}^{j-1} \rho^i \epsilon_{t+j-i} \tag{6}$$

it follows that

$$R_t^{n^*} = \frac{1}{n} \{r_t + (\rho r_t + \epsilon_{t+1}) + (\rho^2 r_t + \epsilon_{t+2} + \rho\epsilon_{t+1})$$

$$+ (\rho^3 r_t + \epsilon_{t+3} + \rho\epsilon_{t+2} + \rho^2 \epsilon_{t+1}) + \ldots.$$

$$+ (\rho^{n-1} r_t + \epsilon_{t+n-1} + \rho\epsilon_{t+n-2} + \ldots + \rho^{n-2} \epsilon_{t+1})\}$$

Hence

$$R_t^{n^*} = \frac{1}{n} \sum_{j=0}^{n-1} \rho^j r_t + \frac{1}{n(1-\rho)} \sum_{j=1}^{n-1} (1 - \rho^{n-j}) \epsilon_{t+j}$$

and on comparing with (4)

$$R_t^{n^*} = R_t^n + \frac{1}{n(1-\rho)} \sum_{j=1}^{n-1} (1 - \rho^{n-j}) \epsilon_{t+j}$$

which can also be expressed as

$$R_t^{n*} = \frac{(1 - \rho^n)}{n(1 - \rho)} \sum_{i=0}^{\infty} \epsilon_{t-i} + \frac{1}{n(1 - \rho)} \sum_{j=1}^{n-1} (1 - \rho^{n-j}) \epsilon_{t+j} \qquad (7)$$

so that R_t^{n*} is decomposed into two terms; the first of which consists of past short-term rate innovations, and the second term involving future innovations. Since the terms are statistically independent the variance of the R_t^{n*} series derived from perfect foresight will be greater than that of the R_t^n derived from taking expectations.

One unsatisfactory feature of the previous methods is the assumption that the short-term rates operate on the long-term rates with unidirectional causality without feedback from R_t^n. Since it seems likely that new information will be at least partly incorporated into both interest rate series, it follows that a more appropriate model would allow for joint endogeneity.

One useful model for such a purpose is the bivariate autoregression, which can also be considered as an unrestricted set of dynamic reduced form equations derived from a structural model. The bivariate autoregression of order p is then of the form

$$\begin{bmatrix} 1 - \alpha(L) & -\beta(L) \\ -\gamma(L) & 1 - \lambda(L) \end{bmatrix} \begin{bmatrix} r_t \\ R_{nt} \end{bmatrix} = \begin{bmatrix} \epsilon_{1t} \\ \epsilon_{nt} \end{bmatrix} \qquad (8)$$

where

$$\alpha(L) = \sum_{j=1}^{p} \alpha_j L^j, \quad \beta(L) = \sum_{j=1}^{p} \beta_j L^j,$$

$$\gamma(L) = \sum_{j=1}^{p} \gamma_j L^j \text{ and } \lambda(L) = \sum_{j=1}^{p} \lambda_j L^j$$

On writing $u'_t = (\epsilon_{1t}\epsilon_{nt})$ it is assumed that $E(u_t) = 0$

and that

$$E(u_t u'_{t-j}) = \begin{cases} \Omega & j = 0 \\ 0 & j \neq 0 \end{cases}$$

These models which do not have any economic structure imposed on them have been popularised by Sargent (1979), Sims (1980) and others and have been shown to be useful in a forecasting context.

Most of the models and tests of the term structure, including the volatility tests of Shiller, and Le Roy and Porter, are predicated on the assumption of the r_t and R_t^n series being covariance stationary. The vector autoregression (8) can be regarded as a finite approximation to an infinite vector moving average process, and it is known from Wold's decomposition theorem that if $(r_t\ R_t^n)$ is a linear, non-deterministic, jointly covariance stationary process, then it will possess an infinite order vector moving average representation which can be approximated by vector autoregression (8). These models have been popularised for forecasting purposes by Sims (1980) and others who have also claimed some success in using them on non-stationary data. Some large sample tests may in fact still be valid when explosive roots occur in these models (see Sims, 1980).

ESTIMATION AND TESTING OF THE RETS MODEL

Before testing the RETS it seems desirable to have as general a model under the alternative hypothesis as possible. For this reason the vector autoregression is used so that the set of all relevant and available information is restricted to consisting of current and past values of the two interest rate series. In order to obtain testable restrictions on the parameters of the model the general procedure is to take expectations at time $t - 1$ throughout equation (1) to give

$$E_{t-1}R_t^n = \frac{1}{n} E_{t-1} \sum_{j=0}^{n-1} r_{t+j} \qquad (9)$$

and to collapse the pth order vector autoregression (8) into the first order system

$$
\begin{bmatrix}
r_t \\
r_{t-1} \\
\cdot \\
\cdot \\
\cdot \\
r_{t-p+1} \\
R_t^n \\
R_{t-1}^n \\
\cdot \\
\cdot \\
\cdot \\
R_{t-p+1}^n
\end{bmatrix}
=
\begin{bmatrix}
\alpha_1 \ \cdots \ \alpha_p\beta_1 \ \cdots \ \beta_p \\
1 \\
\quad p \\
\quad\quad \cdot \quad\quad 0 \\
\quad\quad\quad \cdot \\
\quad\quad\quad\quad 1 \\
\gamma_1 \ \cdots \ \gamma_p\lambda_1 \ \cdots \ \lambda_p \\
\quad\quad\quad\quad 1 \\
\quad\quad\quad \cdot \\
\quad 0 \quad\quad\quad \cdot \quad 0 \\
\quad\quad\quad\quad \cdot \\
\quad\quad\quad\quad\quad 1
\end{bmatrix}
\begin{bmatrix}
r_{t-1} \\
\cdot \\
\cdot \\
\cdot \\
r_{t-p} \\
R_{t-1}^n \\
\cdot \\
\cdot \\
\cdot \\
R_{t-p}^n
\end{bmatrix}
+
\begin{bmatrix}
\epsilon_{1t} \\
0 \\
\cdot \\
\cdot \\
\cdot \\
0 \\
\epsilon_{nt} \\
0 \\
\cdot \\
\cdot \\
\cdot \\
0
\end{bmatrix} \qquad (10)
$$

Or,

$$Y_t = AY_{t-1} + \eta_t$$

As noted by Sargent (1979), equation (9) implies a linear relationship between optimal forecasts of R_t^n and r_t. From equation (10) the minimum mean square error (mse) predictors at time $t - 1$ are given by

$$E_{t-1} R_t^n = g' A Y_{t-1}$$

and

$$E_{t-1} r_{t+l} = e' A^{l+1} Y_{t-1}$$

Thus the RETS model implies $2p$ non-linear restrictions on the $4p$ parameters in the model (8), and are given by

$$r(\theta)' = g'A - \frac{1}{n} e' \sum_{l=1}^{n} A^l = 0 \qquad (11)$$

where $\theta' = [\alpha_1 \ldots \alpha_p \beta_1 \ldots \beta_p \gamma_1 \ldots \gamma_p \lambda_1 \ldots \lambda_p]$, $e' = [\, 1 \; 0 \ldots 0]$ and g' is a $2p$ vector of zeros except for unity in the $p + 1$ element. The approach adopted by Sargent (1979) was to estimate (8) subject to the restrictions (11) by a complicated numerical non-linear Gauss Seidel routine. The approach has been shown, by Tunnicliffe Wilson (1970), to give approximate maximum likelihood estimates. Comparison of the unrestricted and restricted models then allowed Sargent (1979) to compute a likelihood ratio test.

The approach used in this paper is slightly different. In order to test the hypothesis

$$H_0 : r(\theta)' = 0$$

versus

$$H_1 : r(\theta)' \neq 0$$

we can extend and generalise the approach used by Baillie, Lippens and McMahon (1983) when using a Wald statistic to test the EMH in the foreign exchange market. Although the restriction (11) is rather more complicated, we can again use the Wald statistic

$$W = r(\hat{\theta})' \, [D' \, \{\mathrm{cov}(\hat{\theta})\} \, D]^{-1} r(\hat{\theta}) \tag{12}$$

and on generalising a result in Baillie, Lippens and McMahon (1983) a fully parametric expression for D is given by

$$D = \frac{\partial r(\theta)}{\partial \theta} = \begin{bmatrix} -\dfrac{1}{n} \displaystyle\sum_{l=1}^{n} \sum_{j=0}^{l-1} (e'A'^{j}e)\, A^{l-1-j} \\ \hline I - \dfrac{1}{n} \displaystyle\sum_{l=1}^{n} \sum_{j=0}^{l-1} (g'A'^{j}e)\, A^{l-1-j} \end{bmatrix}$$

The unrestricted parameter estimates θ will have the asymptotic distribution

$$\sqrt{T}\,(\hat{\theta} - \theta) \sim N(0, \, \Omega \otimes M^{-1})$$

where T is the sample size and $M = X'X$ with X containing observations on $(r_{t-1}, \ldots r_{t-p}, R_{t-1}^{n}, \ldots R_{t-p}^{n})$.

Under the null hypothesis that the RETS is valid, W will have an asymptotic chi-squared distribution with $2p$ degrees of freedom.

It is also possible to obtain fully efficient estimates of the model under the RETS hypothesis by means of the linearised minimum chi-squared estimator (see Rothenberg, 1973, pp. 23-5). The vector of restricted parameter estimates is $\tilde{\theta}$ and is given by

$$\tilde{\theta} = \hat{\theta} - VD'\,(DVD')^{-1} r(\hat{\theta}) \tag{14}$$

where $\tilde{\theta}$ is the unconstrained (OLS) estimator and

$$V = \mathrm{cov}(\hat{\theta}) = T^{-1}\,(\Omega \otimes M^{-1}) \tag{15}$$

Furthermore the estimator $\tilde{\theta}$ has the asymptotic covariance matrix

$$\mathrm{cov}(\tilde{\theta}) = V - VD'\,(DVD')^{-1} DV \tag{16}$$

which is known to be equivalent to the asymptotic covariance matrix of the constrained maximum likelihood estimator. This constrained estimator is easily and directly computed and has the advantage of avoiding the complicated iterative Gauss Seidel computations employed by Sargent (1979), Hakkio (1981) and others.

When producing forecasts of future short-term rates and estimating and testing statistical models it is, of course, desirable to use as much data as possible in order to achieve statistical efficiency. As far as we know all previous work on the term structure has used data whose sampling frequency coincides with the period of the shortest maturity. We now assume that the frequency of the shortest maturity, associated with r_t, is k times the observation period. The hypothesis of interest then becomes changed from (9) to

$$E_{t-1} R_t^n = \frac{1}{n} E_{t-1} \sum_{j=0}^{n-1} r_{t+kj} \tag{17}$$

and (11) becomes

$$H_0 : r(\theta)' = g'A - \frac{1}{n} e' \sum_{l=0}^{n-1} A^{lk+1} = 0 \tag{18}$$

The Wald statistic (12) goes through as before with D in (13) being replaced with

$$D = \begin{bmatrix} -\dfrac{1}{n} \displaystyle\sum_{l=1}^{n} \sum_{j=0}^{kl} (e'A'^j e) A^{lk-j} \\ \hline I - \dfrac{1}{n} \displaystyle\sum_{l=1}^{n} \sum_{j=0}^{kl} (g'A'^j e) A^{lk-j} \end{bmatrix}$$

EMPIRICAL TESTS OF THE RETS AND COMPARISON OF FORECASTS

Work on the term structure has often been hampered in the past with the difficulty of obtaining high quality data defined on a consistent basis. In this article we take two sets of data – from Salomon Brothers (1982) for the US and from Grant (1964) for the UK.

Sargent (1979) used quarterly data from 1953 (QII) to 1971 (QIV) which are given by Salomon Brothers (1982). The variable r_t is taken as the three-month treasury bill rate and R_t^n is the rate on five-year government bonds, so that $n = 20$ in equation (9). As noted by Sargent, it is necessary to first difference both the variables in order for them to conform to being jointly covariance stationary. We estimated vector autoregressions for lags $p = 1$ to 6 inclusive, from the same number of observations, to enable direct comparison between the fitted models, whereas Sargent's model was only estimated for the case of $p = 4$. Our estimates of the constrained and unconstrained models for $p = 4$ lags are given in Table 8.1. Slight differences between our unconstrained estimates and Sargent's appear to be due to the fact that we omitted two observations in order to obtain model comparisons as stated earlier. In general, the results of our analysis are very close to Sargent's, with both the likelihood ratio and Wald statistics being non-significant. Essential details of all the models, given in Table 8.2, indicate a similar story for the lower order models $p = 1$ to 3. However, as noted by Baillie, Lippens and McMahon (1983), under-fitted vector autoregressions will have residual autocorrelation which may give rise to biased parameter estimates and test statistics, so that it is important to carry out sufficient diagnostic tests on the model in the maintained hypothesis. As shown in Table 8.2, Lagrange Multiplier (LM) and LR test statistics indicate that models with 4 lags or less contain substantial residual autocorrelation, and an LR test rejects at the 1 per cent level the model with 4 lags in favour of a model with 5 lags. Results of estimating a 5th order vector autoregression are given in Table 8.3 and, as shown in Table 8.2, this model now gives rise to highly significant LR and W test statistics. The model does not now appear to possess significant residual autocorrelation and a further model with 6 lags give virtually unchanged results. Thus a carefully specified alternative model gives rise to a clear rejection of the RETS hypothesis; so that an extended information set of past interest rates generates more efficient forecasts.

A further check on these results can be obtained by taking monthly data on these three-month and five-year US bonds. Then $k = 3$ and $n = 20$ in equations (17) and (18) and there are now $T = 225$ observations. As shown in Table 8.4, the data requires a vector autoregression of order 9 or 10 to adequately explain the autocorrelation structure between and within the series. Again the model gives rise to an unambiguous rejection of the RETS hypothesis. Full details of parameter estimates, their standard errors, and so on, in these models are omitted for reasons of space, but are available from the authors on request.

Some standard work on the term structure of UK interest rates was performed by Grant (1964) and Fisher (1966), who based their model on the work of Meiselman (1962). Meiselman assumed an adaptive expectations framework to explain the updating of interest rates expectations and, on the basis of applying this technique to UK Treasury bill rates, Grant (1964) considered that long- and short-term bonds were not always good substitutes, although Fisher (1966) found evidence in favour of the hypothesis. Since the data collected by Grant is very detailed and consists of quarterly observations on UK Treasury bill rates from 1, 2, 3, 4, 5 and

Table 8.1 Estimation of vector autoregression of order 4 on five-year
Government bond and 91-day Treasury bill rate US data

Unconstrained $\hat{\theta}$:

$\hat{\alpha}_1$	$\hat{\alpha}_2$	$\hat{\alpha}_3$	$\hat{\alpha}_4$	$\hat{\beta}_1$	$\hat{\beta}_2$	$\hat{\beta}_3$	$\hat{\beta}_4$
−0.348	−0.318	−0.104	−0.075	0.602	0.401	−0.317	0.196
(0.232)	(0.234)	(0.234)	(0.217)	(0.292)	(0.317)	(0.319)	(0.327)

$\hat{\gamma}_1$	$\hat{\gamma}_2$	$\hat{\gamma}_3$	$\hat{\gamma}_4$	$\hat{\lambda}_1$	$\hat{\lambda}_2$	$\hat{\lambda}_3$	$\hat{\lambda}_4$
−0.276	0.028	0.266	−0.091	0.226	0.089	−0.431	0.029
(0.182)	(0.183)	(0.183)	(0.170)	(0.229)	(0.249)	(0.250)	(0.257)

Constrained $\tilde{\theta}$:

$\tilde{\alpha}_1$	$\tilde{\alpha}_2$	$\tilde{\alpha}_3$	$\tilde{\alpha}_4$	$\tilde{\beta}_1$	$\tilde{\beta}_2$	$\tilde{\beta}_3$	$\tilde{\beta}_4$
−0.071	0.362	−0.185	0.021	0.388	0.319	0.149	0.170
(0.124)	(0.125)	(0.125)	(0.116)	(0.155)	(0.168)	(0.170)	(0.174)

$\tilde{\gamma}_1$	$\tilde{\gamma}_2$	$\tilde{\gamma}_3$	$\tilde{\gamma}_4$	$\tilde{\lambda}_1$	$\tilde{\lambda}_2$	$\tilde{\lambda}_3$	$\tilde{\lambda}_4$
−0.019	−0.009	0.002	−0.002	0.027	0.009	−0.003	0.006
(0.006)	(0.005)	(0.005)	(0.003)	(0.007)	(0.007)	(0.006)	(0.005)

Key: Standard errors are in parentheses under corresponding parameter
estimates.

Table 8.2 Summary of all vector autoregressions fitted to the five-year
Government bond and 91-day Treasury bill rate data

p; the order of the vector autoregression	*Akaike information criteria*	*Wald statistic*	*Likelihood ratio statistic*
1	−248.60	4.62 (0.10)	4.47 (0.11)
2	−254.95	4.49 (0.39)	4.35 (0.37)
3	−250.72	7.71 (0.26)	7.33 (0.31)
4	−246.24	8.30 (0.41)	7.87 (0.45)
5	−262.52	36.76 (0.00)	30.90 (0.00)
6	−260.88	37.38 (0.00)	31.28 (0.00)

Notes: Likelihood ratio (LR) test of model being $p = 4$ versus $p = 5$ was
$LR = 26.78$ (0.00), $LR = 7.01$ (0.15) of $p = 5$ versus $p = 6$.
Key: Significance levels are in parentheses beside corresponding test
statistic.

Table 8.3 Estimation of vector autoregression of order 5 on five-year Government bond and 91-day Treasury bill rate US data

Unconstrained $\hat{\theta}$:

$\hat{\alpha}_1$	$\hat{\alpha}_2$	$\hat{\alpha}_3$	$\hat{\alpha}_4$	$\hat{\alpha}_5$	$\hat{\beta}_1$	$\hat{\beta}_2$	$\hat{\beta}_3$	$\hat{\beta}_4$	$\hat{\beta}_5$
-0.187	-0.408	0.109	0.379	0.153	0.372	0.347	-0.191	-0.219	-1.088
(0.201)	(0.202)	(0.213)	(0.206)	(0.186)	(0.255)	(0.276)	(0.286)	(0.292)	(0.281)

$\hat{\gamma}_1$	$\hat{\gamma}_2$	$\hat{\gamma}_3$	$\hat{\gamma}_4$	$\hat{\gamma}_5$	$\hat{\lambda}_1$	$\hat{\lambda}_2$	$\hat{\lambda}_3$	$\hat{\lambda}_4$	$\hat{\lambda}_5$
-0.149	-0.039	0.286	0.275	0.166	0.046	0.033	-0.349	-0.303	-0.917
(0.156)	(0.157)	(0.165)	(0.160)	(0.145)	(0.197)	(0.214)	(0.229)	(0.227)	(0.218)

Constrained $\tilde{\theta}$:

$\tilde{\alpha}_1$	$\tilde{\alpha}_2$	$\tilde{\alpha}_3$	$\tilde{\alpha}_4$	$\tilde{\alpha}_5$	$\tilde{\beta}_1$	$\tilde{\beta}_2$	$\tilde{\beta}_3$	$\tilde{\beta}_4$	$\tilde{\beta}_5$
-0.057	-0.384	-0.175	0.115	-0.008	0.375	0.332	0.169	0.077	-0.183
(0.126)	(0.127)	(0.135)	(0.129)	(0.116)	(0.158)	(0.171)	(0.178)	(0.179)	(0.173)

$\tilde{\gamma}_1$	$\tilde{\gamma}_2$	$\tilde{\gamma}_3$	$\tilde{\gamma}_4$	$\tilde{\gamma}_5$	$\tilde{\lambda}_1$	$\tilde{\lambda}_2$	$\tilde{\lambda}_3$	$\tilde{\lambda}_4$	$\tilde{\lambda}_5$
-0.023	-0.014	0.005	0.012	0.005	0.047	0.014	0.002	-0.015	-0.031
(0.112)	(0.010)	(0.012)	(0.009)	(0.005)	(0.012)	(0.014)	(0.014)	(0.012)	(0.009)

Key: Standard errors are in parentheses under corresponding parameter estimates.

Table 8.4 Summary of vector autoregression on five-year Government bond and 91-day Treasury bill rate, for monthly, overlapping US data

p	Akaike information criteria	Wald statistic	Likelihood ratio statistic
1	−1206	3.09 (0.22)	3.07 (0.22)
2	−1206	4.11 (0.41)	4.56 (0.35)
3	−1220	11.57 (0.07)	11.26 (0.05)
4	−1220	18.43 (0.02)	17.67 (0.03)
5	−1220	22.74 (0.01)	21.60 (0.01)
6	−1216	25.89 (0.01)	24.44 (0.01)
7	−1226	30.14 (0.01)	28.20 (0.01)
8	−1228	38.84 (0.01)	35.74 (0.01)
9	−1232	49.24 (0.00)	44.40 (0.00)
10	−1232	58.80 (0.00)	52.11 (0.00)
11	−1227	61.33 (0.00)	54.17 (0.00)
12	−1224	63.39 (0.00)	55.90 (0.00)
13	−1218	62.98 (0.00)	55.58 (0.00)

Notes: Diagnostic tests and model comparisons suggested $p = 9$ as being the most satisfactory model.

Key: Significance levels are in parentheses beside corresponding test statistics.

Table 8.5 Summary of vector autoregressions estimated from Grants's UK Treasury bill rate data

Maturity times Short-rate		Long-rate	Order of vector autoregression	Wald	Likelihood ratio
1	and	2	3	14.72 (0.02)	14.31 (0.02)
1	and	3	2	15.63 (0.00)	15.06 (0.00)
1	and	4	1	27.49 (0.00)	25.19 (0.00)
1	and	5	2	32.51 (0.00)	29.37 (0.00)
1	and	6	1	26.29 (0.00)	24.18 (0.00)
2	and	4	6	19.96 (0.07)	19.16 (0.07)
2	and	6	1	24.63 (0.00)	22.76 (0.00)
3	and	6	2	12.00 (0.02)	11.58 (0.02)

6 years or more in maturity time, from 1922 to 1962 inclusive, it seems worthwhile testing the RETS theory on this data. Table 8.5 presents a summary of the results of analysing 1-year bonds against 2, 3, 4, 5 and 6; 2-year bonds against 4 and 6; and 3-year bonds against the 6-year bonds. For 7 out of 8 cases it is possible to reject the RETS model in favour of the more general vector autoregression. Although there is some evidence that the model holds between 2- and 4-year bonds. For reasons of space Table 8.5 only presents a summary of the results; again full details of the estimated models are available from the authors on request.

Apart from the feature of rejecting the RETS theory, our results also illustrate the type of problems that emerge when information is neglected and the vector autoregression attenuated at too short a lag. As with Sargent's study on the quarterly US data, a model with only 4 lags will possess substantial residual autocorrelation and the resulting hypothesis tests may be considerably misleading.

It is also interesting to consider if the models where R_t^n is hypothesised to be a distributed lag of current and past r_t, so that no feedback occurs from R_t^n to r_t, are valid. Such a situation of unidirectional causality is equivalent to $\gamma_j = 0, j = 1, 2, \ldots p$ in model (8); which can simply be tested by a Granger (1969) type causality test. Thus the second equation of (8) was estimated with and without the constraint $j = 0; j = 1 \ldots p$, for all the Salomon Brothers and Grant series of data. In all cases it was found possible to reject the constraint implying the short- and long-term rates were jointly determined.

Finally, it may be of interest to know the relative forecasting abilities of the various models that were estimated. The one step ahead forecasting mse for long-term rates was estimated for (a) a scalar autoregression on past long-term interest rates, (b) the distributed lag-type model given by equation (2), (c) the vector autoregression estimated subject to the RETS constraint, and (d) the unrestricted vector autoregression so that R_t^n is being explained by current and past r_t and R_t^n. The results are given in Table 8.6 for Sargent's data and show that the unrestricted vector autoregression generally provides significantly smaller one-step-ahead forecast mse than the other methods.

It is particularly interesting to note that the vector autoregression estimated under the relatively tight RETS constraint often performs much worse than the autoregressive or distributed lag models. Presumably the parameter restrictions implied by the RETS are extremely restrictive on the parameter space. Also, gains from the unrestricted vector autoregression are far more pronounced when using quarterly, rather than monthly, data.

Table 8.6 One step ahead forecast mse from various models of US government bonds

Quarterly data

Method	No. of lags	p = 4		p = 5		p = 6	
		mse	% gain	mse	% gain	mse	% gain
Autoregression		0.2307	19.3	0.1735	24.4	0.1735	25.1
Distributed lag on 91-day Treasury bill rates		0.2205	14.0	0.1846	32.3	0.1840	32.7
Vector autoregression under RETS constraint		0.2175	12.5	0.2145	53.8	0.2136	54.0
Unrestricted vector autoregression		0.1934	–	0.1395	–	0.1387	–

Monthly data

Method	No. of lags	p = 4		p = 9		p = 13	
		mse	% gain	mse	% gain	mse	% gain
Autoregression		0.06327	5.1	0.06080	8.3	0.6164	11.2
Distributed lag on 91-day Treasury bill rates		0.06401	6.4	0.06070	8.2	0.6160	11.1
Vector autoregression under RETS constraint		0.06294	4.6	0.06304	12.3	0.6251	12.8
Unrestricted vector autoregression		0.06018	–	0.05612	–	0.5543	–

Key: % gain is the percentage increase in mse from using a particular method compared to predicting from the unrestricted vector autoregression.

CONCLUSIONS

The general approach of applying the EMH to bond market data gives rise to the RETS model. For US and UK data, the model is found not to be supportable by the data. This could be due to suboptimal forecasts being made of future short rates, or could be due to the existence of a time-varying liquidity premium. Obviously further work on modelling risk, and examining suboptimal expectations schemes, is required in order to throw more light on why the RETS breaks down, although, to pin down exactly why it is failing may be a very difficult task. The simple distributed lag-type relationship popularised by Modigliani and Shiller (1973) and others is generally found to be inferior to the bivariate autoregressive model. Although the unrestricted bivariate autoregression may give a better forecast of the future long-term rate than the RETS autoregression, it is possible that the RETS autoregression provides a forecast that is adjusting for the time-varying risk premium in some manner.

Finally it should be noted that, following Begg (1984) the rejection of the simple expectations theory in combination with rational expectations may be due to an inappropriate asset equilibrium model under certainty-equivalence.

References

Baillie, R. T., Lippens, R. E. and McMahon, P. C. (1983) 'Testing rational expectations and efficiency in the foreign exchange market', *Econometrica*, 51: 553-63.
Begg David, K. H. (1984) 'Rational expectations and bond pricing: modelling the term structure with and without certainty equivalence', *Economic Journal*, 94: 45-58.
Fama, E. (1970) 'Efficient capital markets: a review of theory and empirical work', *Journal of Finance*, 25: 383-417.
Fildes, R. A. and Fitzgerald, M. D. (1980) 'Efficiency and premiums in the short term money market', *Journal of Money, Credit and Banking*, 12: 615-29.
Fisher, D. (1966) 'Expectations and the term structure of interest rates and recent British experience', *Economica*, 33: 319-29.
Flavin, M. A. (1983) 'Excess volatility in the financial markets: a reassessment of the empirical evidence', *Journal of Political Economy*, 91: 929-56.
Granger, C. W. J. (1969) 'Investigating causal relations by econometric models and cross spectral methods', *Econometrica*, 37: 424-38.
Grant, J. A. G. (1964) 'Meiselman on the structure of interest rates: a British test', *Economica*, 31: 51-71.
Hakkio, C. S. (1981) 'The term structure of the forward premium', *Journal of Monetary Economics*, 8: 41-58.

Le Roy, S. and Porter, R. (1981) 'The present value relation: tests based on implied variance bounds', *Econometrica*, 49: 555–74.

Lucas, R. E. (1971) 'Expectations and the neutrality of money', *Journal of Economic Theory* 4: 103–24.

Meiselman, D. (1962) *The Term Structure of Interest Rates* (Englewood Cliffs, New Jersey: Prentice-Hall).

Modigliani, F. and Shiller, R. J. (1973) 'Inflation, rational expectations and the term structure of interest rates', *Economica*, 40: 12–43.

Modigliani, F. and Sutch, R. (1966) 'Innovations in interest rate policy', *American Economic Review* (Papers and Proceedings) 61: 178–97.

Muth, J. F. (1960) 'Optimal properties of exponentially weighted forecasts', *Journal of the American Statistical Association*, 55: 299–306.

Muth, J. F. (1961) 'Rational expectations and the theory of price movements', *Econometrica*, 29: 315–35.

Rothenberg, T. J. (1973) 'Efficient estimation with *a priori* information', (Yale University Press).

Salomon Brothers (1982) *An Analytic Record* (New York: Salomon Bros).

Sargent, T. J. (1979) 'A note on maximum likelihood estimation of the rational expectations model of the term structure', *Journal of Monetary Economics*, 5: 133–43.

Sargent, T. J. and Wallace, N. (1975) 'Rational expectations, the optimal monetary instrument and the optimal money supply rule', *Journal of Political Economy*, 83: 24–54.

Shiller, R. J. (1979) 'The volatility of long-term interest rates and expectations models of the term structure', *Journal of Political Economy*, 87: 1190–1219.

Shiller, R. J. (1981) 'Alternative tests of rational expectations models: the case of the term structure', *Journal of Econometrics*, 16: 71–87.

Sims, C. A. (1980) 'Macroeconomics and reality', *Econometrica*, 48: 1–48.

Tunnicliffe Wilson, G. T. (1970) 'The estimation of parameters in multivariate time series models', *Journal of the Royal Statistical Society*, B: 73–85.

9 Did High-Powered Money Rule the Roost? Monetary Policy, Private Behaviour and the Structure of Interest Rates in the United Kingdom: 1972–77*

Christopher J. Green

Asset Price Expectation Formation (APEX) equations are derived by inverting theoretically plausible asset demand functions under the maintained assumptions of continuous market clearing and unbiased expectations. In this paper, I argue that APEX equations can be used in empirical research aimed at circumventing the Lucas critique. The results of this work suggest that the mean-variance model with rational expectations can explain a significant proportion of the movement in UK asset returns during 1972–7. The results also suggest that the authorities' avowed strategy of pegging short-term interest rates was correctly perceived by private agents and incorporated into their estimate of the covariance matrix of asset returns. A by-product of this study is that descriptive models of the variance of a time series do not necessarily contain any information about the risks and welfare losses actually incurred by agents facing this data.

INTRODUCTION

The portfolio approach of Tobin and Brainard (1968) has long appeared to offer an attractive methodology for the empirical modelling of asset markets. In practice, the approach has proved to have some major draw-

*I thank Juliette Thomas for excellent secretarial assistance.

backs. First, it introduces a large number of structural parameters which, even if they are identified, are nevertheless extremely difficult to estimate or interpret with much precision (Green, 1984a). Estimated interest rate substitution effects in asset demand equations frequently have implausible signs and magnitudes or are statistically insignificant. This is not altogether unexpected in a setting in which interest rates are highly correlated with one another and in which interest rates and asset holdings are determined simultaneously in continuously clearing markets.

A second and more serious problem with portfolio models is posed by the way in which they are invariably estimated and used. The focus of interest is typically on estimating asset demand functions; these asset demands are then inverted and the result is described as showing the effects on interest rates of exogenous shocks to asset supplies in the context of a freely-clearing market. It is my contention that this way of proceeding is fundamentally incorrect: if asset supplies (and private preferences) are the exogenous processes which determine interest rates, then the regression of an asset quantity on interest rates is not meaningful since it amounts to regressing an exogenous variable on a collection of endogenous variables. In asset markets which continuously clear, it is far from obvious which variables can be regarded as predetermined within a regression framework.

A third and final problem with the Tobin–Brainard approach is shared by any methodology which interprets the decision rules of private agents (in this case, the asset demand functions) to be parametrically invariant. The Lucas (1976) critique suggests that the parameters of private decision rules will, in fact, alter in response to variations in the policy regime faced by the private sector. The effect of regime changes on expectations is just one possible route by which such changes may alter the private sector's decision rules. Any modelling strategy aimed at studying the effects of different monetary policy regimes needs to take some account of this problem.

In a recent paper (Green, 1985), I developed the idea of *asset price expectation formation (APEX) equations*. The idea owes a great deal to pioneering work by Frankel (1982, 1985) and Frankel and Dickens (1984). Put simply, APEX equations are derived by inverting theoretically-plausible asset demand functions under the maintained assumptions of continuous market clearing and unbiased expectations. Under these assumptions, APEX equations turn out to be regression equations which can be estimated by standard techniques. Restrictions implied by theory can likewise be tested in particularly straightforward ways. In principle, the APEX method-ology offers a constructive resolution of *all* the major problems listed above.

In my paper (1985), the main focus of interest was in using the methodology to test the mean-variance model. It turned out that UK data provided strong support for mean-variance portfolio behaviour and Sharpe–Lintner–Black asset pricing (for example, Sharpe, 1964) under constant relative risk aversion and rational expectations. On that occasion the data consisted of comprehensive monthly integrated balance sheets and flows of funds for the United Kingdom covering the period 1972–7 and aggregated into four assets: equities, foreign currency denominated, government securities, and liquid assets, the latter being a consolidation of all short-term paper. In the present study I use essentially the same dataset, but in a way intended to illustrate the structural properties of the APEX methodology.

APEX equations are derived from the mean-variance model. As this model provides a structural, optimising framework for studying asset demands and price determination, it can, in principle, be used as the basis for empirical work that seeks to avoid the Lucas critique. In portfolio demand functions based on the mean-variance model, the structural parameters do not appear in a straightforward way (see Parkin, 1971), and it is the demand functions themselves which perforce have therefore to be treated (incorrectly) as parametrically invariant. In contrast, the structural parameters of the mean-variance model appear in the APEX equations in a relatively simple way. Parameter restrictions implied by specific regimes can therefore be tested directly. Green and Keating (1985) have derived equations which can be used to estimate the mean-variance model across regime changes. Their technique involves a reparameterisation comparable to that used in the derivation of APEX equations but, unlike the APEX methodology, assumes, as an approximation, that asset prices are non-stochastic. The APEX methodology avoids the need for such an assumption, and hence permits us to examine the implications of policy regimes in a completely rigorous way.

The specific set of questions which I address in this paper is among the oldest in monetary economics. It is concerned with the role of monetary policy in general and the quantity of money in particular in determining the level and structure of interest rates. The policy regime I am concerned with is the pegging of short-term interest rates. Did the authorities peg short-term interest rates in the policy regime of the early-to-mid-1970s? What were the implications of the authorities' activities: did they stabilise or destablise other interest rates?

It should be emphasised that, in this study, these questions are addressed within a relatively narrow framework. First, they are construed as questions about the implications of a particular policy regime and not about the effects of a change in regime. Secondly, they are addressed within the framework of a relatively simple linear model of asset pricing of which the mean-variance model (with adjustment costs) is a special case. I test for mean-variance efficiency, adjustment costs and rational expectations along with the tests for the implications of short-term interest rate policy. My investigation of interest rate policy is conditioned on acceptance of the mean-variance model. This relatively narrow focus is impelled to a large extent by the Lucas critique. Parameters which are invariant under regime changes have to be derived from optimising models and more than one such model could be applicable to UK asset markets. The mean-variance model is, however, widely accepted and my previous paper (1985) found 1972–7 data to be consistent with mean-variance efficiency. Furthermore, the focus of the analysis makes possible a direct comparison between the results of this paper and my 1985 study; this comparison turns out to be of interest in its own right.

The plan of the paper is as follows.

In Section 2 I set out the general APEX methodology. The narrative here follows closely that of Green (1985). In Section 3 I consider in detail the nature of the interest rate policy with which I am concerned: the theoretical isssues, the authorities' views, and the general nature of my proposed tests. I also draw attention to a flaw in descriptive models of the variance of time series data. The data is outlined in Section 4. Section 5 sets out the empirical methodology. Here some care is taken to specify the exact interpretation of the proposed tests and the manner in which they are nested in a more general model of asset pricing. I also show that the analysis in the present paper is related in a simple way to that in my previous (1985) paper. In Section 6 I discuss briefly the estimation and testing problems. Finally, Section 7 contains the empirical results and some concluding remarks.

ASSET PRICE EXPECTATION FORMATION (APEX) EQUATIONS

The notation is as follows:

$x_t = n \times 1$ vector of portfolio shares

W_t = Wealth at market value (a scalar)

hence $x_{jt}W_t$ = the market value of holdings of asset j at time t

$\mu = W_{t-1}/W_t$

$\mathbf{Y}_{t+1} = n \times 1$ vector of actual 'gross' asset returns

each $Y_{jt+1} = (C_{jt} + P_{jt+1})/P_{jt}$

with C_{jt} =coupon on the j'th asset at time t

$P_{jt} =$ the price of the j'th asset at time t

$_tY_{jt+1} = (C_{jt} + {}_tP_{jt+1})/P_{jt}$ is the expectation formed at time t of

Y_{jt+1}
i is a conformable vector of ones.

I assume away aggregation problems by adopting the convenient fiction of a representative agent who chooses a vector of portfolio shares (**x**) to:

maximise $U = U(M, V, C)$ (1)

subject to $\mathbf{i}'\mathbf{x} - 1 = 0$ (2)

$U(\ )$ is the usual second-order approximation to the expected utility of some arbitrary function of wealth. The arguments of $U(\ )$ consist of:

Subjective expectation of wealth $M = {}_t\mathbf{Y}'_{t+1}\,\mathbf{x}_tW_t$

Subjective variance of wealth $V = \mathbf{x}'_t\Sigma\mathbf{x}_tW_t^2$

Adjustment costs $C = (\mathbf{x}_t - \mu\mathbf{x}_{t-1})'\Psi\,(\mathbf{x}_t - \mu\mathbf{x}_{t-1})W_t^2$

Σ is an $n \times n$ subjective covariance matrix of asset returns
Ψ is an $n \times n$ matrix of adjustment costs.

I follow the widely-used approach of treating this as a one-period optimisation problem though, strictly speaking, the presence of adjustment costs (with $\partial U/\partial C < 0$) makes such an approach questionable. I assume too that adjustment costs are proportional to (the square of) the net change in asset holdings. Two other plausible specifications are that such costs are proportional to (the square of) the change in portfolio shares or the net cash acquisition of assets (see Friedman, 1977, for a detailed discussion of these issues).

Following my 1985 paper, I assume constant relative risk aversion. In the present model, the second-order approximation to the Pratt-Arrow coefficient of relative risk aversion is:

$$\frac{-2W_t \partial U / \partial V}{\partial U / \partial M} = \gamma \text{ (a constant)} \tag{3}$$

I also assume 'constant relative aversion to adjustment costs' implying that:

$$\frac{-2W_t \partial U / \partial C}{\partial U / \partial M} = \delta \text{ (a constant)} \tag{4}$$

Maximising (1) subject to (2) by choice of x and imposing constant relative risk aversion and aversion to adjustment costs yields as asset demands:

$$x_t = Z_t Y_{t+1} + \delta Z \psi \mu x_{t-1} + \Omega^{-1} i (i' \Omega^{-1} i)^{-1} \tag{5}$$

$$\text{with } Z = \Omega^{-1} - \Omega^{-1} i (i' \Omega^{-1} i)^{-1} i' \Omega^{-1}$$

$$\Omega = \gamma \Sigma + \delta \psi$$

It is in this general form that portfolio demand functions are most commonly estimated (see, for example, Green, 1984a and Keating, 1985).

The next step is to assume that asset markets are continuously cleared by freely-moving prices. Under the assumptions which have been made, setting asset demands equal to asset supplies, and solving for prices, is now equivalent to inverting equations (5). To do this, note first that the matrix Z is singular; this is just another way of stating that an *n* market model can determine only $n - 1$ asset prices. Therefore, we first partition (5) into the first $(n - 1)$ rows and the remaining n'th row:

$$\begin{bmatrix} x_{1t} \\ x_{nt} \end{bmatrix} = \begin{bmatrix} Z_{11} & Z_{1n} \\ Z_{n1} & Z_{nn} \end{bmatrix} \begin{bmatrix} {}_t Y_{1t+1} \\ {}_t Y_{nt+1} \end{bmatrix}$$

$$+ \delta \begin{bmatrix} Z_{11} & Z_{1n} \\ Z_{n1} & Z_{nn} \end{bmatrix} \begin{bmatrix} \Psi_{11} & \Psi_{1n} \\ \Psi_{n1} & \Psi_{nn} \end{bmatrix} \mu \begin{bmatrix} x_{1t-1} \\ x_{nt+1} \end{bmatrix} + \begin{bmatrix} \theta_1 \\ \theta_n \end{bmatrix} \tag{6}$$

Here

$$x_t = \begin{bmatrix} x_{1t} \\ x_{nt} \end{bmatrix} \text{ is } \begin{bmatrix} n - 1 & x & 1 \\ 1 & x & 1 \end{bmatrix}$$

$$Z = \begin{bmatrix} Z_{11} & Z_{1n} \\ Z_{n1} & Z_{nn} \end{bmatrix} \text{ is:} \begin{bmatrix} n - 1 & x & n - 1 & n - 1 & x & 1 \\ 1 & x & n - 1 & 1 & x & 1 \end{bmatrix}$$

$$\theta = \Omega^{-1} i \, (i' \Omega^{-1} i)^{-1} = \begin{bmatrix} \theta_1 \\ \theta_n \end{bmatrix} \text{ is:} \quad \begin{bmatrix} n-1 & x & 1 \\ & 1 & x & 1 \end{bmatrix}$$

and other vectors and matrices are partitioned conformably. Dropping the last row of (6), premultiplying by Z_{11}^{-1} (which is non-singular) and rearranging gives:

$$_t Y_{1t+1} - i_t Y_{nt+1} = (\Omega_{1n} - i\omega_{nn}) - \delta \, (\Psi_{1n} - i\psi_{nn})\mu + \hat{\Omega} x_{1t} - \delta \hat{\Psi} \mu x_{1t-1} \tag{7}$$

with

$$\hat{\Sigma} = \Sigma_{11} - i\Sigma_{n1} - \Sigma_{1n} i' + ii' \, \sigma_{nn}$$

$$\hat{\Psi} = \Psi_{11} - i\Psi_{n1} - \Psi_{1n} i' + ii' \, \psi_{nn} \tag{8}$$

$$\hat{\Omega} = \gamma\hat{\Sigma} + \delta \, \hat{\Psi}$$

Equation (7) is the fundamental theoretical result. It shows that the vector of expected asset returns relative to the return on the numeraire can be expressed as linear combinations of current and lagged portfolio shares, the inverse of the rate of change of wealth, and a vector of constants reflecting the risk and costs of adjustment associated with the numeraire. Note that the share of the numeraire asset does not appear on the right-hand side as it has been eliminated using the wealth identity (2).

To give an economic interpretation to (7) recall that the main assumptions are:

1. One period optimisation.
2. Constant relative aversion to risk and to adjustment costs.
3. Continuous market clearing.

Assumption (3) is particularly important as it legitimises the inversion of the asset demands. In contrast to traditional portfolio models therefore, continuous market clearing is a maintained (untestable) hypothesis. Given these three assumptions and some hypotheses about expectations and about asset supplies equations (7) provide an implicit set of solutions for $n - 1$ current asset prices: $p_{1t}, \ldots, p_{n-1t}$. However, in a regression context, these solutions are no more useful than the asset demands (5). I therefore make the additional assumption:

4. Asset price expectations are unbiased (*not* rational) and (by virtue of the representative agent assumption) homogenous.

This implies that the subjective expectation of wealth (*M*) is identical to the mathematical expectation of wealth. It implies too that actual asset returns (which contain asset prices) provide information about expected returns, subject to a measurement error. Thus:

$$_t\mathbf{Y}_{1t+1} - \mathbf{i}\,_tY_{nt+1} = \mathbf{Y}_{1t+1} - \mathbf{i}\,Y_{nt+1} - (\epsilon_{1t+1} - \mathbf{i}\epsilon_{nt+1}) \tag{9}$$

where $\epsilon'_{t+1} = (\epsilon'_{1t+1} : \epsilon_{nt+1})$ is a vector of white noise errors with covariance matrix defined as:

$$\diagdown\!\!\!\diagup = E_t\,(\epsilon_{t+1}\,\epsilon'_{t+1})$$

$$\widehat{\diagdown\!\!\!\diagup} = E_t\,(\epsilon_{1t+1} - \mathbf{i}\epsilon_{nt+1})\,(\epsilon_{1t+1} - \mathbf{i}\epsilon_{nt+1})'$$

Hence:

$$\widehat{\diagdown\!\!\!\diagup} = \diagdown\!\!\!\diagup_{11} - \mathbf{i}\diagdown\!\!\!\diagup_{n1} - \diagdown\!\!\!\diagup_{1n}\mathbf{i}' + \mathbf{i}\mathbf{i}'\lambda_{nn}$$

Here I am using E_t as the mathematical expectation conditional on information at time t; and $\diagdown\!\!\!\diagup$ is partitioned to conform with the definitions (8).

Combining (7) and (9) gives:

$$\mathbf{Y}_{1t+1} - \mathbf{i}Y_{nt+1} = (\Omega_{1n} - \mathbf{i}\omega_{nn}) - \delta(\Psi_{1n} - \mathbf{i}\psi_{nn})\mu$$
$$+ \hat{\Omega}\mathbf{x}_{1t} - \delta\hat{\Psi}\mathbf{x}_{1t-1} + (\epsilon_{1t+1} - \mathbf{i}\epsilon_{nt+1}) \tag{10}$$

Since the expectations $(_tY_{t+1})$ are based on information available at time t, it is clear that the errors in (10) are uncorrelated with the right-hand side variables, whatever the nature of the processes determining asset supplies. Therefore (10) constitutes a set of regression equations which can be estimated by ordinary least squares (OLS).

If expectations were rational, it would also be true that agents' subjective covariance matrix would coincide with the true covariance matrix of the data. The subjective covariance matrix of relative returns is $\hat{\Sigma}$; the objective covariance matrix, conditional on information at time t, is found by operating on (9) to get:

$$E_t(\mathbf{Y}_{1t+1} - \mathbf{i}Y_{nt+1} - {_t}\mathbf{Y}_{1t+1} + \mathbf{i}_tY_{nt+1})(\mathbf{Y}_{1t+1} - \mathbf{i}Y_{nt+1} - {_t}\mathbf{Y}_{1t+1}$$
$$+ \mathbf{i}_tY_{nt+1})' = \widehat{\diagdown\!\!\!\diagup}$$

Equality of $\hat{\Sigma}$ and $\widehat{\diagdown\!\!\!\diagup}$ amounts to constraints between the coefficient matrix difference $(\hat{\Omega} - \delta\hat{\Psi}) = \gamma\hat{\Sigma}$ and the covariance matrix of regression residuals $\hat{\psi}$. These two matrices should be proportional, with the factor of proportionality equal to the coefficient of relative risk aversion. Clearly, these are testable, though non-standard restrictions.

MONETARY POLICY, MONEY, AND INTEREST RATES

It is widely accepted that 'money' gains its importance in large part because the nominal return on money is exogenously fixed, usually at zero (see Tobin, 1969 and Niehans, 1978). A sketch of the argument is as follows. Since the rate on money is fixed, an exogenous change in the supply of money can be accommodated only by changes in the (endogenous) rates of interest on all other assets. In contrast, an exogenous change in the supply of any non-monetary asset can be accommodated to some extent by a change in the own rate on that asset. Hence, changes in the generality of interest rates play a lesser role in response to a change in the supply of non-monetary assets than they do in response to a change in the supply of money. Thus, with some imprecision of language, it can be said that money determines the *level* of interest rates; relative asset supplies and other factors determine the *structure* of rates. In this sense, money can be said to 'rule the roost'.[1]

In this argument 'money' is identified as those assets whose returns are exogenously fixed. Since 1971, the payment of interest at market-related rates has spread to a wide variety of assets in the UK including current accounts at banks. This effectively narrows the compass of the theoretical argument to refer solely to high-powered money.

The theoretical basis for the argument consists of a picture of freely-clearing asset markets in which asset supplies are set exogenously by the monetary authority, and asset demands are treated as a parametrically-given set of private decision rules, often characterised by the assumption of gross substitutability. In this setting, when the authorities peg any interest rate, they create an additional class of assets whose rate is exogenously fixed and which can be freely converted into cash. In such a regime, the sense in which high-powered money rules the roost is weakened in two respects. First, the impact on interest rates of changes in the supply of money is quantitatively smaller than it is in a regime in which the rates on all non-monetary assets are freely flexible. Secondly, a change in the level of the interest rate which is pegged will itself change all other interest rates. On this interpretation, if the authorities stabilise one interest rate, it helps reduce interest rate volatility in the market as a whole; it also increases the authorites' leverage over the whole rate structure (see Brainard, 1964, and Green, 1982).

As Green and Keating (1985) have pointed out, however, key elements in this argument do not survive the Lucas critique in a wide class of optimising models. Specifically, agents who are mean-variance optimisers are concerned about the subjective covariance matrix of asset returns. If the authorities switch from controlling the supply of an asset to pegging its rate of return, their action will alter the *actual* covariance matrix of asset returns. At one extreme, it is possible that this change will not affect agents' perception of the subjective covariance matrix of returns. If the policy is announced and understood, however, such an outcome appears unlikely; some change in agents' subjective perception of the covariance matrix seems certain to occur. At the other extreme, rational agents will compute the new actual covariance matrix and use this in calculating the mean-variance trade-offs which they (correctly) perceive that they face.

If agents are rational and their behaviour is determined by the true covariance matrix of asset returns, the effects of changes in policy regimes are drastically different from those predicted by models in which decision rules are parametrically given. Green and Keating consider the example of the authorities pegging deterministically the three-month nominal rate of interest. If agents are rational, such a peg has no effect at all on the stochastic properties of asset prices apart from, trivially, on the asset whose price is pegged. However, it remains true that a change in the level of the rate which is pegged will affect all other interest rates.

It follows from this discussion that there are two distinct questions to be answered about monetary policy in the period 1972–7. First, what were the authorities actually doing, and secondly, what were they perceived by the market to be doing?

As a preliminary, it seems clear that interest rate policy was actually and was believed to be directed at *nominal* interest rates. There is no reason to believe that any attempt was made to peg *real* interest rates.

In recent years, the monetary authorities have been increasingly forthcoming about their activities. The introduction of Competition and Credit Control clearly involved a greater degree of market determination of interest rates. However, the effect of this was generally thought to impinge largely on the gilt-edged market. Throughout the 1960s and the 1970s monetary policy was 'aimed for periods of stability in short-term rates, interrupted by discrete adjustments by the authorities' (Bank of England, 1982, p. 87.). It seems reasonable, therefore, to suppose that the authorities believed that they were pegging short-term nominal interest rates. However, it should be noted that the authorities never publicly espoused the view expounded above, that stability of short rates would help stabilise interest rates in general. If anything, they viewed causation as running in the opposite direction: 'If more volatility [of interest rates] was inevitable, greater flexibility in the administration of short-term rates seemed appropriate'. (Bank of England, 1982, p. 88.)

What we have to say about the market's perception of the authorities' actions depends to a large extent on whether they viewed the interest rate peg as stochastic or deterministic. *A priori*, it is hard to see the purpose of a stochastic peg. However, whether or not the peg was perceived to be deterministic depends entirely on the information which was available to the market about the authorities' intentions during the whole period of pegging, and particularly prior to changes in the rate which was being pegged. Within the mean-variance framework, all relevant information about agents' knowledge of interest rate policy is contained in their subjective means and covariance matrix. Thus, what the authorities were actually doing is essentially secondary to what agents thought they were doing. It should, however, be emphasised that this 'bootstraps' property is a characteristic of the simple mean-variance model in the present context, and is not necessarily true of more complex models of asset pricing.

This reasoning has important implications. To determine the effects of interest rate policy over the period of concern, we need to study the market's subjective means and covariance matrix. The APEX methodology *assumes* unbiased expectations; but agents' subjective covariance matrix $(\hat{\Sigma})$ is *estimated* from the data (up to a factor of proportionality equal to the coefficient of relative risk aversion: γ). Tests for the effects of interest rate policy therefore amount to tests on the structure of the estimated coefficient matrix $(\gamma\hat{\Sigma})$ conditional on the prior acceptance of mean-variance efficiency.

Before describing the exact nature of such tests it is worth comparing this methodology with descriptive models of the variance of time series data. Advocates of such models frequently imply that they contain information about uncertainty and welfare losses incurred by the private sector (Engle, 1983). In fact such models contain no information at all about uncertainty and welfare because they cannot discriminate between deterministic and stochastic series. In the present study, the level at which the short-term rate was pegged changed over time; it is therefore possible to compute a 'variance' of the pegged rate using time series data. On its own, however, this computed 'variance' contains no information about the private sector's perceived foreknowledge of changes in the pegged rate. Such information *is* available from the subjective covariance matrix estimated using the APEX methodology. Thus, a strength of this methodology is that it delivers independent estimates of the subjective and objective covariance matrices and permits the correct checks to be made on their consistency.

THE DATA

The data are described in detail in Green (1982, 1984a). As indicated in the introduction to this paper, they consist of monthly integrated balance sheets and flows of funds together with monthly rates of return covering the period 1972 (7)–1977(11).

There are five assets: equities, foreign currency denominated, government securities, interest-bearing liquid assets (IBLAs), and high-powered money. High-powered money consists of currency in circulation and held by banks, together with bankers' non interest-bearing deposits at the Bank of England.[2] IBLAs include all remaining short-term paper including bank deposits and loans, bills, special deposits and national savings.[3] The sum of IBLAs and high-powered money is equal to 'Liquid Assets' as defined in my previous (1985) paper. The other three assets are the same as in that paper. As far as possible all assets are valued at market prices. Thus, equities are valued using Tobin's q; foreign currency using the dollar-sterling spot exchange rate; and bonds using a specially constructed price index which is consistent with the underlying maturity structure of the bond stock. Banks' holdings of securities are adjusted from book value to market value using formulae derived from their accounting procedures (for further details see Green, 1982).

The portfolio shares are those of the consolidated private sector: consisting of banks and other financial intermediaries, the non-central-government public sector, companies, and households. The supply of assets by the monetary authorities and the overseas sector (the remaining two sectors) is assumed to be exogenous. This assumption of exogenous asset supplies is clearly artificial, but it is a convenient starting point, and it is planned to relax the assumption at a future stage in the research.

The rates of return are actual one-month yields as defined in Section 2. For equities the 'coupon' is equivalent to the dividend yield and the price is Tobin's q. The return on foreign currency denominated assets consists of the three-month eurodollar rate adjusted to a one-month basis and modified by the actual change in the dollar-sterling exchange rate.[4] The average coupon on government bonds is generated as a by-product of the procedure used to estimate the average valuation ratio (price) of the stock of bonds. For liquid assets, the return is the three-month local authority rate adjusted to a one-month basis. The three-month rate is chosen in preference to the one-month rate for two reasons. First, three months were thought to correspond more closely to the average maturity of IBLAs. Secondly, and more important, choice of the one-month rate would trivialise the tests. The decision period of the model is equal to the monthly periodicity of the data. Clearly, the nominal rate on one-month assets held for one month is by definition a deterministic return. If tests do not reveal it to be so, it is a fault of the test procedure and not a meaningful empirical discovery. In contrast, the three-month rate is a stochastic return if the holding period is one month, unless of course the evolution of that rate is governed by a deterministic rule: this is precisely the issue that we seek to resolve in this work.

It is, in fact, instructive to compare the volatility of these nominal one-month return series over the period with which we are concerned. A suitably normalised measure of volatility is the coefficient of variation. As shown in Table 9.1, the return on IBLAs is the second most volatile of the return series. Of course, the coefficient of variation is not the only possible measure of volatility. However, the point is clear: the variability of an asset return measured directly from its time series may contain no information at all about the riskiness of the associated asset.

Table 9.1 Coefficients of variation of nominal
one-month returns: 1972(7)–1977(11)

IBLAs	46.100
Bonds	4.675
Foreign currency	6.658
Equities	88.360

The four rates of return are all modified to be expressed as real rates using the retail price index to compute the expected rate of inflation. The numeraire asset is high-powered money with rate of return equal to minus the expected rate of inflation. The rate of inflation is therefore assumed to be determined outside asset markets and this seems reasonable.

Referring back to equation (10), it can be seen that the model will consist of four regression equations with left-hand side variables consisting of the differences between the one-month return on IBLAs and that on high-powered money; the one-month return on bonds and that on high-powered money; the one-month return on foreign currency denominated assets and that on high-powered money; the one-month return on equities and that on high-powered money. A moment's reflection will convince the reader that these relative real interest rates are, in fact, identical to the four nominal returns: on IBLAs, bonds, foreign currency, and equities. Implicitly, the regressions seek to explain the one period ahead expectations of the price of IBLAs, the price of bonds, the spot exchange rate, and the price of equity. The explanatory variables in each equation consist of: the shares of IBLAs, bonds, foreign-currency denominated assets, and equities in private sector wealth; these shares lagged one period and rescaled by the inverse of the change in wealth (W_{t-1}/W_t); the inverse of the change in wealth; and a constant.

EMPIRICAL METHODOLOGY

The maintained hypothesis is provided by equations (10) but ignoring restrictions implied by any particular interpretation of the coefficients. These equations state that asset returns relative to the numeraire can be expressed as a vector of constants plus linear combinations of current and lagged portfolio shares and the inverse of the change in wealth. The first step is to estimate these equations without restrictions on the coefficients.

As the data are seasonally unadjusted, these initial regressions include seasonal dummies. As it happens, the data easily accept the restrictions that all the seasonal dummies have zero coefficients in all the equations. (Other, milder, restrictions on the seasonals were also tested and accepted.) In principle, there is no difficulty in retaining the seasonals and testing them at later stages in the analysis. However, it does severely reduce the degrees of freedom available in estimation. It was found that the presence or absence of seasonals did not affect the results of subsequent tests in any substantive way. Accordingly, the tests on the seasonals are reported as logically prior to all other tests in the analysis.

The next step is to test restrictions implied by the mean-variance model with adjustment costs. According to this model, $\hat{\Sigma}$ is a subjective covariance matrix (of the relative returns $Y_{1t+1} - iY_{nt+1}$) and $\hat{\Psi}$ consists of the parameters of a quadratic form. Thus, mean-variance efficiency with (quadratic) adjustment costs requires that $\hat{\Sigma}$ and $\hat{\Psi}$ each be symmetric and positive semi-definite. These are the usual symmetry restrictions, though, as is apparent from a comparison of (5) and (10), they are available here in a much more convenient form than is usually the case in portfolio demand models. Symmetry of $\hat{\Sigma}$ and $\hat{\Psi}$ is easy to test separately but symmetry of either is not nested in symmetry of the other alone. As shown in my paper (1985), symmetry and positive semi-definiteness of $\hat{\Sigma}$ and $\hat{\Psi}$ are sufficient restrictions for testing the hypothesis of mean-variance efficiency and the Sharp-Lintner-Black CAPM with adjustment costs.

At the next stage, I test whether agents perceive the nominal return on IBLAs (call it y_1) to be generated deterministically. If y_1 is perceived to be deterministic, the associated subjective variances and covariances are all zero. What about adjustment costs? In analysing the case of an interest rate peg, Green and Keating (1985) assumed that the corresponding adjustment costs were also zero. I have been unable to find a compelling argument either to support or rebut this assumption. Adjustment costs are likely to be related to some extent to the costs of information gathering and processing (see Green, 1984b). A deterministic interest rate peg provides considerable information to the market. Accordingly, it seems not unreasonable to associate zero adjustment costs with the interest rate peg and this is the assumption I adopt. In summary then, the test that the return on IBLAs (Y_1) is generated deterministically requires that:

$$\hat{\sigma}_{11} = \hat{\sigma}_{12} = \hat{\sigma}_{13} = \hat{\sigma}_{14} = 0; \text{ where } \hat{\Sigma} = |\sigma_{ij}|$$

$$\hat{\psi}_{11} = \hat{\psi}_{12} = \hat{\psi}_{13} = \hat{\psi}_{14} = 0; \text{ where } \hat{\Psi} = |\psi_{ij}|$$

The APEX methodology assumes as a maintained and untestable hypothesis that expectations are unbiased. As indicated earlier, however, it is straightforward to test whether agents' subjective covariance matrix $(\hat{\Sigma})$ coincides with the true covariance matrix of the data $(\hat{\Lambda})$. These matrices are equal if the covariance matrix of regression residuals $(\hat{\Lambda})$ is proportional to the coefficient matrix $(\gamma\hat{\Sigma} = \hat{\Omega} - \delta\hat{\Psi})$, with the factor of proportionality equal to the coefficient of relative risk aversion. This may be interpreted as a test for rationality of expectations. Since $\hat{\Lambda}$ is a covariance matrix, these restrictions are nested in the symmetry of $\hat{\Sigma}$. Thus, logically, a test for mean-variance efficiency *and* rationality of expectations is more restrictive than one for mean-variance efficiency alone. Note that, in this framework, rejection of rationality does not imply rejection of unbiasedness (which is untestable). A finding that agents were transparently not using the true covariance matrix in their decisions, would, in my view, impel some doubts about the assumption of unbiasedness, but it would by no means be fatal to this assumption.

The final phase of tests consists of checking that agents are *not* risk neutral $(\gamma \neq 0)$. These are separate non-nested tests though each one is nested in some of the previous tests. A test for risk-neutrality is particularly important. Risk-neutral agents are indifferent among deterministic and stochastic asset returns. We can only use the behavioural content of the model to distinguish deterministic and stochastic returns if agents are in fact risk-averse. To establish this, it is necessary not only to test the structure of the estimated $\hat{\Sigma}$ but also to be certain that portfolio shares do contribute in a significant way to the explanation of asset returns.

The proposed tests cannot be nested in a unique way. There are a large number of possible test routes from the most general model (excluding seasonals which are tested at the outset) to the most restrictive. The most restrictive hypothesis states that portfolio shares do not contribute significantly to explaining asset returns which are, accordingly, indistinguishable from white noise. The hypotheses can, however, be ordered in a manner which is guided by the underlying economic theory being tested. The key to establishing a manageable number of test routes lies in the interpretation to be placed on the restrictions associated with the deterministic generation of y_1 ($\hat{\sigma}_{1i} = \hat{\psi}_{1i} = 0$). These restrictions cannot be given the economic interpretation we require unless the symmetry restrictions associated with the mean variance model are also accepted. The economics therefore suggests testing symmetry before deterministic Y_1; statistical considerations clearly require a check in the other direction as well. Economic considerations also imply that the tests for symmetry and deterministic Y_1 should be logically prior to the remaining tests. If Y_1 is stochastic then the model remains one consisting of five assets and four endogenous returns; if, however, Y_1 is pegged deterministically, then high-powered money and IBLAs have identical risk characteristics and the model collapses to one of four assets and three endogenous returns.[5] If the model does collapse to four assets, then it becomes identical to that studied in my previous paper (1985). Thus, the present study also provides a simple check on one aspect of the aggregation scheme chosen for that study.

The nesting of the proposed tests is set out in Figure 9.1. This also shows the degrees of freedom at each level of nesting. The degrees of freedom for tests of more restrictions than symmetry depend on whether y_1 proves to be deterministic. Accordingly, in the lower part of the figure, two sets of degrees of freedom associated with five (5) and four (4) assets respectively are shown. For testing multiple hypotheses the degrees of freedom have to be cumulated along the chosen test route. Thus symmetry of $\hat{\Sigma}$ involves 6 restrictions; of $\hat{\Sigma}$ and $\hat{\Psi}$ 12 restrictions. Clearly there remains scope for ambiguity in the test results but this is inherent in any procedure where the tests do not have a unique order of nesting. Moreover, it should be noted that I have investigated the outcomes of testing along a great many more routes than those actually reported in this paper. These investigations did not uncover any more ambiguities than those which are reported here.

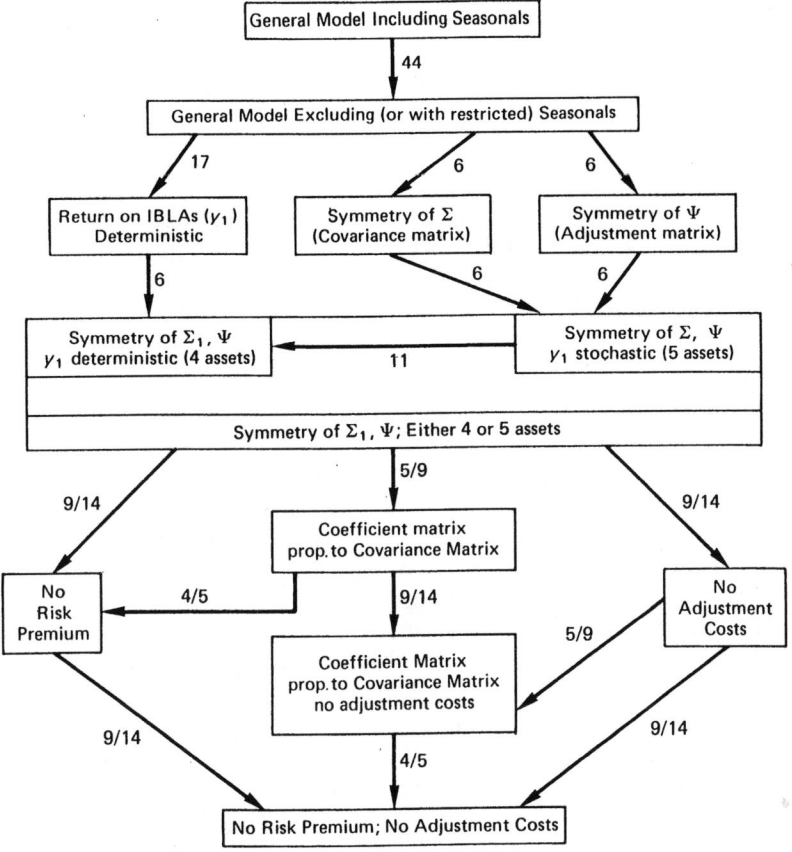

Figure 9.1   Test schema for asset price expectation formation model (showing degrees of freedom)

ESTIMATION PROCEDURES

With one important exception, the restrictions to be tested are linear, though some are cross-equation restrictions calling for a systems estimator under the null hypothesis. The main estimation and testing problem concerns the rational expectations restrictions which require that the difference between two matrices of coefficients be proportional to the error covariance matrix of the equations. These are non-standard non-linear restrictions which are awkward to impose in estimation. Provided our interest lies mainly in testing the proposed restrictions rather than in estimation under the null hypothesis, a natural and relatively easy procedure is a sequence of Wald Tests. This only requires estimation of the unrestricted model.

One problem with using the Wald test is that it is known to be too large in small samples; indeed this is also true, though to a much lesser extent, of the likelihood ratio test (see Berndt and Savin, 1977). Monte Carlo evidence appears to suggest that a degrees of freedom adjustment is sufficient to make the likelihood ratio test the correct size, whereas such an adjustment is less effective for the Wald test which tends to remain too large (see Bewley, 1983).

These difficult issues cannot be resolved in the present paper. In carrying out hypotheses tests I adopted the following procedures. First, the model was estimated under all possible null hypotheses except those involving the rational expectations restrictions. The method of estimation was Full Information Maximum Likelihood (FIML) which, in many cases, was equivalent to OLS on each equation separately. Next, likelihood ratio tests were carried out in accordance with the testing structure given in Figure 9.1 on all hypotheses not involving the rational expectations restrictions. These were supplemented wherever appropriate by Wald Tests. Finally the $(T - K)/T$ small sample correction of Bohm, Rieder and Tintner (1980) was made to both the Wald and likelihood ratio statistics. (Here, T = number of equations, K = number of regressors in each equation). It is these small sample corrected statistics which are reported subsequently. In all cases where a comparison could be made, the small-sample-adjusted likelihood ratio and Wald statistics gave the same accept/reject decision. The only restrictions which are tested exclusively with the Wald statistics are those implied by rational expectations. As these restrictions are all accepted, no amount of further (downward) correction to the Wald statistics in this case would affect the results of this paper.

EMPIRICAL RESULTS

The results of estimating the unconstrained model are shown in Table 9.2. The Lagrange Multiplier (LM) tests for simple third-order and vector first-order autocorrelation suggests that the general model fails to whiten the residuals of the government bond equation and, to some extent, the equity equation. Further investigation of more restricted models suggested that this may, in part, have been caused by overfitting. Of course, a variety of other explanations are possible. A likely candidate is that the specification of adjustment costs needs some reconsideration: the problems in the

Table 9.2 Estimated coefficients of unrestricted model*

	Constant	$\dfrac{L_t}{W_t}$	$\dfrac{G_t}{W_t}$	$\dfrac{E_t}{W_t}$	$\dfrac{D_t}{W_t}$	$\dfrac{L_{t-1}}{W_t}$	$\dfrac{G_{t-1}}{W_t}$	$\dfrac{E_{t-1}}{W_t}$	$\dfrac{D_{t-1}}{W_t}$	$\dfrac{W_{t-1}}{W_t}$	R^2	LMS	LMV
UL_{t+1}	0.031 (1.07)	-0.084 (1.75)	0.001 (0.02)	-0.045 (1.53)	0.081 (1.78)	0.039 (1.34)	-0.029 (0.70)	0.014 (1.99)	-0.050 (1.25)	-0.000 (0.19)	0.433	5.075 (72.0%)	7.629 (89.4%)
UG_{t+1}	0.363 (0.21)	-1.355 (0.48)	1.882 (0.63)	-1.123 (0.66)	2.596 (0.97)	1.187 (0.70)	-2.382 (0.97)	0.892 (2.11)	-2.255 (0.96)	-0.043 (0.43)	0.409	22.122 (100%)	14.800 (99.5%)
UE_{t+1}	-0.345 (0.11)	7.269 (1.43)	12.615 (2.35)	-0.492 (0.16)	2.552 (0.53)	-4.805 (1.57)	-11.498 (2.58)	0.925 (1.21)	-5.038 (1.19)	-0.343 (1.90)	0.455	6.653 (84.5%)	15.021 (99.5%)
UD_{t+1}	1.735 (2.12)	-1.773 (1.30)	-2.882 (2.01)	-1.626 (1.96)	0.967 (0.75)	-0.773 (0.95)	0.767 (0.65)	-0.035 (0.17)	0.771 (0.68)	0.018 (0.38)	0.375	2.879 (42.2%)	1.659 (20.2%)

*Excluding seasonals; 't' ratios in parentheses.

Definitions: L_t, G_t, E_t, D_t = Market values of private sector holdings of interest-bearing liquid assets (L), Government bonds (B),

Equities (E). Net foreign currency assets (D).

W_t = Private Sector Net Worth = $L_t + G_t + E_t + D_t$ + High-Powered Money.

$UL_{t+1}, UG_{t+1}, UE_{t+1}, UD_{t+1}$ = One-month-ahead returns on IBLAs, bonds, equities and foreign currency assets

(respectively) less the one-period-ahead return on high-powered money.

LMS χ^2 (4): LM test for simple 4th-order auto-correlation.

LMV χ^2 (4): LM test for vector 1st-order auto-correlation.

residuals were mostly in the first-order auto- and cross-correlations. As I plan on a more comprehensive investigation of adjustment costs in future work, the specification of the maintained model was thought to be tolerable for the purposes of the present exercise; and no attempt was made to improve the specification by further arbitrary overfitting and the use of additional lags.

The results of hypotheses tests on the unconstrained model are presented in Figure 9.2 which is drawn on broadly the same basis as Figure 9.1. Now however, continuous lines linking hypotheses refer to hypotheses which are accepted at the 95 per cent level. Broken lines refer to hypotheses which are rejected at this level. The small sample adjusted likelihood ratio (L) and Wald (W) statistics and their significance levels are also shown.

According to these tests, symmetry of the matrices of covariances and adjustment costs is accepted by the data. The hypothesis that the three-month rate is perceived as being generated deterministically is also accepted, irrespective of which test route is chosen. This implies that high-powered money and IBLAs have identical risk characteristics and a four asset, three-return model is appropriate. This also provides confirmation of the modelling strategy adopted in my paper (1985). It means that the results of that paper on rational expectations and adjustment costs are directly applicable here. These results are summarised briefly in the lower left and lower middle part of Figure 9.2. They show that the data are consistent with rational expectations (the estimated $\gamma\hat{\Sigma}$ is proportional to the estimated $\hat{\Lambda}$) and zero adjustment costs. However, the data decisively reject the hypothesis that agents are risk-neutral (that is, that there is no risk premium).

Although the hypothesis that the three-month rate is perceived as being stochastic is rejected, it is nevertheless of interest to carry out a parallel set of hypothesis tests on the five-asset model 'as if' the three-month rate were stochastic. The results of these tests which are not reported in detail, parallel almost exactly the results of the similar tests on the four-asset model. In the lower right of Figure 9.2 we show that the five-asset model accepts the restrictions of zero-adjustment-costs and decisively rejects the restrictions implied by risk-neutrality.

The main difference between the results of the four- and the five-asset tests was that, in the five-asset model, the rational expectations restrictions ($\hat{\Sigma} = \cdot\hat{\Lambda}$) were rejected no matter which test route was chosen. The test for rational expectations involves a combination of several restrictions. However, it is straightforward to compute the standard errors of each of the restrictions separately. When these were examined, it transpired that

227

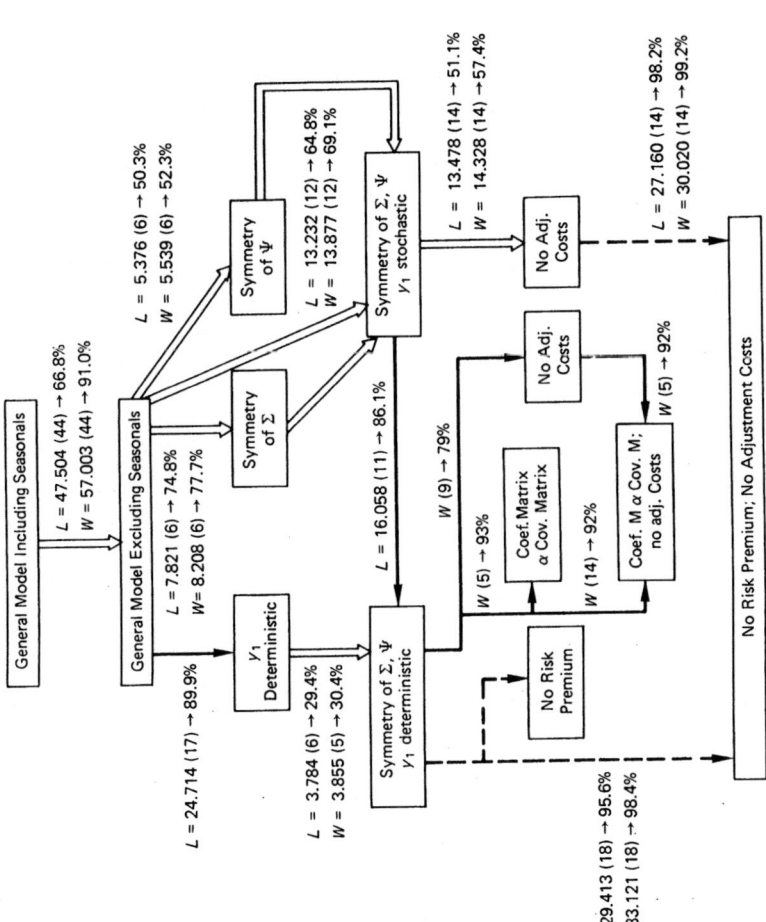

Figure 9.2 Wald and likelihood ratio tests: mean-variance efficiency and deterministic returns

the restrictions being rejected consisted solely of those associated with the covariances of the three-month rate:

$$\hat{\sigma}_{11} = \hat{\lambda}_{11} ; \hat{\sigma}_{12} = \hat{\lambda}_{12} ; \hat{\sigma}_{13} = \hat{\lambda}_{13} ; \hat{\sigma}_{14} = \hat{\lambda}_{14}$$

These restrictions are rejected precisely because, in this form, the test does not have a meaningful behavioural content. Though it is possible to use the historical time series data to compute the 'variance' of the three-month rate, the test on the corresponding row and column of the subjective co-variance matrix shows that agents do not, in fact, perceive the three-month rate to be a stochastic series; it is, rather, thought to be deterministic. These findings underline the earlier argument that descriptive models of the variance of a time series do not necessarily contain any information about the risks actually incurred by agents facing such data.

What finally then do these analyses show? The first point to emphasise is that the present work is intended mainly to be illustrative of how the APEX methodology may provide methods for meeting the Lucas critique; it does not pretend to be the last word on asset pricing in the UK. On the theoretical side, there are more general models of asset pricing than the simplest mean-variance model. On the empirical side, the model is not wholly 'data-consistent', though the main source of trouble would seem to involve the specification of adjustment costs where theoretical guidance is conspicuously lacking. Taking the results at face value, they suggest that the mean-variance model with rational expectations is capable of explaining a significant proportion of the movement in UK asset returns during 1972-7. They suggest, too, that the strategy avowedly pursued by the authorities of pegging short-term interest rates did influence private behaviour over this period.

One might be tempted to go further: if the demand for high-powered money appears 'unstable' over this period, it is because of the actions of the authorities, not the vicissitudes of the private sector; if the authorities did believe that controlling high-powered money would destabilise short rates, and thereby destabilise interest rates throughout the capital market, then the second part of the proposition is without foundation. Manifestly, this study does not justify such strong conclusions. However, I would argue that it has provided a basis for believing that past experience can provide some clues about the way capital markets will behave in the face of regime changes. Clearly there is still much work to be done.

Notes

1. There is a variety of ways in which money may be thought to 'rule the roost' as far as interest rate determination is concerned. Another well-known context is provided by the debates over classical and loanable funds theories of interest rate determination. I do not claim exclusive rights to the aphorism; I do however claim that the interpretation in the present paper is of interest in its own right.
2. 'Bank of England' is a consolidation of the Banking Department and Issue Department.
3. There was insufficient information to enable me to distinguish between interest-bearing and non-interest bearing current accounts. However, bank customers mostly received a notional rate of interest on current accounts to set against their bank charges.
4. Green (1982, 1984a) explains why it is preferable to use the dollar-sterling rate rather than a weighted average exchange rate.
5. In this case, high-powered money is dominated by IBLAs and separate demands for high-powered money and IBLAs cannot be justified with reference to the mean-variance model.

References

Bank of England (1982) 'The role of the Bank of England in the money market', *Bank of England Quarterly Bulletin*, March, pp. 86–94.

Berndt, E. R. and Savin, N. E. (1977) 'Conflict among criteria for testing hypotheses in the multivariate linear regression model', *Econometrica*, 45: 5.

Bewley, R. A. (1983) 'Tests of restrictions in large demand systems', *European Economic Review*, 20: 257–69.

Brainard, W. C. (1964) 'Financial intermediaries and a theory of monetary control', *Yale Economic Essays* 4(1). Reprinted as Chapter 4 in Hester, D. D. and Tobin, J. (eds) (1967) *Financial Markets and Economic Activity* (London: Wiley, pp. 91–141).

Bohm, B., Rieder, B. and Tintner, G. (1980) 'A system of demand equations for Austria', *Empirical Economics*, 5: 129–42.

Engle, R. F. (1983) 'Estimates of the variance of US inflation based upon the ARCH model', *Journal of Money, Credit and Banking*, 15: 286–301.

Frankel, J. A. (1982) 'In search of the exchange risk premium: a six-currency test assuming mean-variance optimization', *Journal of International Money and Finance*, 1: 255–74.

Frankel, J. A. (1984) 'Portfolio shares as 'beta-breakers': a test of CAPM', *Journal of Portfolio Management*, forthcoming.

Frankel, J. A. and Dickens, W. T. (1984) 'Are asset demand functions mean-variance efficient?', *National Bureau of Economic Research Working Paper no. 1113* (revised).

Friedman, B. M. (1977) 'Financial flow variables and the short-run determination of long-term interest rates', *Journal of Political Economy*, 85: 661–89.

Green, C. J. (1982) 'Monetary policy and the structure of interest rates in the United Kingdom: a flow of funds model 1971–77', unpublished PhD dissertation, Yale University.

Green, C. J. (1984a) 'Preliminary results from a five-sector flow of funds model of the United Kingdom 1972–77', *Economic Modelling*, 1: 304–26.

Green, C. J. (1984b) 'Interest parity: a time series approach', *Manchester University Department of Economics*, Discussion Paper, No. 32.

Green, C. J. (1985) 'Asset demands and asset prices in the UK: there is a risk premium', Paper presented at The Money Study Group Conference, September.

Green, C. J. and Keating, G. B. (1985) 'Capital asset pricing under alternative policy regimes', *London Business School*, Discussion Paper, 157 (November).

Keating, G. B. (1986) 'The financial sector of the LBS model', in Currie, D. (ed.) *Advances in Monetary Economics* (London: Croom Helm).

Lucas, R. E. (1976) 'Econometric policy evaluation: a critique, *Journal of Monetary Economics* (supplement) 5: 19–46.

Niehans, J. (1978) *The Theory of Money* (Baltimore: Johns Hopkins Press).

Parkin, M. J. (1970) 'Discount house portfolio and debt selection', *Review of Economic Studies*, 37: 469–97.

Sharpe, W. F. (1964) 'Capital asset prices: a theory of market equilibrium under conditions of risk', *Journal of Finance*, 19: 425–42.

Tobin, J. (1969) 'A general equilibrium approach to monetary theory', *Journal of Money, Credit and Banking*, 1: 15–29.

Tobin, J. and Brainard, W. C. (1968) 'Pitfalls in financial model building', *American Economic Review Papers and Proceedings*, 57: 99–122.

10 Variability in Some Major UK Asset Markets since the Mid-1960s: An Application of the ARCH Model*

Rodney Dickens

1 INTRODUCTION

This paper represents the first results of a continuing project attempting both to describe and to explain yield and price volatility in asset markets in the UK and in other major industrialised countries. This paper confines itself to the first part of the project, using relatively high frequency weekly data to describe the volatility in the UK gilts, interbank, foreign exchange and share markets since the mid-1960s. One reason for interest in the volatility of these markets is, as with interest in the variance of inflation, because of the cost imposed on risk averse agents by increased variability; while even risk neutral agents will face higher costs in a more variable market, if the higher volatility reduces their ability to forecast the mean of the process.

Until recently, conventional variance measures, including moving variance about moving mean (MVAMM) estimators, have generally been employed in the literature to describe volatility in asset markets.[1] A more rigorous variance estimator has been developed by Engle (1982) to model

*I am indebted to Professor Charles Goodhart who initiated this research project, has overseen its progress, and provided helpful comments. A discussion with Professor Robert Engle on the technical aspects and results of this paper was much appreciated, as were comments received on an earlier draft from Dr Mike Stephenson and Dr Peter Robinson. Ongoing discussions with Dr David Barr have been invaluable in shaping this paper. The usual disclaimers apply.

Paper presented at the Money Study Group Conference, Brasenose College, Oxford, 11–13 September 1985.

the heteroskedasticity - time dependence of the variance - frequently observed in the residuals of ordinary least squares (OLS) estimated equations. The technique operates by modelling the residuals as autoregressive conditional heteroskedastic (ARCH) processes which Engle (1982, p. 98) defines as 'mean zero, serially uncorrelated processes with non-constant variances conditional on the past, but constant unconditional variances'. This methodology can be applied to describing the variability of time series data as Engle (1980) has done for US inflation.

The major advance of the ARCH approach over conventional variance estimators is that it measures the dispersion around the conditional mean rather than that about the sample mean. The problem with the latter approach as pointed out by Engle (1980, p. 3) in relation to the measurement of the variability of inflation is that

> even when the inflation rate is on a steady climb, which can easily be predicted, the variance will appear to be high. The [MVAMM type] estimates, therefore, attribute some of the changes in observed inflation to unanticipated surprises where they should properly be considered part of the mean or anticipated inflation.

In contrast, the conditional mean of the series is the anticipated level of the series as derived from the 'appropriate' econometric equation.

Other advantages of the ARCH approach include the empirical estimation of the appropriate order of the variance function using the ARCH test statistic and, while some restrictions are still placed on the values of the coefficients in the ARCH variance function, the data are allowed to help determine them rather than arbitrarily imposing constant weights as in MVAMM estimators.

The high frequency of the data used in this study has made the collection of data an expensive process and effectively ruled out, at least in the first stages of this exercise, the possibility of econometric modelling of the conditional mean of the data series. Instead, univariate time series models have been fitted which, as it turns out, is not necessarily a second-best approach. The literature on the theoretically-expected behaviour of interest rates and asset prices suggests that *approximate* martingale behaviour of such series, especially when high frequency data are employed, is reasonable; in which case the majority of the change in the series from this week to the next will be unanticipated on the basis of currently available information.

The use of univariate conditional mean equations plus the *approximate* martingale behaviour of the data series reduces the advantage of the ARCH model over the MVAMM estimator in terms of the mean specification. However, the other benefits quoted for the ARCH approach remain. The results from both estimators are compared to check on the gains from employing Engle's ARCH technique.

A further more detailed description of the ARCH model, and how it has been applied to the data employed in this study, as well as a comparison of the ARCH and MVAMM estimators, is contained in Dickens (1986). The remainder of the paper is ordered as follows: Section 2 describes the data and investigates whether relationships exist between the means and variances of the series; in Section 3 the conditional mean functions are estimated and the frequency distributions of the series are reviewed; Section 4 reports the ARCH test results for determining the order of the ARCH variance functions and presents the conditional variance functions; the resulting variance series are discussed in Section 5 and compared with MVAMM variance estimates; a brief summary of the paper is contained in Section 6 as well as some discussion of envisaged extensions of the investigation of volatility in asset markets.

2 THE DATA AND MEAN-VARIANCE PROPORTIONALITY

2.1 The Data

One series has been chosen to represent each of the four asset markets mentioned above, these are: (1) calculated gross redemption yields on 20-year gilts (RG20); (2) 3-month interbank interest rates (RIB3); (3) the *Financial Times* 500-share price index (FT500); and (4) the US$/£ spot exchange rate (ER$£). All series have Wednesday observation weekly frequencies. In the case of the two-interest rate series and the share price index, the data period spans from the fortieth Wednesday of 1966 (1966.40 which is 5 October 1966) to the twelfth Wednesday of 1985 (1985.12 which is 20 March 1985). The exchange rate series covers the period 1972.26 (28 June 1972 – the first Wednesday the foreign exchange market opened after sterling was fully floated) to 1985.12 (20 March 1985). The two data periods have 964 and 665 observations, respectively. A data appendix is available on request from the author.

2.2 Proportionality

The scale of measurement of a series can itself introduce heteroskedasticity of a nature this paper does not intend to explain. In the case of FT500, because it is a nominal price index and the sample period was one during which significant inflation was experienced, its variance will exhibit a natural tendency to increase with its mean over the sample period. A similar tendency for the variance to increase over the sample period would also be expected for the increments of FT500. Options to overcome this problem include using a real share price index, or converting the series into holding period yields; both options requiring additional data. The high frequency used in this research project has made the acquisition of data an expensive process and so effectively precluded these options.[2]

A common time series framework for approaching the question is described by McLeod (1983, pp. 11-18 to 11-24). It involves first observing a standard deviation-mean plot (SMP) for subsamples of the dataset to identify whether such proportionality exists, then applying a power transformation to the data if it is considered appropriate. These were calculated for each series using calendar year subsamples. The SMP for RG20 is shown in Figure 10.1. The others are available on request from the author.

The plots for RG20 and FT500 show definite tendencies for the standard deviation to increase with the mean of the series, while no obvious relationships are discernible for RIB3 and ER$£. The correlation coefficients between the annual means and standard deviations confirm these visual interpretations: RG20, 0.676; RIB3, 0.202; FT500, 0.584; and ER$£, 0.125.

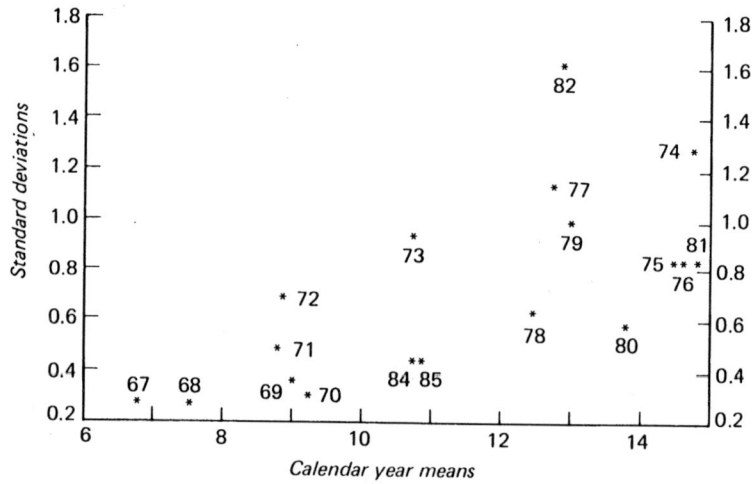

Figure 10.1   Standard deviation-mean plot for RG20

The reason for the proportionality in RG20 seems less obvious than that in FT500. Like FT500 it has a nominal base, although as it is already stated as a rate of return one would not expect it to exhibit a higher degree of proportionality than FT500 as the higher correlation coefficient indicates.[3] If one were to look for an explanation, rather than discount the apparent relationship as non-causal and a quirk of the sample period, the obvious one would seem to be that over the sample period inflation expectations dominated the behaviour of RG20 and that these expectations were more volatile the higher the expected rate of inflation.[4] Such an argument is certainly not new, nor undisputed.

Whatever the explanation, from a statistical point of view RG20 displays significant proportionality, suggesting a corrective transformation is required to account for this source of heteroskedasticity before applying the ARCH technique. While there seems little ground for objecting to such a transformation for FT500, there may be some objection to handling a series which is already specified as a yield in the same manner. This potential disquiet has been pre-empted by applying all subsequent data-handling techniques to both RG20 and the transformed series. This approach is equivalent to explaining the total variability in two stages: the variance of the transformed series indicating the contribution of the underlying ARCH process, and the difference between that and the variance of the original series being attributable to the cause(s) of the proportionality.

The natural logarithm (log) is a commonly-used variance stabilising transformation, although it represents only one strength of the power transformation which is of the form:

$$Z_t^\lambda \quad \text{, when } \lambda \neq 0$$

$$\log_e Z_t, \text{ when } \lambda = 0$$

where Z_t = value of time series at time t, λ = power transformation, and the relationship being assumed to exist between the standard deviation (σ) and mean (μ) of the series is of the form $\sigma = k\mu^{1-\lambda}$.

In Figure 10.2 the SMP is presented for $\log_e$RG20 (LRG20). The correlation coefficient between the mean and variance is still moderately positive at 0.395, although stronger transformations[5] (that is, $\lambda < 0$) would have little impact on reducing the correlation without introducing potentially serious distortions to the data because of the role of the 1967, 1968 and 1982 observations in determining the size of the correlation coefficient – for the remaining years the log transformation almost completely removes the relationship.

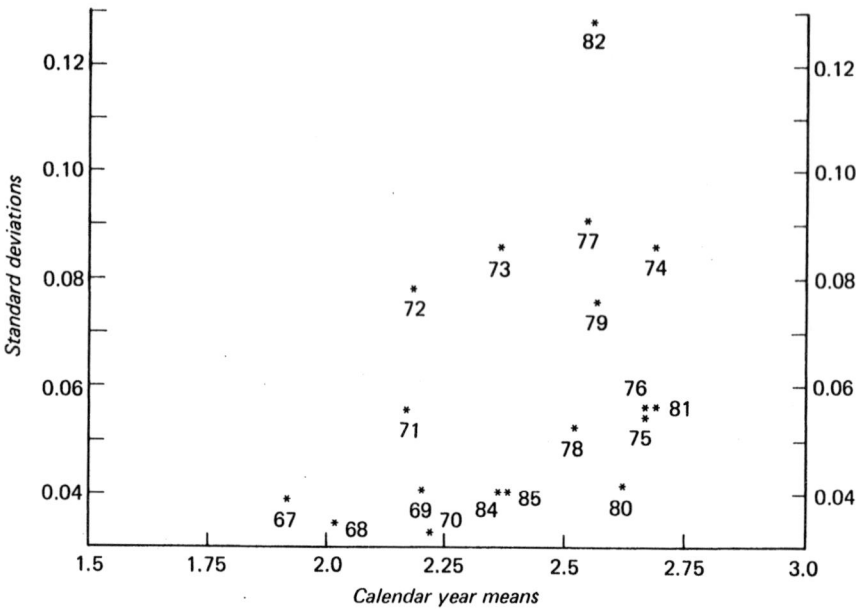

Figure 10.2   Standard deviation-mean plot for the natural logarithm of RG20

In the case of FT500, the log transformation was too strong, replacing the positive relationship with an equally significant negative one - the correlation coefficient was −0.616. Subsequently weaker transformations were employed until the one which effectively removed the proportionality was found. The resulting choice was $\lambda = 0.4$. The correlation coefficient for FTP4 - the transformed series - is still negative at −0.337, although if the observations for 1974 and 1975 are ignored, the correlation drops to 0.023.[6]

3   CONDITIONAL MEAN FUNCTIONS AND SAMPLE DISTRIBUTIONS

3.1   Conditional mean functions

An important consideration before attempting to fit univariate models to estimate the conditional means, is whether the series are stationary; if not, then the t values, and so on, in any levels form equations are suspect. The autocorrelation and partial autocorrelation functions (henceforth termed correlograms) were calculated up to order 52 for each series and clearly indicated non-stationarity in all cases. Figure 10.3 shows the result for RG20 up to order 26.

The usual approach to modelling non-stationary series is to first difference them and then, assuming the differenced series are stationary, fit a model to the increments of the series. If the increments are uncorrelated, then the level form series follow martingale or random walk processes; and

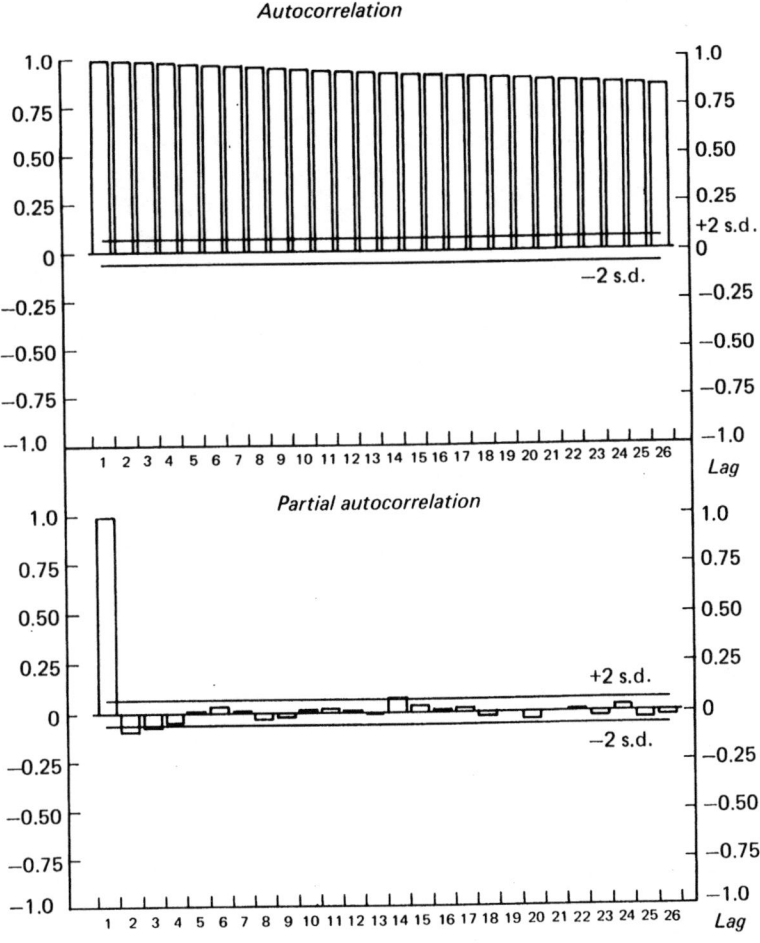

Figure 10.3   Autocorrelation and partial autocorrelation plots for RG20

the conditional mean estimates in any given period would simply be the previous period's level for each series.

In the three differenced interest rate series (DRG20, DLRG20 and DRIB3) the first order autocorrelation and partial autocorrelation coefficients, as well as second order for DRG20 and thirteenth order for both DRG20 and DLRG20,[7] are outside the two standard deviation confidence intervals, indicating that there remains some systematic behaviour in these series. The transformed and differenced share price series DFTP4 has a significant second order coefficient, although subsequent discussion in subsection 3.4 reveals that the significance of this second order correlation is due to two 'outlying' observations two periods apart. The first differenced exchange rate series DER$£ has significant third and fourth order coefficients, although, given that the time series method of evaluating the sigma levels slightly overstates significance, they are marginal.

This paper does not seek to investigate the chosen asset markets for efficiency. As is documented in the literature,[8] a finding that spot rates do not exactly follow martingale or random walk processes does not provide unambiguous evidence against the market efficiency hypothesis. Thus a finding of correlation in the differenced series could indicate that one or any combination of the following apply, *inter alia*: (1) risk premia exist and are autocorrelated; (2) equilibrium returns are autocorrelated; (3) the cost of acquiring such information exceeds any benefits its limited explanatory power provides; (4) frictions and non-competitive elements exist.

There are two reasons in the present context for wanting to model the remaining systematic behaviour: first, to model the conditional mean of the differenced series (one of the main advances of Engle's ARCH approach); and secondly, because ARCH processes are serially uncorrelated – any correlation remaining in the series could bias the ARCH test in favour of rejecting the null hypothesis of no ARCH effect.

On the basis of the correlograms of the differenced series, and from experimentation with potential alternative models, autoregressive (AR) specifications were chosen to remove the correlation remaining in these series. The equations chosen are presented in Table 10.1, while the correlogram for DRG20 is shown in Figure 10.4. The initial approach adopted was to overfit the models when in doubt, to ensure that no correlation remained which might trigger spurious ARCH test results. Experimentation revealed that the overfitted models returned very similar ARCH test results to the parsimonious models, so the latter were preferred. All equations include constants to ensure that the residuals, which are used in the ARCH test, are zero mean.

239

Table 10.1 Conditional mean equations for asset market series: full data set

| Dependent variable | Constant | Lags on dependent variables | | | | | R^2 (F statistic) | Skewness (acceptance range) | Kurtosis (acceptance range) | Sample period |
| | | 1 | 2 | 3 | 4 | 13 | | | | |
		(t values are in parenthesis)								
DRG20	0.00379 (0.55)	0.1175 (3.64)	0.0816 (2.53)	—	—	-0.1024 (3.20)	0.0337 (11.00)	-0.360 (0.159)	6.54 (2.68, 3.32)	1967.5 to 1985.12
DLRG20	0.00047 (0.85)	0.1257 (3.91)	—	—	—	-0.0901 (2.80)	0.0238 (11.56)	-0.424 (0.159)	6.14 (2.68, 3.32)	1967.5 to 1985.12
DRIB3	0.00565 (0.46)	0.1357 (4.24)	—	—	—	—	0.0184 (17.99)	1.473 (0.158)	11.80 (2.68, 3.32)	1967.1 to 1985.12
DFTP4	0.00693 (2.48)	—	0.1015 (3.16)	—	—	—	0.0103 (9.98)	0.193 (0.159)	4.76 (2.68, 3.32)	1967.1 to 1985.12
DER$£	-0.00164 (1.83)	—	—	0.0834 (2.13)	0.0842 (2.15)	—	0.0149 (4.98)	-0.099 (0.191)	4.69 (2.62, 3.38)	1972.31 to 1985.12

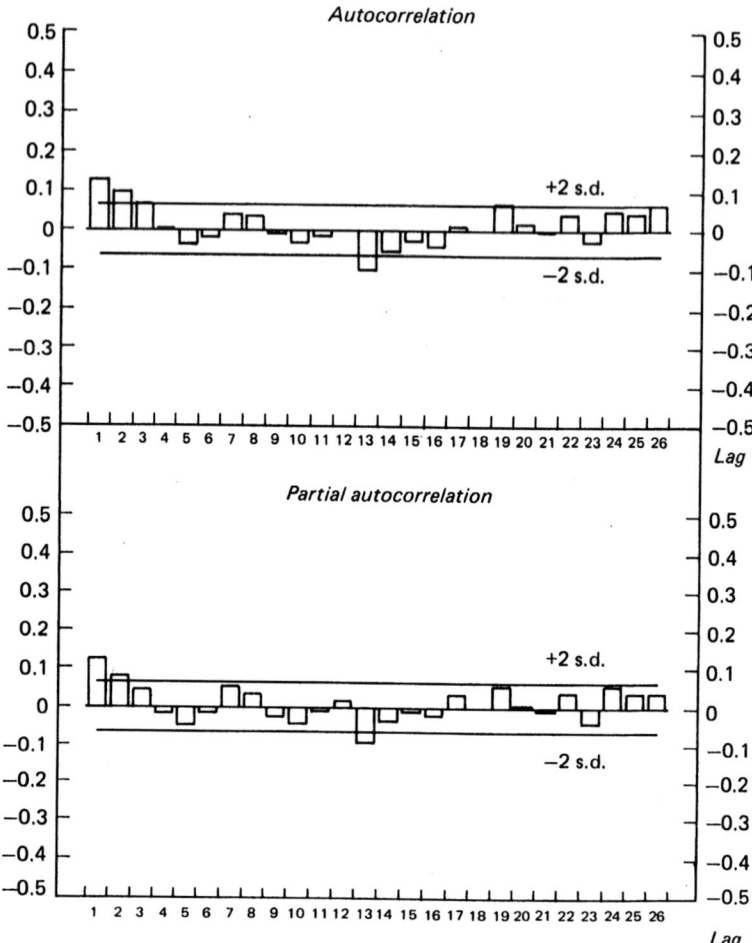

Figure 10.4   Autocorrelation and partial autocorrelation plots for DRG20

The residual correlograms of the mean model are not presented, but have been checked for the presence of significant correlation and were found to be white in that respect.

Of interest in the results reported in Table 10.1 is the significant skewness evident in the errors of all but the equation for the exchange rate. The measure of kurtosis also rejects normality in all equations' residuals. Identical characteristics are evident in the differenced series themselves and, in part, inspired the subsequent consideration of their frequency distributions.

3.4   Sample frequency distributions and the 'outlier' problem

To get a better picture of the distributions underlying the sampled data than relying on the summary statistics reported in Table 10.1, frequency distributions based on 0.5 standard deviations intervals either side of the sample mean have been plotted for the differenced series. That for DRIB3 is shown here in Figure 10.5. The solid line included in the chart shows the theoretical normal distribution based on the sample mean and variance.

All sample distributions, as can be seen in the case of DRIB3, are more peaked *and* assign higher probabilities to extreme observations than the normal distribution. This leptokurtic property of the sample distributions was observed in daily common stock returns by Fama (1977, p. 26), and in daily returns from asset futures markets by Taylor (1985, p. 719). In discussing this result Fama notes that the work of Mandelbrot (1963) showed that distributions of security returns data, and possibly many other economic variables, will display the leptokurtic property.

The 'bodies' of the distributions are largely symmetric for all series, while each distribution except that for DER$£ has one tail clearly longer than the other. It was found that rejection of symmetry for DRG20, DLRG20 and DFTP4 arises because of 2, 4 and 2 extreme observations,

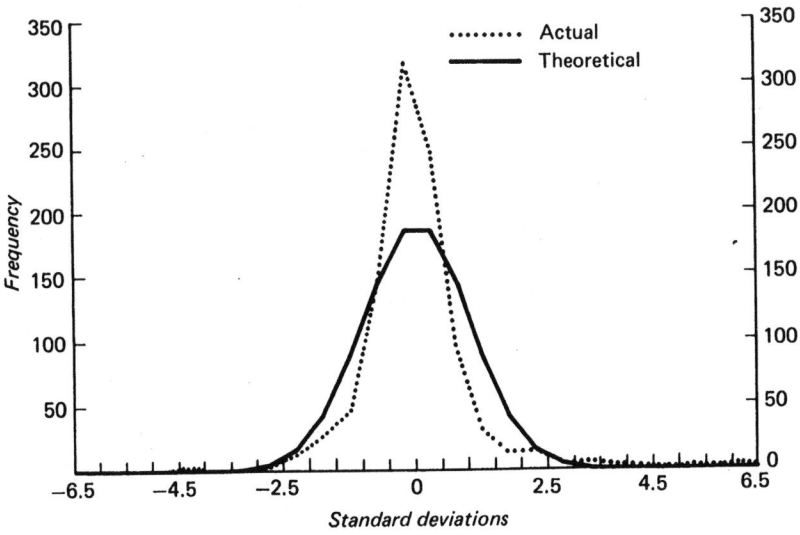

Figure 10.5   Frequency distribution for DRIB3

respectively, in one tail of each distribution. This is out of a total of 963 observations per series. In the case of DRIB3, the removal of 6 observations in the long tail reduces the skewness significantly, but does not completely remove it.

The identification of the observations making up the long tails of the distribution is reasonably straightforward. In all cases, based on the 0.5 standard deviation intervals, there is at least one interval of zero frequency between the extreme values and the rest of the distribution, and the frequencies of the short tails go to zero in the same or one earlier interval.

The non-normality of the distributions certainly reduces the discriminatory powers of tests based on the normality assumption, which includes the ARCH test. Little can be done to cure the samples of their leptokurtosis and, if only to the extent that the leptokurtosis in the sample distributions would appear to be a common feature of such data, it seems of less concern than the skewness. It would also appear from the discussion of the impact of non-normal parent populations on statistical tests contained in Yule and Kendall (1965, p. 486), that a skewed parent will be more damaging to the effectiveness of such tests.

Discarding the extreme observations on statistical grounds is one possibility. However, it would be preferable to have a plausible economic explanation for excluding them as well as a statistical justification. For this reason, and the fact that the outlying observations do have a very significant impact on some of the results,[9] considerable thought has been given to the 'outlier' problem.

The main explanations considered potentially responsible for the skewness are: (1) the population distributions underlying the series, whether stationary or time dependent, are skewed; (2) the observed data for each series are generated by more than one underlying process, and the distributions of the different processes could be either stationary or evolving, and either symmetric or skewed; (3) the observed data come from one process for which the population distribution is symmetric, but it is time dependent and evolving – possibly in terms of all its moments – too rapidly for even weekly observations to be able to characterise realistically its state at any period.

If (1) is correct, and the underlying population is 'markedly' skewed, then all tests set up on the assumption of normality of the parent population would be flawed; or, at least, their ability to discern between alternative hypotheses would vary significantly from the stated confidence levels, and we could not correctly interpret the results of the tests of heteroskedasticity with much confidence.

If (2) is the correct interpretation for any one market, and the observations classified as being outliers – as well as some observations included in the body of the distribution – come from a secondary process, then, subject to the additional assumption of symmetry of the non-outlier distribution, it would seem that variance estimates excluding the outliers would put a lower bound on the level of variance perceived by the market. Similarly, including the outliers should put an upper bound on the market's perception of variability.

If the secondary process is the result of discrete policy interventions or regime changes, for example, which occur relatively infrequently and, once having occurred, the market does not perceive an increased probability of their occurrence in subsequent periods; then, once the regime change has been observed, the market's variance estimate should not increase from the level suggested by the underlying process determining the series, plus that due to the very small probability of a large discrete policy-induced jump in any one period. This is aside from the possibility of widened forecast confidence intervals because of uncertainty about how any new system will operate. In this instance, the variance estimates excluding the outliers would be closest to the market's estimates. At the other extreme, if the market expected such discrete policy interventions to be clustered, then, once one had been observed, the market would attach a far higher probability than the long run probability of observing another one in the near future. If so, their variance estimate would increase significantly, and this would favour inclusion of the outliers in any variance estimate.[10]

If (3) is more realistic, then any estimate of the population mean and variance based on the sample information may provide information in terms of the direction in which they are evolving, but will be unreliable for making accurate comparisons of states of the population distribution over time. Unlike option (2), it would not be possible to put bounds on the possible values of the population parameters.

In terms of interpreting the results presented in the rest of the paper, option (2) combined with a symmetry assumption is certainly the most attractive of a bad choice. It does not give an unambiguous answer how to treat the outliers, but it does leave the existing econometric techniques largely intact and allows bounds to be placed on the behaviour of the variance. In practice, which extreme is likely to be more accurate will probably depend on the nature and timing of each policy intervention, assuming this is the predominant cause of the outliers. Examples of relationships between outliers and policy actions are the floating of sterling in 1972 and the first budget of the Conservative Government in June 1979, which were both associated with over two percentage point jumps in RIB3, as were the reintroduction of the minimum lending rate (MLR) in January 1985, and a one-and-three-quarter percentage point increase in the MLR in November 1973.

The 'outlier' problem is closely linked with the question of the causes of volatility in asset markets and, while the latter is clearly pertinent to a description of volatility, investigation of the issue in greater depth must await subsequent research. In terms of this paper, the option taken has been to assume that there are two processes determining each series, and to report the results for the two extreme cases. Where the outliers are excluded the assumption is that the market fully discounts them in their forecast confidence intervals; where they are included it assumes they believe the occurrence of an outlier significantly increases the likelihood of observing another one in the near future. If the two process assumption is reasonable, then reality should lie somewhere between these two extremes.

The correlograms of the differenced series excluding the outliers have been estimated and, based on these, the new mean equations reported in Table 10.2 were fitted. All subsequent tests applied to the full dataset conditional mean model residuals are also applied to the residuals of these models.

The remainder of this section is devoted to a brief discussion of the outlying observations themselves. In Table 10.3 all increments outside the three standard deviation interval are listed. The outliers identified for each series are underlined in the table.

Not surprisingly there is a general tendency for the large increments to be concentrated in the early 1970s, while none appear in the period 1966 to 1971. The exchange rate is the exception to the first observation, with the most volatile period in terms of large increments being in 1979. There is not a clustering of large increments in any year in the 1980s for any of the series, although other than the exchange rate, which last experienced a 'large' weekly change in 1981, the 1980s have certainly not been exempt from sizeable changes.

Of particular note in Table 10.3 is the relationship indicated between the share price series and the two interest rate series. All of the large increments in DFTP4 coincide approximately with large changes of the opposite sign in one or other of DRG20 and DRIB3 – the honours shared almost evenly between the two.

The lack of correlation between the large increments in DRG20 and DRIB3 is very interesting: in only two periods do they coincide – 1976.41 and 1983.2. It was felt that this warranted further investigation, and so for each period when an outlier was observed in one of the series, it was

Table 10.2 Conditional mean equations for asset market series: excluding 'outliers'[1]

Dependent variable	Constant	Lags on dependent variables			R^2 (F statistic)	Skewness (acceptance range)	Kurtosis (acceptance range)	Sample period
		1	2	13				
		(t values are in parenthesis)						
DRG20	0.00598 (0.89)	0.1063 (3.29)	0.0794 (2.46)	-0.0859 (2.67)	0.0272 (8.82)	-0.086 (0.159)	5.49 (2.68, 3.32)	1967.2 to 1985.12
DLRG20	0.00070 (1.34)	0.1041 (3.24)	—	—	0.0108 (10.52)	0.076 (0.158)	4.41 (2.68, 3.32)	1966.43 to 1985.12
DRIB3	-0.00624 (0.57)	0.1576 (4.94)	—	—	0.0248 (24.44)	0.395 (0.158)	6.89 (2.68, 3.32)	1966.42 to 1985.12

1. The 'outliers' are excluded from the differenced series by setting them equal to zero, which is very close to the mean for each series. A mean model is not presented for DFTP4 because it is white noise with respect to its serial correlation properties.

Table 10.3 Large increments in UK asset market series[1]

DRG20 Week	Data	DRIB3[2]	DLRG20 Week	Data	DRIB3 Week	Data	DRG20[2]	DFTP4 Week	Data	DER$£ Week	Data
1974 25	0.68	0.35	1975 7	-0.056	1972 25	2.31	0.34	1973 49	-0.265	1973 7	0.087
44	0.66	0.28			1973 30	1.69	0.38	1975 5	0.523	1974 5	0.071
46	0.78	0.15	1977 39	-0.080	31	1.31	0.02	7	0.409	1976 10	-0.102
1975 2	-0.85	-0.59	41	0.053	32	1.31	0.27	17	0.323	1978 1	0.074
4	-0.80	0.09	1979 9	-0.088	34	1.37	0.09				
7	-0.82	-0.25	1980 3	-0.060	46	2.47	0.61	1981 38	-0.290	1979 27	0.068
1976 41	0.75	1.59	1982 33	-0.091	1974 10	1.25	0.21			38	-0.076
1977 39	-0.52	0.00	41	-0.084	15	-0.57	-0.11			47	0.070
1979 9	-1.19	-0.62	1983 2	0.076	1976 17	1.53	0.36	1984 28	-0.296		
27	-0.75	-0.03	1984 32	-0.067	21	1.31	0.58	32	0.307	1981 26	-0.081
45	0.70	0.50			37	1.19	0.38				
1980 3	-0.86	0.06			41	1.59	0.75				
1982 33	-1.12	-0.72			1977 4	-1.55	-0.13				
41	-0.90	-0.90			48	2.24	0.20				
1983 2	0.87	1.19			1979 24	2.03	0.44				
1984 32	-0.76	-0.79			1981 39	1.56	0.31				
					1983 2	1.19	0.87				
					1984 28	2.31	0.36				
					1985 3	2.05	0.36				
Mean	0.00378		0.00042			0.00649			0.00764		-0.00203
standard deviation	0.21505		0.01723			0.38180			0.08662		0.02288

1. Large observations are defined as those that are more than three standard deviations either side of the sample mean. The underlined observations are those that have been defined as 'outliers'.
2. The data in these columns are included for a comparison with the values of the other differenced interest rate series when the latter are outside the three sigma interval.

compared with the contemporaneous observation for the other differenced interest rate series. This comparison is included in Table 10.3 (see columns 3 and 8). In only 2 of the 35 periods of the comparison do the two rates move in opposite directions (1975.4 and 1980.3, both periods when the long rate exhibited a large change), and in both cases the change in the non-outlier series was very close to zero. So while the timing of the large observations in DRG20 and DRIB3 do not coincide consistently, the qualitative nature of the behaviour is almost identical.

4   ARCH TEST RESULTS AND ESTIMATION OF ARCH VARIANCE FUNCTIONS

4.1   ARCH test results

The ARCH test for a pth order ARCH process involves regressing the squared residuals from the conditional mean equation against a constant and the first p lags of themselves. The R^2 from this equation multiplied by the sample size is asymptotically distributed as *chi*-squared with p degrees of freedom under the null hypothesis of no significant ARCH effect.

The results from applying the ARCH test for orders 1 up to 52 to the residuals of the estimated mean models are presented in Table 10.4 for the models based on the full datasets, and in Table 10.5 for the models which exclude the outliers in the four series DRG20, DLRG20, DRIB3 and DFTP4.

In the cases of the mean model residuals for DRG20, DLRG20 and DFTP4, other than for the first order in some instances, the ARCH statistics are highly significant at the 1 per cent level for all orders up to 52 for both the full dataset and when the outliers are excluded. The residuals from the exchange rate equation are significant at the 5 per cent level for orders 2 to 6 and 9 to 14, but none are significant at the 1 per cent level. None of the orders for the residuals of DRIB3 come close to being significant even at the 5 per cent level when the full dataset was used, while they return highly significant statistics at the 1 per cent level when the six outliers are excluded. As the outliers were far more extreme in the case of DRIB3, it would therefore seem reasonable to conclude that they masked a strong underlying ARCH process.

Possible explanations for the relatively weak ARCH process evident in the residuals for DER$£ are: that this series displays considerably less heteroskedasticity than the other series do over the same sample period;

that, if heteroskedasticity is present, it is of a non-ARCH nature; alternatively, the other series might not return such highly significant ARCH test results if they were tested over the shorter sample period available for DER$£.

The third possibility seemed quite plausible because the sample period for DER$£ excludes the relative tranquillity of the late 1960s and early 1970s which is included in the sample periods for the other series. However, testing the other series over the shorter sample period showed this not to be the explanation. Tests of heteroskedasticity carried out, but not reported here, based on comparing variances calculated over subsamples of the datasets for all the series, indicated that the first possibility was the most likely.

If the ARCH statistics presented in Tables 10.4 and 10.5 were taken at face value, they suggest ARCH processes for most of the series in excess of

Table 10.4   ARCH test statistics for the residuals of the full dataset mean models[1]

Order of test (p)	Asset market series[2]					χ_p^2 (0.05)	χ_p^2 (0.01)
	DRG20**	DLRG20**	DRIB3	DFTP4**	DER$£		
1	3.87	0.56	2.43	<u>18.13</u>	1.05	3.84	6.64
2	<u>22.86</u>	<u>10.52</u>	2.70	<u>49.78</u>	6.78*	5.99	9.21
3	<u>31.45</u>	<u>15.21</u>	2.70	<u>50.09</u>	<u>9.58*</u>	7.82	11.35
4	<u>35.27</u>	17.00	6.12	51.63	<u>11.16*</u>	9.49	13.28
5	<u>41.86</u>	<u>23.07</u>	7.91	52.20	11.29*	11.07	15.09
6	<u>42.05</u>	23.07	8.24	60.41	12.92*	12.59	16.81
7	42.06	23.07	8.38	<u>60.95</u>	<u>13.55</u>	14.07	18.48
8	<u>56.96</u>	<u>51.32</u>	9.40	61.53	13.78	15.51	20.09
9	<u>58.02</u>	<u>51.59</u>	9.43	63.09	<u>18.51*</u>	16.92	21.67
10	<u>63.80</u>	52.46	9.67	<u>66.47</u>	<u>18.68*</u>	18.31	23.21
11	64.63	53.85	10.24	67.55	19.81*	19.68	24.73
12	64.64	53.86	12.51	<u>73.80</u>	23.52*	21.03	26.22
13	<u>72.52</u>	<u>63.19</u>	13.12	<u>74.12</u>	<u>23.71*</u>	22.36	27.69
14	<u>73.05</u>	<u>63.98</u>	14.73	74.39	23.84*	23.69	29.14
15	73.34	64.26	15.37	74.43	24.12	25.00	30.58
16	73.57	65.44	23.02	75.31	24.18	26.30	32.00
17	73.75	65.92	23.15	76.39	24.38	27.59	33.41
18	<u>82.69</u>	<u>72.89</u>	23.21	76.51	24.42	28.87	34.81
19	<u>89.64</u>	<u>78.95</u>	23.33	77.94	24.73	30.14	36.19
20	<u>89.77</u>	79.53	23.74	77.47	24.75	31.41	37.57
21	91.49	80.29	26.86	77.72	24.97	32.67	38.93
22	91.73	80.57	27.27	77.74	25.75	33.92	40.29
23	92.23	80.62	27.28	77.78	26.77	35.17	41.64

Order of test (p)	DRG20**	DLRG20**	DRIB3	DFTP4**	DER$£	χ^2_p (0.05)	χ^2_p (0.01)
24	93.70	83.04	27.28	77.87	27.23	36.42	42.98
25	94.26	83.49	28.57	77.89	27.36	37.65	44.31
26	94.27	84.11	29.04	81.80	27.55	38.89	45.64
27	94.67	84.69	36.53	86.47	27.57	40.11	46.96
28	97.16	86.16	37.35	86.47	28.01	41.34	48.28
29	97.18	86.45	37.36	86.63	32.67	42.56	49.59
30	97.29	86.77	37.44	86.72	32.67	43.77	50.89
31	97.30	86.89	38.66	86.73	33.39	44.70	51.31
32	97.71	87.19	39.17	87.08	33.40	45.91	52.61
33	98.68	87.94	39.78	87.23	39.00	47.12	53.90
34	100.91	89.00	39.93	87.26	39.82	48.32	55.18
35	100.94	89.26	40.87	87.46	40.07	49.52	56.46
36	101.73	89.73	40.88	87.58	40.94	50.71	57.74
37	102.63	91.22	41.97	87.60	41.43	51.91	59.01
38	103.01	91.22	41.33	88.23	43.64	53.10	60.28
39	103.59	91.97	41.33	88.24	43.64	54.29	61.55
40	103.77	93.20	41.47	88.86	44.89	55.47	62.81
41	105.21	94.11	41.58	89.25	44.98	56.66	64.07
42	105.98	94.94	42.39	89.55	45.88	57.84	65.33
43	107.04	95.88	42.63	89.56	45.27	59.02	66.58
44	107.63	96.28	44.29	90.46	45.34	60.20	67.83
45	108.22	97.32	44.38	92.42	46.27	61.37	69.08
46	117.96	101.58	44.85	92.58	46.35	62.55	70.32
47	118.16	101.92	45.80	93.03	47.01	63.72	71.56
48	118.16	101.95	47.40	93.03	50.18	64.89	72.80
49	118.76	102.06	47.53	93.14	50.27	66.05	74.04
50	119.06	102.11	47.53	93.38	53.13	67.22	75.28
51	119.08	102.12	48.68	93.43	53.18	68.39	76.51
52	120.55	103.18	48.68	93.46	53.23	69.55	77.74

Notes: * Significant at 5 per cent level.
　　　　** Significant at 1 per cent level. In the case of DRG20, DLRG20 (except p = 1 for both series) and DFTP4, the ARCH statistic is significant at the 1 per cent level for all orders.
1. The residuals are those for the equations presented in Table 10.1 for the respective asset market series. The sample periods used for the tests for the first four series starts in 1967.2 while for the exchange rate series it starts in 1973.31. The last observation for all samples is 1985.12. The respective sample sizes are 898 and 608.
2. The figures underlined in the table are where the ARCH statistic is both significant (at either 5 or 1 per cent levels) and where the highest order lag in the equation returned a significant coefficient as measured by its t value.

Table 10.5 ARCH test statistics for the residuals of the mean
models excluding 'outliers'[1]

	Asset market series[2]			
Order of test (p)	DRG20*	DLRG20*	DRIB3*	DFTP4*
1	9.85	9.59	26.83	18.82
2	49.58	24.77	39.24	20.67
3	64.50	27.24	40.40	21.34
4	66.90	34.11	65.11	33.74
5	77.63	48.10	67.51	33.88
6	77.66	48.29	69.56	48.87
7	77.68	48.29	69.78	49.17
8	81.50	50.36	74.53	52.35
9	86.31	54.15	74.55	54.88
10	101.76	63.92	78.90	55.14
11	102.42	64.41	79.09	55.91
12	102.59	64.57	79.66	55.93
13	115.72	66.09	79.78	57.09
14	115.83	66.10	81.38	57.69
15	116.17	66.61	84.97	58.79
16	116.19	69.94	85.41	59.89
17	116.21	70.04	85.66	60.41
18	117.27	70.68	85.66	61.52
19	122.22	70.68	86.10	61.99
20	122.33	70.78	90.91	62.10
21	122.33	70.83	92.34	63.27
22	122.52	70.99	92.38	64.67
23	123.57	71.08	92.39	64.71
24	124.42	72.18	93.92	67.08
25	125.41	72.18	97.71	67.09
26	126.29	73.34	97.89	67.13
27	126.29	73.38	97.89	68.14
28	132.77	77.38	98.38	68.80
29	133.51	77.64	98.79	71.37
30	134.88	77.85	98.93	72.10
31	134.96	78.73	99.14	73.37
32	135.54	78.93	111.32	74.54
33	138.68	80.94	115.12	74.59
34	140.26	83.52	116.54	74.74
35	140.29	83.53	119.31	75.35
36	140.31	83.55	121.19	77.37
37	140.42	83.64	121.20	77.44
38	141.61	84.65	121.42	77.48
39	141.30	84.66	122.00	77.71
40	141.82	85.04	122.38	77.71

Order of test (p)	DRG20*	DLRG20*	DRIB3*	DFTP4*
41	145.99	87.30	123.96	77.74
42	146.69	87.32	124.82	77.78
43	147.03	88.00	124.85	77.84
44	147.21	88.03	124.97	80.96
45	147.82	88.20	125.01	86.57
46	147.82	88.43	128.56	86.58
47	151.68	89.70	130.73	86.77
48	152.31	91.11	130.95	86.78
49	152.48	91.54	133.60	88.04
50	153.97	91.67	134.16	88.06
51	154.21	91.74	134.21	88.59
52	158.94	95.98	134.26	88.59

Notes: *   All orders for all series are significant at the 1 per cent level.
1. The ARCH tests are applied to the residuals of the conditional mean equations presented in Table 10.2 for the respective asset market series except DFTP4. In the case of DFTP4, where no mean model was needed because the series did not display significant serial correlation, the tests are applied to the series itself. The same periods used were 1967.42 to 1985.12 for DLRG20 and DRIB3 (910 observations), 1968.2 to 1985.12 (898 observations) for DRG20, and 1967.41 to 1985.12 (911 observations) for DFTP4.
2. The figures underlined in the table are where the ARCH statistic is both significant and for which the highest order lag in the equation returned a significant coefficient as measured by its t value.

order 52. This conclusion is based on the fact that the calculated test statistics exceed the critical *chi*-squared value at this order. However, the nature of the ARCH test is such that significant lags of the squared residuals in the ARCH test equation can effectively 'carry' insignificant higher order lags – significance measured by the t values of the lags' coefficients in the test equations. The 'appropriate' order of the equation is therefore not the highest order for which the ARCH test is significant, but the highest order at which the lagged squared residuals add significantly to the explanatory power of the equation.

It was decided to use the usual F test for the relevance of additional regressors to determine the appropriate order of the ARCH test equations.[11] In practice the ARCH test decides which orders are relevant for consideration, then the F test is applied to these to determine which is the highest order of relevance.

When testing was carried out up to order 52, it was found in all cases that the highest order of significance did not exceed 20. This suggests that investigation of orders beyond 52 would be unlikely to alter the orders of the ARCH processes chosen for the residuals. Two strengths of the F test have been applied. In the case of DER\$£ a 1 per cent rule for determining the relevant order rejects all orders, suggesting that none add significantly to the explanatory power of the equation including only a constant on the RHS. This is not surprising since the ARCH test results are only significant at the 5 per cent level. A 5 per cent rule is therefore applied for the exchange rate series, while a 1 per cent rule is applied for all the other series as a first approach.

The F test results for the full dataset ARCH tests are presented in Table 10.6, while the results for the series excluding the outliers are presented in Table 10.7. In both cases the F tests have been applied to the orders underlined in Tables 10.4 and 10.5, respectively. The underlined orders are those where the ARCH statistic is both significant and where the coefficient on the highest ordered term of the squared residuals in the ARCH test equation returned a significant t value.

The F test results reported in Table 10.6 indicate that the respective orders appropriate for the ARCH processes of the full dataset mean model residuals for DRG20, DLRG20, DRIB3 and DFTP4 are 19, 19, 0^{12} and 12. None of the higher orders for DER\$£ add significantly to the explanatory power of the second order ARCH equation at the 5 per cent level – the nearest is order 12 where the calculated F statistic is 1.70 compared to a 5 per cent critical value of 1.84. Strict application of the stated rule would accept a weak ARCH process of order 2 for the residuals of DER\$£. However, a supplementary method suggested by Professor Engle for employing the data to discern between two different orders was applied, and it did in fact favour the twelfth order equation over the second order specification. The method is considered in the next section.

The removal of the outliers from the data does not alter significantly the ARCH test results for DRG20, DRIB3, and DFTP4, when compared to the marked impact on the results for DRIB3. The respective orders of the ARCH processes considered most appropriate for DRG20, DLRG20 and DFTP4, decline from 19, 19 and 12 for the full dataset as reported in Table 10.6, to 13, 10 and 6, as reported in Table 10.7 when the outliers are excluded. There is a moderate difference between the length of the orders chosen for the two datasets, although the impact of this difference on the ARCH variance estimates is minor when compared with the impact on the variance series of removing the outliers.

Table 10.6   F test results to determine the appropriate order of the ARCH processes for the full dataset asset market series[1]

Comparison of order X relative to order Y (X/Y)	Asset market series			
	DRG20	DLRG20	DFTP4	DER$£[2]
2/1	–	–	33.40**	–
3/2	8.87**	4.75*	–	2.82
4/2	–	3.28*	--	2.21
4/3	3.95*	–	–	–
5/2	–	4.26**	–	–
5/3	5.42**	–	–	–
6/2	–	–	2.83*	1.55
8/5	5.32**	9.89**	–	–
9/2	–	–	–	1.70
10/2	–	–	2.23*	–
10/8	3.64*	–	–	–
12/2	–	–	2.58**	1.70
13/8	3.38**	2.51*	–	–
18/8	–	2.30*	–	–
18/13	2.19	–	–	–
19/8	–	2.69**	–	–
19/13	3.10**	–	–	–
26/12	–	–	0.61	–
27/12	–	–	0.91	–
46/19	1.14	0.90	–	–

Notes: * Significant at 5 per cent level.
     ** Significant at 1 per cent level.
     1. The F tests are applied to the R^2s of the stated order ARCH test equations for which the relevant ARCH statistics are presented in Table 10.3. The Table 10.3 results apply to the residuals of the full dataset mean models.
     2. The F statistic which comes closest to being significant at the 5 per cent level relative to the base equation of order 2 was for order 12 where the calculated value is 1.70 compared to a critical value of 1.84.

The F test results reported in Table 10.7 for DRIB3 show that applying the 1 per cent rule implies an appropriate order of 32. There is a possibility that the thirty-second order correlation in the squared residuals could be due to almost significant correlation in the levels of the residuals at the same order. The previous highest order which passed the 1 per cent rule is 4. However, order 10 was significant at around the $2\frac{1}{2}$ per cent level when

Table 10.7   F test results to determine the appropriate order of the ARCH processes for the asset market series excluding 'outliers'[1]

Comparison of order X relative to order Y (X/Y)	Asset market series			
	DRG20	DLRG20	DRIB3[2]	DFTP4
2/1	41.87**	15.56**	12.93**	—
3/2	15.99**	—	—	—
4/1	—	—	—	5.14**
4/2	—	4.82**	13.86**	—
5/3	7.14**	—	—	—
5/4	—	14.68**	—	—
6/4	—	—	—	7.93**
8/4	—	—	2.54*	—
8/5	1.40	—	—	—
9/5	2.37	1.59	—	—
10/4	—	—	2.49*	—
10/5	5.38**	3.36**	—	—
13/10	5.26**	—	—	—
15/4	—	—	1.96*	—
19/13	1.23	—	—	—
20/4	—	—	1.75*	—
25/4	—	—	1.69*	—
28/10	—	0.79	—	—
28/13	1.29	—	—	—
32/4	—	—	1.81*	—
33/32	—	—	4.19*	—
41/13	1.23	—	—	—
45/6	—	—	—	0.99
46/32	—	—	1.32	—

Notes: * Significant at the 5 per cent level.
** Significant at the 1 per cent level.
1. The F tests are applied to the R^2s of the stated order ARCH test equations for which the relevant ARCH statistics are presented in Table 10.4. The Table 10.4 results apply to the residuals of the mean models which exclude the 'outliers'.
2. The F statistic which comes closest to being significant at the 1 per cent level between orders 4 and 32 is at order 10 where the calculated value is 2.49 compared to a critical value of 2.82.

compared with order 4. The method suggested by Professor Engle for further discriminating between competing orders was applied to orders 10 and 32, and in this instance favoured the shorter lag, so it was adopted.

The lengths of the ARCH processes found for the asset market series would seem to provide some information on how long volatility shocks persist. This question, or more particularly that of the serial correlation in estimates of stock market volatility, was addressed by Poterba and Summers (1984). Their finding of only weak serial correlation prompted them to observe that:

> These shocks can therefore have only a small impact on stock market prices . . . since changes in volatility affect expected required rates of return for only short intervals. These findings lead us to be skeptical of recent claims that the stock markets' poor performance during the 1970s can be explained by volatility-induced increases in risk premia, as suggested by Malkiel (1979) and Pindyck (1984). They also lead us to doubt that fluctuations in risk premia associated with changing return volatility can account for much of the observed variation in stock prices. The finding that volatility is not highly serially correlated is puzzling in light of Black's (1976) observation that stock market returns and changes in volatility are negatively correlated (Poterba and Summers, 1984, p. 1).

The relatively short lengths of the ARCH processes reported in this paper could be interpreted as support for the Poterba and Summers finding of weak serial correlation of volatility. However, even if it does, their contention that weak serial correlation necessarily implies only a small impact of volatility shocks on returns does not appear to be the full story. The impact of changes in volatility – as a proxy for changes in risk premia – on market returns, would seem to rely not only on how long volatility shocks persist but also on the quantitative impact of the shocks on returns while they do persist and the frequency of such shocks.

4.2 ARCH VARIANCE FUNCTIONS

The ARCH model, as applied in this study, is as follows for an $AR(1)$ conditional mean equation and a conditional variance equation of order p:

$$X_t - X_{t-1} = \beta_0 + \beta_1 (X_{t-1} - X_{t-2}) + \epsilon_t \tag{1}$$

$$\epsilon_t^2 = \alpha_0 + \alpha_1 \epsilon_{t-1}^2 + \alpha_2 \epsilon_{t-2}^2 + \ldots + \alpha_p \epsilon_{t-p}^2 \tag{2}$$

Engle (1980, p. 6) points out that to be a sensible specification (2) – the conditional variance function of the ARCH test – must satisfy certain stationarity and non-negativity constraints. In the first instance the sum of the estimated coefficients on the ϵ_{t-i}^2s must not exceed unity, while non-negativity of the variance estimates can only be ensured if none of these coefficients are negative.

The stationarity condition is satisfied in all instances. However, in all unrestricted ARCH test equations negative coefficients and negative variance estimates arise. To overcome this problem Engle's two parameter model, which imposes a linearly declining lag structure on the conditional variance equation, was adopted.[13] In this case (2b) replaces (2) as the variance specification:

$$\epsilon_t^2 = \alpha_0 + \alpha_1 \sum_{i=0}^{p-1} (p - i) \, \epsilon_{t-i-1}^2 \sum_{j=0}^{p-1} (p - j) \tag{2'}$$

As well as being superficially justifiable on the basis of economic theory, the declining lag structure was not altogether in dispute with the data. The unrestricted equations invariably returned the most significant – and positive – coefficients on the first four lags, while most lags after the first half dozen were insignificant. The main contrast with the unrestricted lag structures, aside from negative coefficients, was the tendency in the latter for a lag to pop up significant after several insignificant ones.

Using the orders of the ARCH processes identified for the residuals of the differenced series mean models in the last section, restricted ARCH variance functions were estimated in the form of (2b), and are reported in Table 10.8.

All equations have significant constant terms, the relevance of which becomes particularly important in the comparison of the ARCH and moving variance about moving mean (MVAMM) variance functions in the next section. The loss of explanatory power due to the restrictions is indicated by the smaller ARCH statistics returned for the restricted equation. Only in the case of DER\$£ is the restricted equation ARCH statistic not significant. This is not surprising given that the statistic for the unrestricted equation was itself only significant at the 5 per cent level. Of the other restricted equations, only the ARCH statistic for the full dataset equation for DLRG20 dropped below the 1 per cent level of significance, although it was only marginally under, with a calculated value of 36.11 compared to a critical value of 36.19.

As already highlighted in the previous section, the orders of the equations excluding the outliers are up to half the length of the full dataset

Table 10.8 Restricted ARCH variance functions

Asset market series[1]		Estimated coefficients		Equation order	ARCH statistic		Sample period (sample size)
		Constant (t value)	Summation[2] variable (t value)		Unrestricted equation	Restricted equation	
DRG20	Full dataset	0.01752 (3.55)	0.6204 (7.97)	19	89.64**	59.56**	1967.21 to 1985.12 (931)
	excluding 'outliers'	0.01641 (4.08)	0.6234 (9.60)	13	115.72**	83.86**	1967.21 to 1985.12 (931)
DLRG20	Full dataset	0.0001384 (4.12)	0.5335 (6.12)	19	78.95**	36.11*	1967.21 to 1985.12' (931)
	Excluding 'outliers'	0.000139 (5.79)	0.4823 (7.14)	10	63.92**	48.43**	1967.21 to 1985.12 (931)
DRIB3	Excluding 'outliers'	0.06269 (5.34)	0.4667 (7.17)	10	78.90**	48.79**	1967.22 to 1985.12 (930)
DFTP4	Full dataset	0.003614 (5.20)	0.5235 (7.73)	12	73.80**	56.35**	1967.3 to 1985.12 (949)
	Excluding 'outliers'	0.00464 (8.22)	0.3547 (6.00)	6	48.87**	34.80**	1967.3 to 1985.12 (949)
DER$£	Full dataset	0.0003441 (5.38)	0.3452 (3.57)	12	23.52*	12.56	1972.43 to 1985.12 (648)

Notes:
* Significant at the 5 per cent level.
** Significant at the 1 per cent level.
1. The dependent variables are the squared residuals of the relevant equations presented in Tables 10.1 and 10.2
2. The summation variable takes the form

$$\sum_{i=0}^{k-1} (k-i)\, e_{t-i}^2 \sum_{j=0}^{k-1} (k-i)$$

where k is the order reported in the third column of the table and e_{t-i}^2 is the ith lag of the dependent variable.

equations. This indicates that the outliers played a major part in causing the higher order correlations between the squared residuals of the mean models.

5   ARCH AND MVAMM VARIANCE ESTIMATES

5.1   Comparison of ARCH and MVAMM variance estimates

The ARCH and MVAMM variance series to be discussed have all been plotted with the weekly data summarised into quarterly average series. The result for DFTP4 are exhibited in Figure 10.6. The others are available on request. As mentioned in Section 1, and discussed at greater length in Dickens (1986), the difference between the specifications of the ARCH and MVAMM variance estimators is reduced considerably when the latter is applied to the first difference of the asset market series. Barr (1984, p. 4) suggests measuring the variability of the first differenced series in his investigation of exchange rate variability. The argument being that, on the basis of the 'fairly common finding that the exchange rate follows a random walk', the change in the series is fully unanticipated.

Three potentially important differences still remain however: the ARCH variance function contains a constant; the weights in the ARCH specification (the α_i in (2) above) depend on i unlike the constant weights in the MVAMM specification; the order of the ARCH variance function (p) is chosen on the basis of the ARCH test, while there is no obvious method for choosing the lag length for the MVAMM specification (k). The implications of these differences are discussed in Dickens (1986).

Prior to observing the ARCH test results, the choice of window length for the MVAMM estimator was an arbitrary one. In the event a window length of 13 weeks was adopted, which, in light of the orders suggested by the ARCH test results, removes much of the potential difference between the two estimators from this source. However, without knowledge of the ARCH results - assuming they can in fact be taken as a good indication of the 'appropriate' lag length - a window length of a year, or even five years, may have been chosen justifiably. Such large differences in order could give the two estimators quite different profiles, especially in the face of large observations.

Turning to the actual variance estimates, the results for DFTP4 are generally representative of those for all the series. Comparison of the respective full dataset ARCH and MVAMM variance estimates for each series suggests that their 'cyclical' behaviour is very similar in terms of the

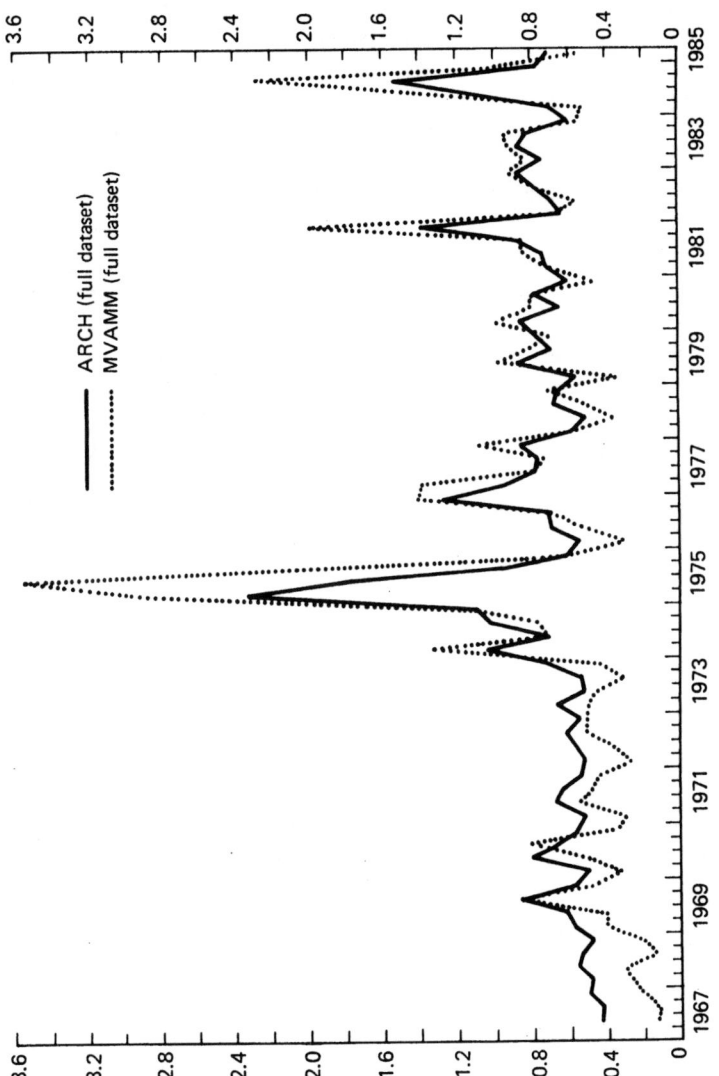

Figure 10.6   ARCH and moving average (MVAMM) variance functions for DFTP4 (quarterly averages)

period in which peaks, troughs, and turning points occur, and generally in the relative magnitudes when peaks are compared with peaks and troughs with troughs. The major difference is when the relative magnitudes of peaks and troughs are considered. In the case of DFTP4 the ARCH peaks exceed the trough levels by factors ranging from 2 to 3, while comparable factorial differences for the MVAMM estimates are 3 to 6. The equivalent ARCH and MVAMM factor ranges for the extreme case of DER$£ are 1.5 to 2 and 3 to 5, respectively.

To the extent that the extra rigour of the ARCH estimator is accepted, then the ARCH estimates are more accurate in terms of their absolute magnitude and for peak-to-trough comparisons of changes in the level of variability. This result, combined with the fact that the similarity in the timing of the cyclical behaviour of the variance series from the two estimators was in part a result of the fortuitous choice of lag length for the MVAMM estimator, suggests that the ARCH route has significant advantages over the conventional MVAMM type techniques; even when its main advantage – the conventional mean specification – is effectively discarded. There is, of course, the question of cost effectiveness. The ARCH technique as adopted in this paper would not seem to be too restrictive for general practice as long as moderate computer facilities are available.

5.2   The ARCH variance estimates

The discussion that follows has been based almost entirely on a visual inspection of the charts showing the results, as opposed to an interpretation of the variance series in light of either known and relevant UK and international events or of a theoretical framework. The description is limited in this way because, as already indicated, explanation of the causes of variability is outside the domain of this paper; rather being the intended topic for further work. Limited space has meant that only a selection of the charted results are included here, a full set being available on request. In Figure 10.7 the full dataset ARCH variance series are plotted for DRG20, DFTP4 and DER$£, as well as the results for DRIB3 excluding outliers. In Figure 10.8 the full dataset variance series for DFTP4 is compared with the series derived after the exclusion of the identified outliers.

The over-all conclusions drawn for the asset markets analysed are:

1.   In the period 1967–72 the variance estimates are by far the lowest and most stable for any similar length subperiod, while in all four markets they increase significantly above these levels in either 1973 or 1974. This is also the period of greatest cross-market similarity in the

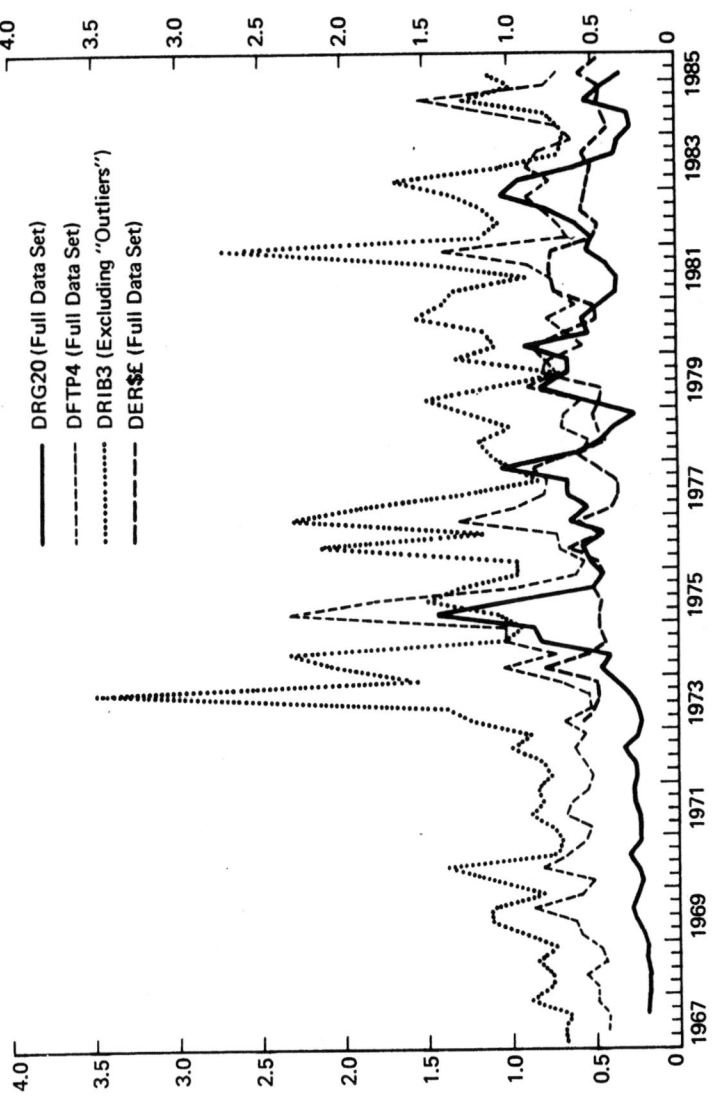

Figure 10.7   ARCH variance functions for DRG20, DFTP4, DRIB3 and DER$ £ (quarterly averages)

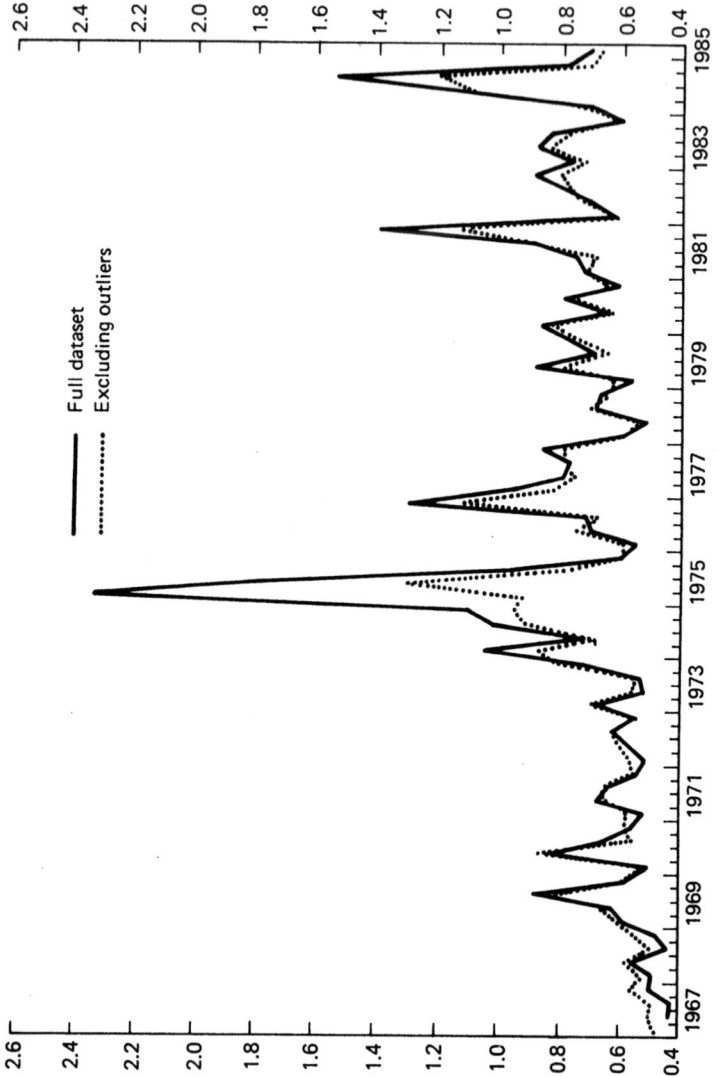

Figure 10.8 ARCH variance functions for DFTP4 (quarterly averages)

behaviour of the variance series, with the cyclical pattern in DRIB3 and DFTP4 almost identical over this period, and that for DRG20 also quite similar to these two series.

2. The dramatic increase in variability in the early to mid-1970s lasted for between 6 and 18 months in the various markets before returning to levels similar to those experienced in the 1967-72 period; or, as in the case of DRG20, while still remaining at approximately double the magnitude of the earlier levels, being closer to them than the peak levels experienced in 1974-5. The peaks experienced in this first major upturn in variability were easily the highest peaks over the whole sample period, the exceptions being DER$£, and DLRG20 when the outliers were excluded.

3. Over the remainder of the sample period each market experienced three or four cyclical-type movements in variability, with transition from trough to peak levels and vice versa, when they did occur, generally being rapid. The duration of the cycles range from one to six quarters based on the quarterly average data. The levels in the trough were generally similar within each series, and not unlike the 1967-72 levels, although the post 1973-5 peak levels are well above all levels in the 1967-72 period.

4. The first half of the 1980s has been very similar to the second half of the 1970s in terms of the frequency and magnitude of peaks and troughs for all series.

5. At the end of the sample period - 1985.1 - the variance estimates were at or near the trough levels for most series, generally having just descended from minor peaks in 1984. The only exception to this is the MVAMM estimates for DRIB3; here, because of an outlier in 1985-1, the variance estimate at the end of the period is near the average peak level.[14]

A comparison of the ARCH variance estimates based on the full dataset with those excluding the outliers has been made. These indicate the following:

1. There are no ARCH estimates for DRIB3 over the full dataset and so, with little loss of relevance, the ARCH estimates which exclude the outliers are instead compared with the MVAMM estimates. This is an interesting case because it is the only series for which exclusion of the outliers removes whole 'cycles' in the variance estimates: dramatic increases in the MVAMM variance estimates in 1972.3, 1978.1, 1979.3, 1984.3 and 1985.1 are in each instance due to a single outlier. Probably the most relevant of these instances is near the end of the

sample period when two outliers occur. Their inclusion produces variance estimates for the period 1984.3 to 1985.1 at least as large as any since the early 1970s, while their exclusion suggests the variance over this period was not much above the level experienced during the period 1967-72. The ARCH estimates, excluding the outliers for all other series, have peaks occurring in mid/late 1984 – of a relatively minor nature for DRG20 and DER\$£, but one of the largest for DFTP4. This could indicate the appropriateness of including some proportion of the influence of the outliers in DRIB3 in this instance.

2.   The outliers in the other series, as with the remaining outlier in DRIB3, do not themselves cause variability cycles, instead occurring in periods of generally higher variability. They do, however, greatly change the impression of the magnitude of the increase in variability, with the variability estimates on average doubling when the outliers are included.

3.   As visible in Figure 10.8, the exclusion of the two outliers in DFTP4 dramatically reduces the variance estimates for 1975, suggesting that the peak of the variability cycle in 1974-5 was not significantly higher than the three subsequent periods of high variability. Also the factorial differences between the post- and pre-1973 peaks in variability reduce from the range 1.5 to 3, to 1.3 to 1.5; implying for DFTP4 that the post-1973 period was not so different from the earlier period as the full dataset variance estimates suggest.

The final consideration before making cross-market comparisons is the results for DRG20 and DLRG20. The peaks and troughs are identical for the full dataset ARCH variance estimates of these series, although two major differences emerge: first, in the case of DLRG20, unlike DRG20, the peak levels of the 1974-5 cycle do not dramatically exceed those in subsequent cycles; and secondly, in the 1975-7 trough the estimates for DRG20 – unlike those for DLRG20 – do not return to the level of most other troughs. These two differences arise because it is during the 1974-7 period that RG20 is generally at its highest, and so the logarithm transformation would be expected to have its major impact on reducing the variance in this period.[15]

Cross-market comparisons of the variance estimates are based on consideration of the cross-series correlation coefficients, contemporaneous linear regression relationships of the weekly series excluding outliers, and consideration of Figure 10.7.

Based on the correlation coefficients reported in Table 10.9, other than the moderate positive correlation between the variability in DRG20 and DFTP4 (0.40 over the full sample period), none of the correlation co-

Table 10.9   Cross-market correlation coefficients of weekly ARCH variance estimates (excluding 'outliers')[1]

1968.1 to 1985.12	*DRG20*	*DRIB3*	*DFTP4*
DRIB3	0.153	–	–
DFTP4	0.400	0.226	–
1973.1 to 1985.12			
DRIB3	0.007	–	–
DFTP4	0.306	0.141	–
DER$£	−0.092	0.183	0.032

1. The correlation coefficients are calculated over two sample periods. The longer of the two is representative of the full sample period, while the shorter represents the period subsequent to the floating of sterling.

efficients – and especially those between DRG20 and DRIB3 – are as large as some might have expected.

Taking the ARCH variance series for the share market as the dependent variable and regressing it against the other ARCH variance series over both the floating exchange rate subsample and the full sample period returns equations (3) and (4), respectively. The regressions are run on the weekly series and exclude the outliers, and the series are indicated by a 'V' before their usual name. They suggest that the correlations between VDFTP4 and both VDRG20 and VDRIB3 are in fact statistically significant, while the variability in the exchange rate has no part in 'explaining' variability in the share market.

$$VDFTP4 = \underset{(8.22)}{0.279VDRG20} + \underset{(3.49)}{0.047VDRIB3} + \underset{(0.93)}{0.064VDER\$£} + \underset{(12.14)}{0.529}$$

$$R^2 = 0.114; F = 27.32; DW = 0.35; 1973.1 \text{ to } 1985.12 \qquad (3)$$

$$VDFTP4 = \underset{(12.26)}{0.328VDRG20} + \underset{(5.55)}{0.062VDRIB3} + \underset{(20.34)}{0.505}$$

$$R^2 = 0.188; F = 103.43; DW = 0.34; 1967.1 \text{ to } 1985.12 \qquad (4)$$

If VDRG20 is chosen as the dependent variable, then the correlation between it and VDRIB3 is positive and statistically significant over the full dataset, but it is not significant over the exchange rate subsample. VDFTP4 is a significant positively correlated explanatory variable in both samples, while the coefficient on VDER$£ is significant but negative. VDRIB3 and VDRG20 are both significant when VDER$£ is taken as the dependent variable, although the coefficient on VDRG20 is negative. Perhaps if one were to posit a negative relationship between variability in the exchange rate and either of the interest rates, it would most likely be with the short-term rate, on the grounds that the authorities might try, under some policy regimes, to vary short rates in order to maintain exchange rate stability. The explanation of the negative coefficient on VDRG20 will have to wait for the intended investigation of international asset market volatility.

As indicated by the correlation coefficients and equations (3) and (4), the relationships between these variance series are not strong. This seems to contrast with the description of over-all similarity in the behaviour of all the variance series given above. Reference to Figure 10.7 reveals some instances where the cyclical upturns in the variability series coincide after 1973, although there are almost as many where there is no coincidence. These results, however, implicitly assume any relationship must be contemporaneous and linear. There may also be excluded relevant explanatory variables. For these reasons, care must be taken in interpreting the 'results' of this brief examination of cross-market variability.

A potentially useful method of internalising such comparisons in the ARCH specification is to include cross-market covariance terms in the ARCH variance equation. In such a way a variance-covariance matrix type system of equations could be built up which would be more consistent with the portfolio approach to modelling asset demand. This type of approach was suggested in Engle, Lilien and Robins (1984, p. 19).

6   CONCLUSION

In this paper Engle's (1982) ARCH model has been employed to describe the variability of yields and prices in four major UK asset markets. Compared with conventional methods of describing variability in time series, such as moving variance about moving mean (MVAMM) estimators, the ARCH approach provides some welcome methodological rigour without being too unwieldy a technique to be useful in practice.

The general impression of asset market volatility since the mid-1960s, based on observation of the plotted quarterly variance series, is one of quite similar over-all behaviour over the sample period in the four chosen markets. Variability was relatively low, stable, and co-ordinated up until

the early 1970s, when the most variable period in the sample was experienced. More distinct 'cycles' in variability were in evidence after this
period, with trough levels generally around the level experienced in the
1967-72 period and, while not as high as the peaks reached in the first
major cyclical upturn in variability in the 1973-5 period, the peak levels
were well in excess of the trough levels.[16] Movements from trough to peak
levels, when they occurred, were generally very rapid. This was in part the
result of 'outlying' observations in the differenced series – the data being
handled in differenced form because examination of the autocorrelation
and partial autocorrelation plots of the levels form series clearly indicated
non-stationarity. The influence of only a handful of 'outliers' in the
samples of over 900 observations on the estimation of both the conditional
mean and variance functions was extreme in some instances. Considerable
attention was therefore devoted to the 'outlier' problem.

The variability in the first half of the 1980s appears to have been quite
similar to that experienced in the second half of the 1970s in terms of the
frequency, duration, and magnitude of the 'cyclical' upturns of the variance
series. In all cases except the interbank market, the variance estimates were
at or near the 'trough' levels at the end of the sample period – March 1985
– and it turns out that the divergent result for the interbank market was
the influence of a single 'outlier'.

Except for the pre-1973 period, the over-all impression of similarity of
the evolution of variability in the differenced series breaks down considerably when the timing of specific variability 'cycles' are compared. On the
basis of correlation coefficients calculated between the weekly variance
series, the strongest relationship was between the gilts and share markets
(0.40), with surprisingly little contemporaneous correlation between
variability in the interbank and gilt markets. Regression techniques suggested
that significant, although not particularly strong, contemporaneous
relationships exist between the variance series.

As stated in the introduction, this paper is only the first tangible
evidence of an ongoing project aimed at describing and explaining the
variability of yields and prices in selected international asset markets. The
next step is to apply the ARCH technique to the weekly asset market
series already obtained for the US, West Germany, Japan, France and Italy.
Once this is completed, more detailed cross-market and cross-country
analysis of variability is intended. The other major wing planned for the
larger project is an investigation of the causes of changes in variability,
with particular emphasis on the roles of external shocks and domestic
policy regime changes.

Notes

1. Engle (1980, 1982) and Fama (1977, p. 15) refer to several papers that use conventional variance measures. Other examples include Johnson (1981), Pindyck (1984), Poterba and Summers (1984) and Barr (1984).

2. As Professor Engle suggested, one possibility which would not require extra data is to consider only the capital gains/losses component of the stock market holding period yield. This relies on the empirical finding that dividends series are generally smooth processes relative to the capital gains/losses component of holding yields. As it turns out, this is approximately the series employed.

3. If the 1974 and 1975 observations are excluded, the correlation coefficient for FT500 increases to 0.774; while such tampering should be done with great caution, both years display extreme behaviour in terms of their means and variancies and would appear to mask the strength of the underlying relationship.

4. A supplementary explanation is that adopted by Engle, Lilien and Robins (1984), who approached the matter from the opposite direction. On the assumption of risk averse agents they expect the mean of the excess holding period yield of 6-month US treasury bills over 3-month bills to increase with its variance to compensate for the higher relative risk.

5. The meaning of the word 'stronger' in this context is that the further the value of λ is from unity, in either direction, the more the data are transformed from their original values.

6. Prior to measuring the extent of proportionality in FT500, the natural logarithm of the series was used because of strong priors regarding the existence of proportionality in this series. The results obtained using the log of the series were largely consistent with those subsequently reported for FTP4.

7. The significance of the thirteenth order lag for the gilts series could indicate quarterly seasonality. The twenty-sixth order correlation coefficient for DRG20 is positive, which is consistent with the negative thirteenth order coefficient being indicative of quarterly seasonality, although neither the thirty-ninth nor the fifty-second order coefficients are consistent with this pattern. The possibility of a quarterly seasonal pattern was discussed with a senior official in the Bank who is intimately involved with the gilts market, and, while the possibility of seasonality could not be ruled out, he knew of no reason to expect seasonal behaviour in this market.

8. A selective review of this literature is presented in Dickens (1986).

9. As well as the impact on the mean model fitted to DFTP4 noted above, the removal of the outliers from DRIB3 dramatically changes the ARCH test results for this series.

10. The time dependence of the variances of the underlying and outlier processes should be modelled separately. However, with so few observations identified as potentially coming from a secondary process, separate modelling of the two variances, and their summation

(including allowance for covariation) to give the total measure of variability, is not feasible. The alternative chosen has been to lump the two together, and model them as coming from one process.

11. See Kmenta (1971, pp. 370-7) for a description of the test. Dickens (1986) presents a rationale for choosing this test, and describes its application.

12. *F* test results are not reported in Table 10.6 for DRIB3 because the mean model residuals for this series do not return significant ARCH statistics when tested over the full dataset.

13. See Engle (1980, p. 8; 1982, p. 1002). As Professor Engle suggested, the flexibility of the lag structure can be improved by including linearly declining lagged summation variables of different orders in the same equation. The inclusion of summation variables of two different lengths is also the supplementary method suggested by Professor Engle to decide which was the most appropriate of the two orders.

14. While the discussion of this section is based on the ARCH variance estimates, because full dataset ARCH results were not obtainable for DRIB3, the MVAMM results for DRIB3 were also included in the discussion.

15. The only other period when yields were consistently as high as in the 1974-7 period was in the period 1980 to mid-1982.

16. These comments are not entirely applicable to the exchange rate series because, first – for obvious reasons – the exchange rate data were not collected before 1972, and secondly, the peak levels in the 1979 and 1981 cyclical upturns in variability were not significantly below the 1974 peak – those upturns also lasted twice the length of the 1974 cycle.

References

Barr, D. G. (1984) 'Exchange rate variability: evidence for the period 1973-1982', *Bank of England*, Discussion Paper, 11.

Black, E. (1976) 'Studies of stock price volatility changes', *Proceedings of the 1976 Meetings of the American Statistical Association, Business and Economic Statistics Section*, 117-81.

Dickens, R. R. (1986) 'The ARCH model as applied to the study of international asset market volatility', *Bank of England*, Discussion Paper, forthcoming.

Engle, R. F. (1980) 'Estimates of the variance of US inflation based upon the ARCH model' (San Diego: University of California) Discussion Paper, 80-14.

Engle, R. F. (1982) 'Autoregressive conditional heteroscedasticity with estimates of the variance of United Kingdom inflation', *Econometrica*, 50: 987-1007.

Engle, R. F., Lilien, D. M. and Robins, R. P. (1984) 'Estimating time varying risk premia in the term structure: the ARCH-M model' (San Diego: University of California) Discussion Paper, 85-17.

Fama, E. F. (1977) *Foundations of Finance* (Oxford: Blackwell).

Johnson, D. (1981) 'Interest rate variability under the new operating procedures and the initial response in financial markets', *Federal Reserve Staff Review of Monetary Control Procedures*, January.

Kmenta, J. (1971) *Elements of Econometrics* (New York: Macmillan Press).

McLeod, G. (1983) *Box Jenkins in Practise* (Lancaster: Gwilym Jenkens & Partners).

Malnier, B. G. (1979) 'The capital formation problem in the United States', *Journal of Finance* 34: 291–306.

Mandelbrot, B. (1963) 'The variation of certain speculative prices', *Journal of Business*, 395–419.

Pindyck, R. S. (1984) 'Risk, inflation, and the stock market', *American Economic Review*, 74: 335–51.

Poterba, J. M. and Summers, L. H. (1984) 'The persistence of volatility and stock market fluctuations', National Bureau of Economic Research Working Paper, 1462, September.

Taylor, S. J. (1985) 'The behaviour of futures prices over time', *Applied Economics*, 17: 713–34.

Yule, G. U. and Kendall, M. G. (1965) *An Introduction to the Theory of Statistics* (14th ed) (London: Griffin).